Unreasonable
Doubt

Unreasonable Doubt

Circumstantial Evidence and an Ordinary  in New Haven

Norma Thompson

University of Missouri Press   Columbia and London

University of Missouri Press, Columbia, Missouri 65201
Printed and bound in the United States of America
5 4 3 2 1   10 09 08 07 06

Library of Congress Cataloging-in-Publication Data

Thompson, Norma, 1959–
   Unreasonable doubt : circumstantial evidence and an ordinary murder
in New Haven / Norma Thompson.
      p.   cm.
   Summary: "A murder trial ends in a hung jury because of the reasonable
doubt of a few jurors who, faced with circumstantial evidence, refuse to judge
the accused. Thompson confronts this evasion of judgment through the reex-
amination of the works of Faulkner, Austen, Tocqueville, Plato, and
Aristotle"—Provided by publisher.
   Includes bibliographical references and index.
   ISBN-13: 978-0-8262-1638-0 (alk. paper)
   ISBN-10: 0-8262-1638-2 (alk. paper)
   1. Brazier, Anthony—Trials, litigation, etc. 2. Trials (Murder)—
Connecticut—New Haven. 3. Jury—Connecticut—History. 4. Jury—
Philosophy. 5. Jury in literature. I. Title.
   KF224.B29T48 2006
   345.746'802523—dc22

                                                         2005030815

♾™This paper meets the requirements of the
American National Standard for Permanence of Paper
for Printed Library Materials, Z39.48, 1984.

Designer: Stephanie Foley
Typesetter: Crane Composition, Inc.
Printer and binder: The Maple-Vail Book Manufacturing Group
Typeface: Simoncini Garamond

Publication of this book has been assisted by the Frederick W.
Hilles Publication Fund of Yale University.

To Syl and Bill,

Loving parents who taught me the worth of a single human life.

Contents

Acknowledgments

JURY DUTY IS UNDERRATED. I am privileged to have served as a juror for the state of Connecticut during the fall of 2001, and I am beholden to my fellow jurors who agreed to share their opinions about the experience. I have attempted to be scrupulously fair in recounting our travails in the deliberation room. In order to respect the privacy of those jurors who dissented from the majority view, I have changed their names in this account. Special gratitude goes to State's Attorney Michael Dearington for his generous assistance in researching the case.

Humanistic associations of all sorts are championed in this book. I have been fortunate to participate in many such settings, from panels with my fellow political theorists in national and local political science association meetings, to Liberty Fund conferences, where collegiality and conversation are at a premium. Papers delivered on Plato in New Orleans, on Jane Austen in Chicago, and on manliness in Portland, Maine, have all found their way into this book. I am grateful to the many good friends and interlocutors at these gatherings who have deeply enriched my thinking, especially Todd Breyfogle, Timothy Fuller, Harvey Mansfield, Stephen Salkerer, Arlene Saxonhouse, Jean Yarbrough, Catherine Zuckert, and Michael Zuckert. I have presented portions of this book at workshops at several universities, including Yale, Dartmouth, the University of Denver, and Quinnipiac University, and all of these appearances helped me to sharpen my insights. The Hoover Institution at Stanford University offered me support during summer work, and I would like to thank Director John Raisian and others, including Romayne Ponleithner, for their help during these visits.

Coincidentally, I moved into my home base at the Whitney Humanities Center at the same time that I became a juror in the New Haven County Courthouse. The buildings face each other across Church Street, and when, from time to time, bomb threats empty the courthouse, the judges, lawyers, security guards, and jurors will spill out onto our shared sidewalks. I do not need these physical prompts to feel connected to our judicial system, but I don't mind being reminded how fortunate I am to have been able to meditate about judicial matters within the confines of the Whitney. Its spirited intellectual environment is what a humanities center should be, and rarely is. María Rosa Menocal sets the tone of high energy and purpose and has inspired works of originality and genius from fellows across the disciplines. María, Jane Levin, and Toni Dorfman are in their own category of my inspirational friends at the Whitney. Our weekly luncheons are irreverent and stimulating, and I have benefited immeasurably from conversations there with Don Brown, Bryan Garsten, Tony Kronman, Catherine Labio, Joseph LaPalombara, Kate Stith, and Robert Wokler, among many others. Special mention must go to former fellows Keri Ames and Ryan Hanley for their uncommon insights and advice on early drafts of this work. My coworkers and friends Amerigo Fabbri, Sandra Malan-Bowles, Manana Sikic, and Sue Stout enhance my life at the Whitney in countless ways.

My students at Yale are somehow always at the heart of it all. With special thanks to those onetime students who have blended seamlessly into friends: Winifred Amaturo, Michelle Tolman Clarke, Raluca Eddon, Lt. Ewan Macdougall (who was leading his marines in Iraq as I wrote this book), Jeffrey Morris, and Justin Zaremby. Another cadre of original thinkers and cherished friends—Peter Berkowitz, Patrick Deneen, and Stefanie Nelson—have each taken unconventional routes in academia that parallel, and fortify, my own. My husband, Charlie, as always, was with me on every page, encouraging me to finish my thought and extend my reach.

Unreasonable Doubt was a while in the making. Writing the core story was not difficult, but finding a publisher who was willing to risk the unusual genre was a challenge. It has been a delight to work with the director and editor in chief of University of Missouri Press, Beverly Jarrett, my editor Clair Willcox, managing editor Jane Lago, and editor Susan King. The anonymous readers for the University of Missouri Press were enormously helpful and enabled me to improve this book considerably.

In Dante's *Inferno,* those who do not take a stand or make a judgment are not consigned to hell; somehow they are not worthy of such a dramatic place. No, those sorry souls who stand apart are required to do in death what they did not do in life. Dante's Canto X of *Inferno* describes them incessantly racing about, following a banner on which is written nothing. I may have encountered one or two people in my lifetime whom Dante might have had in mind when he wrote his work. But I am quite sure that no one in my family will be so judged, and for that I am proud. In this, I empathize so much with the families of the victims because my own is so precious to me. My sisters, Kathy and Mary, and brothers, Bill and John, my nieces and nephews, and all the cherished members of my marvelously extended family, have spurred me to my best writing. At the head of it all are my wonderful parents, to whom *Unreasonable Doubt* is dedicated.

Unreasonable
Doubt

Introduction

Jury Stories, Old and New

WHAT IS OUR RECOURSE when the need to judge is crucial, but our understanding is partial? This book is about how great literary and historical texts may help us at such junctures in developing the capacity for prudential judgment.

The specific event that prompted these reflections was fourteen days of jury duty, an experience that was both traumatic and unresolved. Fourteen days was by no means two weeks, not only because those days were spread over almost a full month's time, but also because juror-time is appropriately reckoned day by day, so distinct is each new sitting. The case for which I served as a juror involved the 1998 slaying of Nancy McCloskey in New Haven. It was the second time this case was tried by the state of Connecticut, and, in December 2001, the second time it ended in a mistrial. The case was closed in January 2003 when the defendant pled out and received a fifteen-year sentence. This precluded a third trial, already in preparation.

Other events from this time period intrude and are recounted for being similarly suggestive about the state of American cultural and intellectual life at the turn of the twenty-first century. "This is what happens when you write books," says Nathan Zuckerman, the character who narrates *The Human Stain,* by Philip Roth. "There's not just something that drives you to find out everything—something begins putting everything in your path. There is suddenly no such thing as a back road that doesn't lead headlong into your obsession."[1] For some

1. Philip Roth, *The Human Stain,* 344.

1

time now, all of my back roads have led to a single terminus: the debasement of judgment, the loss of common sense, the call for prudence. All around me, people were getting away with murder.

The great texts to which I will refer are varied and versatile, with authors ranging from Herodotus and Plato to Jane Austen and William Faulkner. These are old friends from the classroom who surprised me in this case by not permitting me to write the book I intended to write. I wanted to write about literary modernism and fragmented memories, on reconstructing the past without the guidance of an omniscient narrator. This was to bring my jury account into line with my academic work (admittedly, in an unusual manner). The book I did write is that and more. It is stranger, and strangely gripping, in the manner of an obsession. Against all plan, I found myself taking up Tocqueville's celebration of the American jury and raising him one. I had thought I was finished with him. Tocqueville spoke glowingly of the jury, and after my difficult experience, I became aware of the force of his insights and the need to update his characterizations. The institution of the jury stands out from every other political institution that Tocqueville identified in *Democracy in America,* as corrective to the democratic ills that he also described in detail. As he saw, the paradigm status of the American jury could not be overstated. The jury's old enemies should not go unrecognized in their new garb.

Who are the jury's old enemies? They are the poet and the sophist, at least if we are to give Plato his due. We must give him the attention he deserves because his *Apology of Socrates* depicts one of the two most momentous jury scenes in the Western world.[2] It is true that *that* jury erred in convicting the accused, unlike mine, which erred in withholding judgment. Perhaps, though, it is appropriate to have the example of a faulty conviction (and wrongful death) looming over the issues I consider in the pages that follow, in the same way that the fear of convicting falsely looms over the consciousness of jurors during deliberation. In any case, *The Apology* is undoubtedly a text concerned

---

2. The other pivotal jury scene is in Aeschylus's *Oresteia.* See also Eva Brann, *The Music of the Republic: Essays on Socrates' Conversations and Plato's Writings,* on why the trial of Jesus is not comparable to that of Socrates and why it is "in a way very revealing for the *Apology*" (46).

with examination, judgment, and self-accounting. Its definition of *reasonable* has not lost its resonance.

As it happens, singly or together, the poet and the sophist are the adversaries of Socrates in nearly all of the Platonic dialogues, not just in *The Apology,* and that is a point of abiding interest to me. Like their modern counterparts, the poet and the sophist oppose philosophic questioning and self-examination with their techniques of ending debate. Before I became a juror in the McCloskey trial in 2001, my freshmen had studied *The Republic* and were already familiar with these Platonic characters. During the trial, I was not permitted to speak to my class about the specifics of the case. But who needed specifics? In seminar one afternoon (I had been liberated early that day by the court), I told my students that the majority of the jurors in this case had two main adversaries; one of these adversaries was a poet and the other was a sophist. There was a general gasp, to which I contributed. Could Plato really be so relevant to this real-life drama? Until I said it aloud, I had not comprehended how precisely the new enemies of the jury mirrored the old. With the passage of time, my conviction only strengthened. Just as my familiarity with Plato helped me to be a better juror, so did my experience as a juror help me to become a better reader of Plato. Both developments pointed to the same conclusion: poet and sophist are alive and well in American society and, in their various expressions of unreasonable doubt, a menace to its prized political institution, the jury.

I

Two Murders, One Trial

The Law-Abiding Citizen

I was summoned for jury duty in the fall of 2001, with my one-day jury service scheduled for Friday, November 9, 2001. From veterans of the process I received the same piece of advice: "bring a book." It was the end of the tenth week of the semester, which put my seminar in the middle of Hannah Arendt's *Eichmann in Jerusalem.* I brought it along in the hopes of preparing for class.

I was charmed by the idea of jury duty: the court began its proceedings at ten o'clock, dispersed for a one-hour lunch at one, and ended promptly at five. That's hardly a day at all, and everyone knows that most jurors on their one-day service are sent home well before closing time. This schedule meant that I would have to miss a Directed Studies lecture given by one of my colleagues but still would be able to make an appearance at the weekly luncheon for fellows at the Whitney Humanities Center, which began with wine at 12:30 and concluded with the speaker's talk ninety minutes later. The Whitney was conveniently located across the street from the New Haven County Courthouse. I held out hope of turning this day to my advantage, as it was necessarily free of students, phones, e-mail, appointments, and meetings. One of my Chicago advisers, James Redfield, a brilliant classicist but something of an unwilling writer, attributed the origin of his eminent book on the *Iliad* to two weeks of jury service in the Cook County Criminal Court building, where, inexplicably, there were no

4

cases to hear. "We spent our days sitting at long tables, a room full of silent men," Redfield related, "It was like being in prison, except that they let us go home at night."[1] So he wrote *Nature and Culture in the Iliad*. I wondered if one could request jury duty?

At ten minutes before ten, the line at the courthouse snaked outside and around the building. There were actually three lines, one for the public, one for jurors, and one for court personnel. The latter were first in priority, and no matter how long others might stand in line, the guards waved through the judges, lawyers, and court reporters. Jurors were next. I began to feel a sense of patriotism. I was here as a citizen, not involved in a legal proceeding myself but at the ready to judge in whatever civil or criminal case might come my way. I recalled Tocqueville. But my patriotic mood battled with another as I made my way through the metal detector and to the ninth-floor juror assembly room. The feeling was vaguely like I had been sentenced to the DMV for an entire day: the long lines, the elevators that did not work, the employees who barked out instructions, the ever-present TV, but, mostly, the waiting.

A talk show blared on channel 8. New Haven nestles between East and West Rock, and there was no cable for the courthouse, so channel 8 is the only option. Most of the jury pool stared blankly at the perky talk show host. I found a seat as far away from the TV as possible and tried to shut out my surroundings. A voice called out suddenly, answering an unheard question, in high volume. Can you hear me now? Another loud rejoinder, and I twirled around to throw an angry stare at the cell phoner. It worked. She glared back but lowered her voice. By now we were being called to attention by one of the marshals. Remove your hats, the judge is on the way. An instructive video would be shown to prepare us. Everyone must pay attention. If anyone was caught not paying attention, the marshal would have to stop the video and go back to the beginning. This was superfluous advice. I remembered hearing about this video. The word was that jurors got so bored by the end of the day that they would *beg* to see the video again. I could see why: it was unintentionally amusing, especially the consoling finish, when we were told not to feel bad if we were not chosen to

1. James M. Redfield, *Nature and Culture in the Iliad: The Tragedy of Hector,* ix.

serve on a jury. It was nothing personal and did not reflect on us. The audience snorted.

All rose for the judge's arrival. He was youngish, and black, as I noticed to my surprise that very few were blacks among the pool of potential jurors. This did not seem to reflect the general population of New Haven. The judge told us that he knew how we must have felt when we got the summons to serve on the jury—sort of how *he* felt when he got the word that it was his turn to instruct us. Anyway, he promised, 90 percent of us would be sent home by the end of the day, and even if we were not picked for a jury, we would have served an important function, for criminals are often scared into a plea bargain by the mere sight of an assembled jury. None of this sounded like Tocqueville's "political virtue," and I was not so sure about the statistic either. The room was less than one quarter filled and appeared to contain no more than fifty people. If the state had more than one case, it looked as if just about everyone would be selected for voir dire. The judge repeated the phrase before he departed: we should not feel bad if we were not chosen. I returned to my book and could not help but note the chapter heading: "Duties of a Law-Abiding Citizen." This day had a preordained feel to it. I was beginning to suspect that I would not be given the occasion to feel bad.

The first list of fifteen was called, and then the second, which included me. We were brought down in a "Jurors Only" elevator to a fifth-floor courtroom. The elevator also carried other court personnel and stopped on intervening floors. Because it held only half our number, we traveled slowly and always in stages. This was the first of many indicators that most juries in Connecticut are made up of six, not twelve, individuals. Once we were finally assembled in the courtroom, Judge Fracasse entered, and we took the juror's oath en masse. The case was murder. The judge had soft white hair and was kindly looking and avuncular. I liked him immediately for his manner and his gravitas. He read the charge: "In the Superior Court for the State of Connecticut, New Haven County, Michael Dearington, State's Attorney for the Judicial District of New Haven, accuses Anthony Bazier of Murder and charges that at the City of New Haven, on or about the 1st day of December, 1998, at about 9:00 p.m., at or near 25 Norton Street, the said Anthony Bazier, with intent to cause the death of Nancy McCloskey, did cause the death, in violation of Section 53a–54a (a) of the Connecticut General Statutes."

Suddenly I sat straight up. The murder of Nancy McCloskey was the other murder reported by the *New York Times* a full three years before this proceeding, along with the murder of Suzanne Jovin. There was a remarkable clarity in my recall of events for December 1998. I was going to be out of here in no time flat.

"An Ordinary Evening in New Haven"

My husband, Charlie, was working in the ground-floor study late Saturday afternoon on December 5, 1998. I was in the kitchen above. The radio news on the hour reported that a female Yale student had been murdered. I rushed down the stairs. "What was her name?" he asked. "Suzanne Rovin—something like that," I said. "Jovin?" Yes, that was it.

Suzanne Jovin, a senior in my department, political science, and Charlie's advisee and student in the seminar for seniors majoring in international studies (she was a double major), had been stabbed seventeen times in the back, on a street corner about two miles north of campus in New Haven's wealthiest neighborhood. Yet only minutes earlier she had been seen at Phelps Gate in the heart of campus. She had just come back from a Friday night pizza party at a nearby church with "Best Buddies," where Yale students served as friends and counselors to a group of the mentally retarded from the local community. Suzanne had been working hard, indeed almost feverishly, on the last draft of her political science senior essay, a major requirement for graduation from Yale. She had told friends that she would be working late that night on her paper, a study of the Al Qaeda terrorist Osama bin Laden. How, in just a few short minutes, could she have gotten two miles away and been savagely murdered?

The newspapers reported the Jovin murder together with the murder of Nancy McCloskey, who was identified in reports as a prostitute. Two women were murdered in New Haven within days of each other, the stories related, but only the Yale case was getting extensive attention. The suggestion was that the death of an elite young woman was significant, while the death of a troubled prostitute was considered routine, as if one life was worth more than the other. Such language disturbed me to no end. Was it me? I had to consider that possibility because I was so frequently out of step with my peers, even on the reading of newspapers. The formulation just seemed so insulting to both women. Political correctness extending beyond death? It got under my skin.

The weather continued to be unseasonably warm on Sunday, December 6, 1998. I was too unsettled about the murder of Suzanne Jovin to concentrate, but when I left my office I was inspired to plant tulips for Suzanne. Surely by the time they bloomed, the case would be solved. When Charlie and I bought our New Haven home, we inherited a beautiful arbor. But I worked all the time, and for years it sat there neglected. With all the teaching, writing, and meetings at Yale, there never seemed to be an afternoon to give over to gardening. Suddenly all of that had changed. Back at home, I weeded furiously, digging up all four boxes. I ignored the crawly things and wondered idly which sides of the bulbs were suppose to face up as I threw them into the ground. I was sure it would work out. I'm never quite sure of the turkey, either, but Thanksgiving never fails. And it did work, at least in the sense that all the tulips started coming up in April 1999. I found little comfort elsewhere, given the fact that the Jovin case was showing no signs of being solved. I clung to my superstition nonetheless, rousing myself into something of a frenzy waiting for the moment each tulip would bloom. Apparently I wasn't alone. Day after day, a flower would reach its moment of glory, and a squirrel would bite its head off. Now it's an annual thing I go through, although I keep trying to change the outcome. I've planted daffodils for purely tactical reasons, spread mothballs and soap, and sprayed red hot pepper on the plants. The ending is the same. Some demonic force carries on, and the ravaged scene reappears. "How is this possible?" my friend, and closest colleague, María Menocal wanted to know. "I mean, physically, how is it possible for them to look so hideous?" Clearly I hadn't been exaggerating. Not twenty yards away were my neighbor's perfect tulip rows, all colors and varieties, all intact and stunningly beautiful.

We were kept involved with the Suzanne Jovin murder case for weeks and months afterward because Charlie had been teaching a course in which Suzanne was enrolled at the time she was murdered.

Many of his students, who had known and loved Suzanne, shared with him their memories and stories of her as well as their speculations about her murder. With his characteristic meticulousness, Charlie kept close, contemporaneous notes of every student version that he heard. His notebooks accumulated over the months, containing certain themes and stories that seemed to form a powerful circumstantial theory of the case. But it was all circumstantial, for neither Charlie nor any of the students who came to talk to him had any direct knowledge or hard evidence that might have been reliable in a murder trial. A few weeks after the murder of Suzanne the situation grew rather bizarre when an assistant professor barged into Charlie's Yale office to declare that he knew who the murderer was: a senior Yale professor of national, indeed international, reputation and one of our best friends. The accuser was obviously and tragically unbalanced, but many more months would pass before he would stop making these allegations. Everywhere were stories, some serious and heartfelt, some imagined and baseless, that would not or should not be allowed to take hold as guideposts to the truth.

Charlie gave me an early Christmas present that year: my own Smith and Wesson .45 Colt. For a period of a couple of days, New Haven had felt like a very dangerous place.

Voir Dire

Three years later, I was reliving all of these memories as I sat in voir dire. *Voir dire* is a "low French" term for the session during which prospective jurors are questioned by the opposing attorneys to determine who would be chosen and who dismissed. Judge Fracasse introduced the prosecutor, Michael Dearington, and the defense attorney, William Bloss, of Jacobs, Grudberg, Belt, and Dow. I had some knowledge not only of this crime but also of the lawyers. I even knew the intern, Chimène, who worked for Michael Dearington, though I didn't put this together until later. She had attended my rhetoric seminar once or twice the previous year, as the girlfriend of one my enrolled students. The case transformed her and made her think about becoming a prosecutor. Perhaps it's not obvious to people outside Yale Law School that her internship with the state's attorney was not a plum

assignment. (Prosecution is practically like the CIA in those parts, politically unpopular.) But Chimène was Canadian and last in line in
terms of being assigned an internship, so the prosecutor's office it
was. Lucky for her! Now she understands the draw of the work. "You
have no idea," she said to me in the aftermath. "You have no idea
what it's like to get to know the family, to sit with them day after day."
She shook her head and didn't say any more. But I had the idea.
Charlie and I had sat with the Jovins, too, in distant Connecticut
towns, in California, when they couldn't bear to step foot in the city of
New Haven. Chimène meant that recovery for the parents, for the
siblings, for the children of a murder victim was not an option.

The names of witnesses who might take the stand were read by the
judge as the events in the courtroom proceeded, and we were asked if
any of the names were familiar. These results were tabulated for our
individual voir dire. We were returned to our small rooms by the elevator as the individual roll call began. According to the original list of
jurors, I was due to be among the very last to be questioned. Each
juror was interrogated for up to forty minutes, so it looked as if my
one-day jury service was going to last a full day after all. When we got
close to 12:30 and the next prospective juror was brought before the
court, the judge dismissed the rest of us for lunch and ordered us to
return by 2:00. I considered my original evaluation of the judge now
to be fully vindicated. It would have been one of those enraging but
perfectly predictable features of the court to have kept us all until the
stipulated time of release, at one o'clock, for no purpose whatsoever.
But we were in good hands. Before leaving, we were reminded to
wear our juror buttons and to maintain a strict code of silence about
the case.

Across the street with a glass of wine in my hands, I was anything
but silent. To whomever would listen, I predicted that there was not a
chance in a million that I would be selected as a juror. Not only was I
a Yale professor (and everyone knows that lawyers sought the ideal
"dull normal," as Charlie's mother used to say), but I knew an awful
lot about this case. Deep down, though, I must confess that I felt a little bad about the prospect of not being chosen, as if it were personal.

The state's attorney for the McCloskey case was the same Dearington whose name had been all over the *New Haven Register* just a week

earlier, when it was revealed (inexplicably, three years later) that male DNA had been found under the fingernails of Suzanne Jovin and that it did not match that of James Van de Velde, the only named suspect in the case. My husband had just been summoned, too, to see if his DNA matched the sample. Van de Velde's counsel was David Grudberg, a colleague of the defense attorney for the McCloskey case, William Bloss. New Haven was a smaller town than I had ever reckoned.

Even as I was predicting confidently to my lunch companions at the Whitney that my jury service would be over within the space of a few hours, I was aware of conflicting signals. I happened to be seated next to Ed Kamens, a professor of East Asian language and literature, who related that he had been the jury foreman for a murder trial the previous summer. That trial lasted three weeks. Here was that fateful quality of the day emerging again. With a far-off look, Kamens added that he still had not put the event behind him.

A Yale professor selected for jury duty? It happens routinely. The things that everybody thought would get you off jury duty most certainly did not. Weeks later, when I compared notes with other people about voir dire, I found that their experiences matched my own. It did not seem to matter so much for jury selection what your job was, provided that you could afford to interrupt your schedule for a week or so. It did not seem to matter so much what you knew about the case, either, or whether you had heard of the lawyers. What mattered was how you answered the follow-up question: would your knowledge prevent you from being impartial in the case at hand? (My lawyer friends demur and assure me that both lawyers ignore the answers.) So when State's Attorney Dearington asked me during voir dire whether there was anything the court should know that might disqualify me from sitting on this jury, my response that I was very close to the Jovin case did not deter him. I added that I remembered the McCloskey murder, that she had been identified in the papers as a prostitute, and that there were drugs involved.

Dearington was unmoved: "Are your feelings about the Jovin case, or how my office handled the case, so strong that they would prevent you from being impartial in the case at hand?" I answered hotly that my feelings about the Jovin case could not be stronger—but he was still waiting. I finished: "But no, that case would not affect my ability to judge fairly in this one." Later, I surmised that Dearington had already decided to accept me as a juror based on how I answered his very first question. "Shall I call you Professor Thompson? Dr.? Mrs.?" I opted for the only one that he did not offer and that was not actually true: "Miss Thompson is fine." This self-abnegation was not rehearsed but acquired through long Catholic training. Possibly Dearington had me pegged.

The next group of questions revealed the contours of the McCloskey case. Would I be able to convict in a case that had no physical evidence but was constituted by circumstantial evidence alone? Would I be able to view graphic photographs of the murder victim? Could I listen to testimony by incarcerated witnesses and consider it potentially credible? Could I bring objective scrutiny to testimony by police officers? My answers were affirmative all the way through. They asked about my relations who are lawyers. We started with my sister Kathy, then a senior research specialist at the American Bar Association Legal Technology Resource Center. That passed. Next I recounted that Charlie also has a JD but had worked only briefly in law. He was in the foreign service for more than twenty years and now taught at Yale. What kind of law did he once practice and why did he stop? Dearington asked. "He was a public defender," I answered, not attending to my own words. "And he told me that he had to give it up because he was too good at helping people who were guilty get away with . . . ." I stopped myself from saying the word *murder* as I became conscious of my surroundings. I glanced up at the accused, who suddenly looked very big, very black, very menacing. "With . . . crime," I finished awkwardly. Yes, that was it, he was too good at helping guilty people get away with crime. Oh, Charlie is going to love this, I thought to myself. Dearington suppressed his amusement. "That will be all, Miss Thompson."

The defense attorney cocked his head, smiling, and said that he had to ask me about what I had just said. "Would your husband's experience affect how you view this case?" I answered quickly: "No, that story says more about my husband than it does about me." On second thought, it says a lot about me that I was practically finished telling the story before I recognized my own bluntness. Furthermore, I may well have missed my chance for a principled dismissal. I didn't think to say that quite apart from Charlie's experience, I was predisposed to agree completely with his sentiment. I did believe that any decent lawyer could enable the guilty to get away with murder, in just about any case based solely on circumstantial evidence.

I might have been let go, if I had managed to articulate my strong belief that advances in modern science have led to impairment in the ability of the general public to make judgments. No one could argue with the gains accrued to the wrongly accused, of course, when scientific testing vindicated their claims to innocence. But I continue to believe that breakthroughs in DNA testing and forensic science offer such attractive visions of certainty that Americans are becoming increasingly incapable of believing any evidence that does not approach that standard. Television shows such as *Forensic Files* and *Cold Case Files* just exacerbate these perceptions because, in those worlds, murders are always solved conclusively and unequivocally by the scientific analysis of a fiber, a bloodstain, or a drop of fluid.

Scientific analysis is one thing, scientism is another. My abhorrence of rational choice methodology in my academic life had emerged from my conviction that a preoccupation with quantifiable evidence could interfere with proper human understanding. Once I had naively believed that those in the Department of Political Science would be interested in politics. I was baffled when events such as the controversial presidential election, the terrorist attacks of September 11, and the Iraq War were met largely with silence. It's the rigor thing, I'm pretty sure. The ground was much more secure over in the Department of Economics where they had formal models of human behavior to debate.[2] Actual human motivations are a little harder to be sure about. Where was the payoff?

Even more distressing in this regard was my experience in the Jovin

2. Just about all humanities and social sciences departments separate into "hard" and "soft" factions. Law schools are no exception. In retrospect, a jury seems to offer the perfect case study for testing the relative capacities and insights of humanistic versus quantitatively inclined inquiries. I thought of this while I was reading a law review article in which the author attempted to measure reasonable doubt and complained about "continuing judicial hostility to attempts to quantify the reasonable doubt standard" (Erik Lillquist, "Recasting Reasonable Doubt: Decision Theory and the Virtues of Variability," 186). We humanists agree that precision is desirable. But we disagree with rational-choice theorists, it seems, on when it is possible.

murder case when, for perfectly good reasons, questions about motive were brushed aside by detectives as irrelevant. Strange to say, Charlie and I and my colleague David Cameron were spending a lot of time with the Yale University police at the beginning of 1999. Just a few steps away from the political science department, the Yale police were a world away from its workings. One morning I attempted to explain the complicated tenure system to Lieutenant Kozak. "There is a ten-year 'ladder,' for me, for example, but it doesn't necessarily go anywhere. It's climb, climb, climb, most likely, to nothing but air." Russ Kozak couldn't believe what I was telling him. "Do you mean to tell me that the university hires people to teach here for ten years and then lets them go? After ten years of service, just lets them go? That's it, good-bye? Nothing more?" His innocence was charming. "It's a hundred times worse," I answered, "for those who have to get by with year-by-year reappointments." The Yale police seemed to appreciate the inside dope ("here comes Nick and Nora Charles"), but they didn't necessarily want to hear all of our accounts of real or purported events. "Aw Jeez, why'd ya hafta tell me that?" was a line put to us more than once.

In voir dire, then, I inadvertently missed my exit line. But I suppose that if I had somehow managed to convey my predilections to the court, Bloss would have come back with: "And are your feelings so strong that they would prevent you from being impartial in the case at hand?" To that I would have had to say no, every case stands alone. As it was, Bloss was satisfied with my answers, and now I was positive, positive that for whatever reasons both of these lawyers wanted me as a juror. Bloss returned to the Jovin case, and I was full of dread. I had taken an oath to tell the truth, and now I was going to have to tell him what my opinions were about Van de Velde. "I'm not going to ask you what your opinions are about Van de Velde," he began. I sank back in a total sweat. Bloss could not know the state of anxiety of this Catholic girl—wholly absorbed by the Jovin murder, knowledgeable about its particulars, opinionated to the extreme—and still under oath. That Irish Catholicism imperils me still: I'm always ready to confess to everything. (Any un-Christian fierceness probably comes from the Abenake side of the bloodline. "An unusually vicious tribe," according to Charlie. "Not to be trifled with.") The rest of the questioning passed uneventfully. The judge asked me to wait in the small room adjoining the court while the lawyers conferred. The knock came, and I was ushered back into the courtroom to receive my further instructions.

Before I was selected as Juror #10, the judge asked me if it would be a terrible inconvenience to sit on a jury for a trial that was scheduled to begin the following Thursday and expected to last five days. This requirement turned out to be the other necessary qualification for becoming a juror in New Haven, aside from the stated ability to be impartial. Could you spare the time? Was your occupation of a suitably nonessential nature? On this score, professors were excellent candidates. If the proposed schedule held, the bulk of the trial would take place during Yale's Thanksgiving vacation. By chance, I was not hosting my extended family for the feast, just Katie, my stepdaughter, and she was the world's easiest guest. She liked eating out as much as I did and always entertained me with her searing psychological observations of my colleagues. It was conceivable that I could finish my jury service without missing a single seminar. The prospect of sacrificing my vacation did not bother me in the least. After all, my penchant for "law and order" was never far below the surface, and, at some level, I always have harbored the desire to be a detective. I like to think that I make a quick study of people (I like to *think* it, despite overwhelming evidence to the contrary). Given that my early reading was in *Encyclopedia Brown,* as in *Encyclopedia Brown Takes the Case,* stories in which a boy detective finds the clues, gets his man, and always solves the case, I considered the possibility that jury duty might even be *fun.* "No," I answered. "It would be no inconvenience at all."

When we assembled as a group for the first time on November 15, I turned my powers of detection toward my fellow jurors. I recognized only one person from my one-day service: Jen, the woman with the cell phone. With embarrassment, I recalled my brusque stare. No more unfriendly gestures, I vowed inwardly; this case was going to require a unanimous decision. Still, I was sure I wouldn't like her, with or without her cell phone, because she seemed to like to hear herself talk. This supposition turned out to be completely mistaken. Later, she told me that she had just closed on a multimillion dollar deal at work, so it was a bit stressful to be out of the office. She did land surveying. "What," I asked, "like Thoreau?" She wasn't sure about that. But in the jury room, she was thoughtful, measured, and more reticent than I. When we were finally dismissed three weeks later, we parted in tears, with hugs, and full of mutual respect. Strike one for the quick study.

I didn't recognize any of the other jurors, but with roll call I heard a name that was very familiar to me: John Faragher. I had never met Johnny Mack Faragher, a distinguished member of Yale's history department, but already I had decided his name was pretty cool. There was the cowboy part of it and the adult refusal to leave behind the diminutive ending. (My brothers used to be "Johnny"—or more accurately, in Rhode Island-speak, "Jawnie"—and "Billy," respectively, but at a certain point the family was informed that it was trouble for anyone who said anything but "John" or "Bill." I preferred the youthful condition—and was suitably pleased when Charlie renamed me "Nori" some time in my thirties.) And I knew that Johnny Mack was friends with my old friend Skip Stout and that my friend María also knew and respected him highly. That was plenty; if this were the same man, I was prepared to like him. Here was another test for my powers of observation. I would figure this one out for myself, without asking. The strapping figure who responded to the name looked like no academic I had ever met; he was large and imposing, beardless, had a booming laugh (not that there would be much occasion to hear it), and carried neither book nor backpack. This guy works for the phone company, I decided. Strike two; it turned out that it was Yale's Johnny Faragher after all. In fairness to myself I should note that before we had reached our first holding pen, Johnny did pull out a book, a tome of some one thousand pages—highly incriminating evidence, if only it had appeared sooner. Time would reveal why Johnny was no ordinary academic. Anyway, within a few moments it was clear that there were two of us on this jury.

Actually, there were four. Soon enough I overheard Yale talk from two other men who did fit the academic bill more precisely: salt-and-pepper beard, medium-to-slight build, confident demeanor, full backpack. David Pease had recently retired from Yale after serving as dean of the art school. An amiable man, David would work tirelessly for group harmony. We struck up conversations easily and shared war stories about our respective departments during the frequent breaks in the trial. Therefore, I assumed, I could trust his judgment. Wrong again! The fourth professor from Yale was Gene Burbank, our only scientist.[3] That made four Yale professors recruited to seek justice beyond a reasonable doubt. Little did I know what kind of justice we might find and what kind might elude us.

3. Gene Burbank is a pseudonym. I have changed the names of all dissenting jurors.

II

The Trial

But when events draw near, or are,
our minds are useless.

DANTE, *Inferno X*

The State of Connecticut v. Bazier

On the opening day of the Bazier trial, the jury was led to the small room adjoining the courtroom to await Judge Fracasse. The marshal would refer to this as the coffee break room, an odd name for this cramped space with no coffee and no heat, where the clock was stuck at 12:04. On sight, I decided that this could not possibly be the deliberation room. It was far too small for us and we shifted uncomfortably around the center table, which seated eight at most. Only after five days of retiring to this room did I admit to myself that it had to be the deliberation room. It was designed for the six-member juries that are the rule in Connecticut for all but capital cases. The saving grace was the window, which offered a splendid view of the city and the university. True, the window could not be opened, but one understood without asking the reason for that. There were two bathrooms, one for men and one for women, connected to the deliberation room. We fastidiously held to the gender distinctions, though, in point of fact, neither room offered much privacy.

Only one juror, Fred the tire salesman (in a way he even resembled the Michelin Man), routinely took a seat at the table, as he rustled through newspapers.[1] They seemed to be old classified and automobile and comic sections of the *New Haven Register* and the *Hartford Courant*. Fred worried me because he appeared morose and antisocial. He never spoke. I kept thinking that we would need everybody's input during the deliberation process. Like most of the jurors, I had brought my own reading for our numerous breaks, and my book of choice—Dante's *Inferno*—raised a few eyebrows. But there would be no reading because we had Kristen. Kristen was an alternate juror, a fact that provided some consolation during her nonstop commentary—about the room, about last night's TV, about TV shows missed during the trial, about her meals, past and future. She was like elevator Muzak, except more intrusive, because she demanded some human response. Soon she began baking for us: cookies, fudge, cake. What is your favorite icing? Do you like Rocky Mountain squares? Should we exchange numbers, and stay in touch? The room was getting smaller. A sharper contrast between chatty Kristen and silent Fred could not be imagined. I changed my mind about Fred and began to grow fond of him. Dante's rings of hell had nothing on our own; it was 12:04, and Kristen was holding court. Take care of yourself, some of the real jurors started urging each other. It was imperative that this jury stay healthy. When Kristen was dismissed, she left a quarter and her phone number. The foreman preserves both to this day.

In the courtroom, the judge instructed us that during the course of the trial, we were not to talk to anyone about the case or about anyone who had anything to do with the case. We were not to let anyone talk to us about the case or about anyone who had anything to do with it. If there was any media coverage of the case, we were not to read, watch, or listen to it. This strangely soothing refrain would be repeated four or five times a day during the trial and deliberation. We were told that it was our duty to decide if the defendant, who had pleaded not guilty, was guilty or not guilty. When we reached a decision, we would say so by our foreperson and say no more. Foreperson? I

1. Fred is a pseudonym. I have changed the names of all dissenting jurors.

winced. The judgeperson continued. We were enjoined kindly to attend to the evidence. Little did we know what a struggle that would
be. But then came the real kicker: the judge admonished us not to
come to any conclusions about the case, even in the privacy of our
own minds, until deliberation began. How's that again? We were to
pay full attention during the trial, to listen intently to all testimony,
but we were to refrain from forming any opinions about the case until
we began deliberating? That was a fascinating injunction, underlining
as it did the peculiar language of the courtroom. Many of the intricacies
of forensic rhetoric are familiar to those who watch television shows
and films—what is admissible, what is leading, what is hearsay—but
from the jury box, the rhetorical situation appeared newly complex.
The judge was telling us in an exaggerated way that the intellectual
exercises of trial and deliberation are separable. The former is silent,
brooding, and inconclusive; the latter is interactive, a little combative,
and judgmental. For a juror, trial thinking must involve a more tentative mode of judging because a juror must be cautious about making
judgments before a trial is finished. But the propensity to judge what
we had heard in the courtroom was present throughout the trial. As
human beings, we naturally try to make sense of anything we hear or
observe. What was immediately captivating was how much more was
expressed by witnesses than their bare verbal responses might seem
to indicate in an exact transcript.[2]

In the state of Connecticut, the jurors' attempts to make sense of
the facts are not aided by the shaping device of an opening statement
by the lawyers. This omission is odd, inexplicable really, as if we were
intended to experience the disorientation of the first pages of a
Faulkner novel. I have grown to love Faulkner's style of writing, but I
still find this situation a little bizarre. Facts and testimony came tum-
bling out without us having the means to understand their place in
the whole narrative. It would have been an entirely different experience—less modernist—if we had had the benefit of hearing the antic-

2. Milner S. Ball likens a trial to a theatrical performance, and he cites Mar-
garet Spillane's argument that the theater "reminds people of a literacy that entertainment technologists have made them forget—the ability to read stories
directly off the living bodies of other human beings" (Ball, "All the Law's a
Stage," 217).

ipated plots. As one jury expert wrote, "It is hard to emphasize the importance of the availability of what might be called 'free narrative' in the opening statement for the American trial; it is essential for an understanding of what American law is . . . [it] freely invites the jury to use the full range of its powers of inquiry in deciding what the event under consideration was . . . [and] it keeps the trial, and so the law, in intimate touch with the full range of moral evaluation."[3] The convention of not having an opening statement seems to put an undue burden on the prosecutor, who is not permitted to get the story line out before the attacks and the deflections from the defense commence. The juror, like the reader of a modernist novel, must struggle toward narrative coherence alone, adrift in the sea of facts requiring interpretation.

The Prosecution

Just the same, the testimony was riveting from the start. The first witness called was Jocelyn McCloskey, the nineteen-year-old daughter of the murder victim, Nancy McCloskey. She was sixteen when her mother was killed. Jocelyn came into the courtroom wearing skintight jeans and looking like a typical teenager, if not exactly like a Yale freshman, not streetwise either. Did she read the same newspaper articles I did, I wondered, about her mother being a prostitute? I started to doubt my recollection of the case; it *had* been three years ago. Jocelyn reported that at the time of the murder she was living with her mother and her mother's boyfriend, Darryl Allen, at 1579 Chapel Street in New Haven. A gigantic map of the area was placed on an easel so that jurors could follow the route. We were expressly warned not to drive to the area to conduct any private investigating on our own. But I could scarcely avoid the neighborhood because it was just two blocks from Cullman Tennis Courts. Johnny knew the neighborhood well, too, as he had raised his family in a home nearby. Mother's Homestyle Kitchen was there, where New Haven went for goat curry, jerk chicken, and collard greens. We could hardly be expected to refrain from those staples. The familiar became laden with significance.

3. Robert P. Burns, *A Theory of the Trial,* 119–20.

Asked her occupation, Jocelyn replied, "babysitter." After the trial was over, I learned that she had taken up the study of criminal law. Jocelyn recounted that on the night of the murder, she and her mother walked over a few blocks to see Jocelyn's father (Nancy's ex-husband). This was Tuesday, December 1, 1998, at about six o'clock. They returned to their own apartment after a short visit. At that point, Jocelyn's mother reportedly told her that she was going to an AA meeting. Did Jocelyn believe this, I asked myself? She said it without flinching. The prosecutor, Michael Dearington, asked her about her mother's substance abuse problem, but Jocelyn did not seem to understand his question. Her response was chilling. Jocelyn seemed detached, almost incredibly so. Was this the repression required of a victim? She shed no tears on the stand. I thought of my own mother, and I could not understand Jocelyn's behavior, for I remember as a young girl worrying that my mother would die before I grew up. How would I ever be able to endure such a calamity? But Nancy McCloskey's death was beyond words and beyond imagining. I was confounded by Jocelyn's composure and curious about the few family members who showed up in the courtroom day after day. Why didn't Jocelyn return? Later I was told that she couldn't, as a witness. But where was Daryl Allen? Jocelyn was only the first witness, and my conjectures about the plotlines were already spinning. We jurors always wanted to know much more than we were told. The parallel with modernist reading struck me again.

Mr. Dearington showed two pictures to Jocelyn. The first was a Polaroid shot, showing a pretty and perky woman in her early thirties, with dark brown hair. She was full of joy and smiled endearingly at the camera. The second appeared to be a mug shot of an angry and coarse woman in her forties, with a blotchy face and a tough sneer. She had about her the look of drug addiction. Her hair was an unnatural orange brown color, and it was crudely cut. She looked like a prostitute. The photos were passed around to the jurors, who sucked in their breath in turn as the realization hit that the photos represented the same woman: Nancy McCloskey. (Nancy was thirty-eight when she was killed.) Jocelyn was asked to identify the woman in each picture. Indifferently, she did so, seemingly without the shock that registered on our faces. In cross-examination by Mr. Bloss, Jocelyn went through the same exercise. The first picture was her mother. The second picture was her mother, a few years later. She'd changed her hair. Jocelyn's demeanor was unaccountably disturbing. Nancy McCloskey was also fourteen pounds heavier in the later picture. What had happened to this woman in the course of her thirties? The jurors peered quizzically at one another. But we were not permitted to speak to each other about the events of the trial. Every day we had to check ourselves a few more times. Self-restraint became more difficult to preserve.

Next on the stand was Johnnie Washington, the first of five major witnesses. She was in some ways the most off-putting witness because of her impact on jurors. This distinction is not bestowed easily on Washington, considering that in this case the four other main witnesses consisted of a drug user and three men in chains. But Washington really did not want to be in court. Uneducated, she was uncomfortable around the lawyers, and she proved to be putty in the hands of the defense. At one point, Washington let it slip that "to be honest, I just didn't want to get involved." Her most common refrain was "I'm not for sure." Yet, however easily her words could be manipulated or twisted, it was difficult to doubt her sightings or her identification of the accused. She was a woman in her fifties who tended to watch what went on in her neighborhood, peering through her curtains, and she also happened to live in a house at 67 Derby Avenue that was strategically crucial to the murder case. The alley on the left side of her house led to the backyard of 25 Norton Street, the murder scene.

Johnnie Washington reported that she had seen Bazier on three separate occasions, including shortly before the murder. A couple of days before December 1, she was returning home and looked down Derby Avenue, toward the intersection of Derby and Norton. There she said she saw Anthony Bazier. When she saw him hanging out on the corner, she decided against going shopping and went back into her house. She was not asked why. Then on the day of the murder, as she parked her car at about 3:30 in the afternoon, she saw Anthony Bazier and Nancy McCloskey in front of her house, and she had to walk around them to enter her home. At about 8:30 P.M., Washington observed the same two figures from inside her house. She claimed that for about twenty minutes they "cussed each other out." She pointedly did not claim to have seen their faces during this interval, apparently intuiting that they were the same people she had seen earlier in the day (my formulation, not hers). The last time she saw them, they were walking down the alley, toward the backyard of 25 Norton Street.

Washington's testimony was crucial for placing the accused in the neighborhood—presumably with some nefarious purpose—and for placing him at the scene with the victim. But her ability to describe what she had seen was poor, and the defense attorney exploited her weaknesses. Her discomfort was palpable. She appeared to be unable to distinguish between left and right; she could not estimate distance in feet; and she referred to the height of Nancy McCloskey's hair. Her description of what Bazier and McCloskey were wearing that night was imprecise, and, as it turned out, it differed from the descriptions given by the other witnesses. Bloss was able to provoke her to affirm statements that were so feeble that they, in effect, canceled out her identification. For instance, she was made to agree that her identification of Bazier was based on his clothing, even though she could recall nothing about what he was wearing on the night of the murder. Doubtless, she had never given much thought to how one human being identifies another, and doubtless, she wanted to say whatever would get her off the stand as quickly as possible. But Bloss was negotiating a fine line, since his verbal maneuvers that left Washington baffled also left jurors wondering whether they were supposed to conclude that her credibility was impaired simply because she wasn't well educated and couldn't speak well. Her testimony was painful to observe, though, there were moments of humor. One of the defense attorney's favorite expressions was "Fair to say?" as in: "Fair to say you only got a quick look?" But the expression only served him if he wanted an affirmative answer. "And so there was no particular reason for you to be paying attention to these two people on this particular day; fair to say?" As always, Washington simply answered, "No, sir." To receive the dutiful "yes," Bloss had to backtrack. "Is, Is what I said fair?" he asked.

When Johnnie Washington was shown the two photographs of Nancy McCloskey, she identified the attractive woman in the Polaroid as the woman she had seen arguing with Bazier. She claimed never to have seen the "other" woman. Mr. Bloss made much of the fact that Washington swore with full certainty that she had never seen the haggard woman in the mug shot. The mug shot of McCloskey, in fact, had been taken just two months before her death. But it was hardly surprising that Washington failed to associate the two pictures with the same woman. Indeed, the jury's reaction to the autopsy pictures of Nancy McCloskey seemed to vindicate Washington's observations about the Polaroid and the mug shot. Horrible as these autopsy photographs were, the woman in them resembled the Nancy of the Polaroid more than she did the woman in the mug shot. To me, the fact that Washington clung to her identification of the first picture only strengthened her credibility. An unflattering photograph is not so out of the ordinary, after all. But other jurors apparently accepted this discrepancy as the first of many indicators of the inherent unreliability of photo identifications.

Washington had picked out a photograph of Bazier on two separate occasions. The first photo array had been shown to her by Detective Adger in December 1998. The second array (with a different photograph of Bazier) had been shown to her by Detective Roberts in February 1999. On both occasions, she also identified another man, Darryl Belton, as looking similar to the man she had seen on the night of the murder. (It was stipulated later that Belton had been imprisoned at the time of the murder.) She picked Bazier out again at the probable cause hearing, and she identified him in the courtroom as well.

Before the other main witnesses were brought forward, Officer Tim Veno from the New Haven Police Department took the stand to describe his role at the scene of the murder. He was the patrol officer who had been flagged down by two black men in the vicinity of 25 Norton Street. According to Officer Veno, one of the men, Charles Randall, reported that he had heard suspicious sounds behind a nearby house. Veno recalled him mentioning "the rustling of leaves" and the noise "of somebody either jumping over a wooden fence or running into a fence, and did I know what that sounded like." But this account sounded feeble and perplexing. Do people really flag down the police because they hear the rustling of leaves? Early in the trial, we jurors were disposed to give to the police the benefit of the doubt.[4] I recalled a question that I was asked during voir dire: would you automatically believe the account of a police officer? "No," I had answered, "not automatically." I'm sorry to say that after the trial, I would think twice before accepting point-blank a police officer's account of an event, at least in New Haven.

Veno described how he followed Randall behind the house at 25 Norton Street, and he testified that in the backyard, he found a woman on the ground with a very weak pulse. She was almost unconscious or completely unconscious, and she had injuries on her face. He called for backup and an ambulance, and he told Randall to stay put. Dearington displayed an oversized photograph of the backyard, and he asked Veno about the numbered yellow stanchions that were visible throughout. The stanchions noted points of interest or where evidence was located. Dearington pointed out the air-conditioning unit. The air-conditioning unit was one of those elements in the story that seemed to float around aimlessly. I kept trying to find a place for it. Did Bazier push McCloskey against it, causing an injury? Was she thrown out of the second-story window, on top of it? Bloss worked effectively to keep these floating elements forever airborne. They made us doubt our reconstruction of the event.

When police backup arrived, Randall was held for questioning. Defense Attorney Bloss asked Veno whether Randall had said anything to him about seeing a man run out of the backyard of 25 Norton Street and then run north. "No." And do you remember if there was an open window on the second floor of the abandoned house above where you found the body? If you remember. "I do." These were seasoned answers: no elaboration, no narrative. Bloss asked Veno if he noticed any blood on Randall's shoes. "No." We subsequently heard that Randall's boots were confiscated, and that one drop of blood was found on them. Bloss asked whether Randall's clothing had been seized.

---

4. It was difficult to warm up to any of the police officers who took the stand. I've concluded that this was because they were trained witnesses, who only answered one step at a time in terms that remained with the immediately perceptible. These were the legal constraints that they had all learned by heart, no doubt the hard way in some cases. "A witness's testimony, with narrow exceptions, must be the report, under oath, of an event that the witness once saw, touched, tasted, felt, or heard and now remembers" (Burns, *Theory of the Trial,* 86).

"Yes." Had the clothing been sent to the forensic lab run by the world-famous Dr. Lee? "No." Not incidentally, Mr. Bloss mentioned Dr. Lee a lot. (This was the same Dr. Lee famously *not* summoned by the New Haven Police to the scene of Suzanne Jovin's murder, until several months had passed.) But really, the world-famous Dr. Lee probably had better things to do than examine Randall's shoes. Remember the old joke about looking for the lost wallet under the streetlight, because the light was better there? The man who flagged down the cop was not everyone's idea of the most likely suspect. We jurors were still struggling to put together a coherent series of events using the narrative offered by the prosecution, but the defense was always seeking to undercut that coherence. Bloss wasn't doing half bad. I wondered how many other jurors saw the defense as trying to interfere with their understanding of the case. (Much later, another juror, Russ, wrote to me that he thought the defense attorney was "very effective" at placing doubt everywhere, although "anyone with common sense could have realized that he had nothing.") I enjoyed the game, but the insinuation seemed preposterous: Randall's action was hardly one to expect of a murderer. In any case, it was soon revealed that Randall was questioned for four hours that night ("they did the good cop, bad cop thing"). Later I discovered that Randall had a relative on the New Haven Police force, and Bloss had been suggesting that for this reason, Randall had been let off the hook as a suspect. But why he should have been a serious suspect in the first place was not clear.

The contours of the story became clearer with the testimony of Miguel Cruz. He testified to being an appliance installer now living in New Jersey. For our purposes, he was the drug addict. He acknowledged as much. I recalled another question from voir dire: would you automatically dismiss the testimony of someone who admitted to taking drugs? I had said "no," and here was the test. (Character matters, as Aristotle teaches us in *Rhetoric,* but it is not the *only* thing that matters. There were those interesting qualifications in the *Nicomachean Ethics:* an addiction reveals weakness, not evil. I liked Cruz, drugs and all. He seemed decent, if a little battered by the world.) Cruz confirmed that he had driven to the neighborhood around Norton Street and Derby Avenue to buy crack cocaine from his dealer, Randall. On the night of December 1, 1998, Cruz parked his car across the street from the Jamaican restaurant "Mother's Kitchen" and signaled to Randall that he wanted to purchase two bags. Randall would testify to selling him six. According to Cruz, as he was standing in front of 25 Norton Street, waiting for the cocaine, suddenly the accused, Anthony Bazier, ran out from behind the left side of the house as Randall ran out from behind the right. The three of them ended up on the sidewalk in the same place at the same moment. Randall's words "to the gentleman," Cruz testified, were "what the fuck were you doing back there?" Cruz continued, "the gentleman said, 'Chill, chill, just handling my business.'" Dearington repeated the expression "just handling my business?" Cruz replied, "Right. At that time I was looking at him, he was jumping up and down, fixing his pants, and putting his jacket over his pants, and zippering his pants, and fixing his belt. He was like, 'Chill, chill. I'm handling my business. I'm cool. I'm cool. I'm cousin to Mother's Kitchen.' That's basically what I heard him say."

Cruz did not mention any physical contact between Bazier and Randall, but he did mention that Bazier was much bigger than Randall. At this point, Cruz was not really sure of what was going on (a fitting appraisal of the jurors' situation as well), but he suspected that he was being set up. Cruz was asked to describe what the accused was wearing that night. He testified that Bazier was wearing a black Starter coat with the words *White Sox* printed on it and baggy slacks that looked like corduroys. "It's hard to describe the color," Cruz added, "'cause I never seen no pants like that before in a long time, like early eighties, late eighties-style pants." Cruz opined that the state of fashion in Connecticut lagged several years behind the state of fashion in New Jersey. He let out a long whistle. "They were cords, kind of mustard color [later he changed it to "diarrhea"], with all different colors, yellow, white, brown, a pattern." Salvation Army, I guessed, recalling the hideous clothing my sisters and I donated in the late 1970s.

Cruz described Bazier as wearing a black hat "with a half stop sign" on it, which was "the only stylish thing he was wearing." This detail puzzled me until the following weekend. About halfway through the Yale-Harvard football game, I gazed out on the crowd and above the sea of hats. It was then that I realized that it was not a literal stop sign that he meant, as I had imagined, but an octagon. The hat that Bazier wore that night was a common ski hat—still stylish among the Ivies in November 2001. But this was Connecticut.

A man named Octible Jones arrived on this scene. I assumed (rightly) that Jones was the man who had been with Randall when he flagged Officer Veno down and who had immediately fled the scene. He would appear as a witness for the defense. According to Cruz, Randall told "his boy" (Jones) to "hold" Bazier while he himself returned to the back of the house. Randall was worried about one thing, his drug stash, and on his way to check his supply, he found Nancy McCloskey in the backyard, "all fucked up," as he put it. He ran back to the street, only to discover that Bazier had sprinted up Norton Street and taken a right onto Chapel Street, out of sight. Cruz ended his account of the murder scene here. He was asked if he had been afraid for his own safety. "No," he replied, "these guys aren't violent. They just try to mess with your head and get you confused, until you leave." Cruz was confused about what was happening, and he left. The next morning, when he heard on the radio that a woman had been killed behind 25 Norton Street, Cruz called his wife to ask her what to do. "She said I had to go to the police." Cruz looked directly at the jury and said, "I had to. I have a daughter." A classic ethical appeal, possibly coached but very convincing.

The police showed Cruz a photographic array, the standard eight-pack. Bazier was not in the first set of photos, but Cruz did identify someone that he knew: Randall. In the second series of eight, he identified Bazier without hesitation as the man who had run out from the left side of 25 Norton Street and who had then sprinted away. Dearington asked Cruz to describe the facial hair of the man he had identified. "It wasn't well kept, like when you don't comb your hair for a while, it gets peazies, all in circles, knots. It's like that." Cruz had an eye for detail and the vocabulary to match it, an especially engaging trait when (the straight man) Bloss attempted to rein in his descriptions.

Cruz remembered some time later that he had encountered Bazier before the night of December 1, 1998. He testified that in the middle of the night, it came to him that Bazier had sold him two "beat bags." Beat bags clearly referred to bogus drugs, for Cruz was claiming that Bazier had cheated him in the past, but this was another new term for me. (This mention of Bazier and drugs was the first one in the trial, and it confirmed my recollection of the case. Bazier and McCloskey were apparently doing drugs when something went awry.) I wondered if this information strengthened the force of Cruz's identification, or not. I concluded that it did. Cruz did not recognize Bazier when he saw him at the murder scene, but he remembered later that he had met him before. I thought about other instances in which the reliability of memory has been called into question. Adult memories of being abused as a child are like that, and God knows that the reliability of memory has been a factor in those cases. But people sometimes went way too far in the other direction, too, toward total disbelief. And even for Cruz, this wasn't a traumatic memory, just an annoying one.

Cruz told the jury that shortly after the murder, before Bazier was arrested, he made what turned out to be a false sighting of Bazier. Cruz was returning home from work on the day that he had gone to the police with his information. As he drove on Chapel near Day Street, he glanced in the direction of a small park, and he thought he saw Bazier. Alarmed, Cruz drove a few blocks to St. Raphael's Hospital, where he notified a police officer. They returned to the park and began to approach the man Cruz had seen. Cruz reported that when they got close enough to hear the man speak, he concluded that he had been mistaken. He saw his teeth, heard his voice, and then wheeled around, saying "that ain't him."

In his cross-examination, Bloss insinuated that Cruz might have a memory problem: "You're certain about all of your testimony here this afternoon, sir?" (Later, Bloss would specifically ask Cruz whether crack cocaine had an impact on his memory. "No," Cruz replied. But Bloss continued this line of questioning. "You just don't remember how many times you bought crack cocaine?" Bloss asked. "No," Cruz responded, "I was never counting.") Bloss concentrated on the physical description Cruz had given of Bazier. Had Cruz told Dearington that the accused was "way taller" than him? Cruz is five feet nine. "You're certain he wasn't 5'10"?" Bloss asked. "I didn't have a measuring stick at that time," Cruz replied, "so I don't know." Cruz had estimated Bazier's weight between 180 and 240 pounds. Bloss provoked him here, too. "I didn't put him on a scale, so I don't know." In the courtroom in 2001, Cruz revised his estimate upward. "He's doin' just fine," Cruz commented, looking at Bazier with contempt. This kind of visceral body language had its effect, for Cruz seemed to shudder when he looked at the defendant.

Cruz could not know how his account of what Bazier was wearing on the night of the murder would differ so dramatically from that of other witnesses. He could not know, in other words, how his testimony was already taking place on more than one level. This kind of awareness heightened jurors' interest and attention. Then Bloss questioned Cruz about the false sighting of Bazier in great detail, to Cruz's visible exasperation. A slight discrepancy emerged between Cruz's account of the false sighting and the police officer's account of the event, regarding how certain Cruz had been in the park. Was it "It ain't him," or was it something more like "I don't think it's him?" This point was belabored to an astonishing length and tended to increase jurors' sympathy for Cruz (needless to say, I am speaking only for the majority here). Bloss insinuated that the police had been negligent, again, in not treating the man in the park, whose name was Chapman, as a suspect. Furthermore, it would turn out that Chapman had a cut on his hand. (Bloss would ask the police if he was interrogated. "No." Were his clothes confiscated? "No." Were his shoes checked for blood? "No." Where was Dr. Lee?) Cruz's park sighting indicated that he was agitated about being a witness, but there didn't seem to be a point in dwelling on the false sighting. But the questioning continued. Suddenly, Cruz spoke very slowly, "What I *do* know is that the man in the park was *not* the guy on Norton Street." He turned to look at the defendant and said that "*that* was the guy *right there.*" This was one of those instances that couldn't be translated effectively into the transcript. To Russ, Cruz's exasperated assertion was one of the most memorable moments in the whole trial. Perhaps Bloss had annoyed us at the same time he annoyed Cruz, or perhaps the intuitive connotations coming out of the account were simply compelling to most jurors.

Next came testimony from the Office of the Chief Medical Examiner, provoking us to consider the order in which evidence was presented. Here was the end of the story that might have seemed to belong at the beginning of the trial, so we would know where we were going. How Nancy McCloskey died was still an unanswered question.

Why should the autopsy report be here? Why now? Its distanced language was specifically designed not to draw conclusions, which was understandable, but its antiseptic character was more than a little unnerving. McCloskey had "abrasions and scrapes, mostly of the right side of the face, little punctate or little tiny circular marks around the cheek, the tip of the nose, just above the upper lip on the right side, and then a fairly large bruise that involved almost the entire right ear and the skin in front of the ear and the scalp behind the ear. On the left side of the jaw she had two dried scrapes or abrasions that were circular in shape with a little bit of bruising around that. On her back there was an area about five inches in diameter, right in the middle of the back, of abrasions that looked like little tiny dots that were in a regular pattern right in the middle of the back that were consistent with perpendicular force or a crushing of the skin."

Dearington asked if the injuries around the head were life threatening. The answer was "not specifically." The most significant injuries and the injuries that caused her death were said to be fractures of the rib cage and severe chest and abdominal injuries. Associated with the fractured ribs on both the right and left side of her body were tears of both the right lung and the left lung, and a collection of about a pint of blood in the right chest cavity. The liver was basically broken in half, and the left kidney was torn. The medical examiner testified that it was a crushing-type blow that caused those injuries, whatever mechanism would compress the body significantly. Just around the spine area in the midback were little tiny punctate or pinpoint marks that were consistent with the crushing of the skin, and he concluded that the force had been applied from the back to the front. Dearington asked if the injury was consistent with a foot having struck the back. The answer was no, not from a single foot. Would it be consistent with a cinder block striking the back? To this question, the answer was yes, if applied with "some force."

On cross-examination, Bloss asked the medical examiner whether he could say within a reasonable degree of scientific certainty that the mechanism that caused Nancy McCloskey's injuries was being struck with a cinder block. No, that much could not be said. Her injuries were consistent with that theory but not specifically to the exclusion of something else. We were shown three appalling photographs, and then, mercifully, the autopsy report was over.

If Miguel Cruz was our master of detail in regard to style, our next witness, Charles Randall, was the alpha male and the main player in this saga. He was the first witness to have been already seated in the witness box when the jury entered the courtroom. There was extra security in the courtroom (more dozing guards), so it was hard to avoid the deduction that witnesses who are incarcerated at the time of a trial are spared the indignity of walking before the jury in chains. Unlike in ordinary cases, we were always dismissed before these witnesses were. Randall was of slight build and average height. In his opening exchanges with Dearington, it was established that he had six felonies to his name. His record was in drug trafficking, carrying a gun without a permit, and violating the terms of his probation. He learned in the course of his initial exchange with Dearington that there was an outstanding warrant out on him as well, for a new probation transgression. Bloss, in turn, would insinuate that Randall was testifying in this trial because he hoped that by doing so he would be let off for this outstanding warrant. But it was difficult to believe that Randall was faking his surprise when he learned about the outstanding warrant.

In the courtroom, Randall identified Bazier as the man he encountered on Norton Street on December 1, 1998. He also picked Bazier out of two separate photo lineups. A different photo of Bazier was used in each of these photo arrays. There was no ambiguity in either identification. But once again, the weak link was the description of Bazier's clothing. When asked to describe what the accused had been wearing that night, Randall gave a third, now comically different, description. Bazier reportedly wore a jacket with Regal Red written on the back, in gray reflective letters. According to Randall, Bazier's coat was red but with darker colors mixed in as well. He had on gray jeans and was not wearing a hat, though his hair was matted down, as if he had recently been wearing one. Randall reported that the first time that he saw Bazier in the backyard of 25 Norton Street, he thought that Bazier was wearing glasses (as he said, something glinted), but when he saw Bazier in the front yard, Bazier was not wearing them.

Randall provided a much fuller version of events than Cruz had, revealing three (not two) episodes behind 25 Norton Street, but he corroborated all the key points of the narrative. At a certain point in his testimony, as Randall described the events of December 1, 1998, the unfolding scene took on cinematic quality. As he and Cruz stood in front of the house making their deal, Randall reported, they both heard noises behind the house, in the form of the rustling of leaves. Randall asked Cruz if he had heard it. "Yeah," Cruz responded. And Randall said, "I'm not going back there. Come back in fifteen minutes." But Cruz wanted his drugs. "Come on man, you scared?" Randall repeated, "I ain't going back there." So Cruz left, according to Randall ("He didn't want to, but he did"), and he returned in approximately fifteen minutes. Randall was twenty-six years old, but suddenly he came across as a boy scared of noises in the dark. A raccoon? He wasn't going to find out. Randall headed toward the package store across the street and ran into his friend Octible Jones. Jones and Randall were standing together on Norton Street when Cruz returned. Jones left, and the next Randall-Cruz episode began. (Cruz had begun his account at this point.) This time, Randall went all the way behind the house. He reported that he saw the accused, kneeling down, as if he was putting something in the leaves or searching for something. Randall thought that Bazier was messing with his drugs and instinctively yelled at him, scaring both of them. Each turned tail and ran to the street. Randall said he ran around the right side of the house, and Bazier ran around the left. I felt as if there was something heartbreakingly childish about this scene, as if Randall and Bazier had been playing a game of hide-and-seek or tag on a hot night—except that there was a crushed body under those leaves. But Randall didn't know that yet.

Randall repeated the account of the three of them in the street, with Randall yelling "what the fuck . . ." to Bazier's "chill, chill, chill" and "cousin to Mother's." Jones arrived and Randall told him to hold Bazier. Randall returned to the backyard, and for the first time, he saw Nancy McCloskey on the ground, lying on her stomach. Randall raced out to the street to find that Bazier had fled. He got Jones to go behind the house with him "to help the lady," who was still alive. Cruz left. Randall and Jones approached McCloskey, who rolled over and tried to stand up. They tried to help her. She moaned "oh, my ribs, my back" and fell back. At this news, I cringed. She could still talk! If only she had said the name of her killer. How many times have I thought the same thing about the murder of Suzanne Jovin? Randall told McCloskey that he would get an ambulance and the police. "No, don't," she pleaded. Then she started to breathe "really strangely" and her eyes rolled backward. Randall and Jones took off to find help.

Randall reported knowing Nancy McCloskey as someone from the neighborhood. He didn't sell drugs to her, but he knew that someone else did because he would see her around a lot, "talking to people." After the police arrived at the murder scene, Randall was taken into a car for questioning. He testified that he demanded to be let out. "The ambulance was there, and they were bringing the girl out, and everyone would think that I did that to that girl." Like Cruz, Randall looked at Bazier as if he was some form of vermin. I found it impossible to deny that some moral system was intact for both of them. The thought occurred to me that given different circumstances, different opportunities, Randall might have become a successful politician, perhaps the mayor of a city like Providence. (What a fine line between charisma and lawbreaking. I thought of Providence's former mayor Buddy Cianci who was doing time in the penitentiary.) With these musings, I acknowledged to myself that I believed the Randall-Cruz story.

Without exactly saying so directly, Dearington disclosed that there had been an earlier hearing of this case, and that Randall had played the critical role in the mistrial. Apparently, once on the stand in the first trial, Randall had not supplied the same vehement testimony against Bazier that he was here. Randall acknowledged that he was "pissed off" at the police at that time. He had asked them repeatedly whether they had a warrant for him, and they had kept saying no. But they served him with a subpoena and a warrant. So he decided not to cooperate. In his first court appearance as a witness in this case, he testified that he couldn't be sure if Bazier was the same guy he saw on December 1, 1998. A breakdown in the moral system, no doubt, but not unprovoked. Dearington also asked him if he were afraid of being labeled a "snitch." Randall replied in his noncommittal way, "Yeah."

In his cross-examination of Randall, Bloss attempted to impugn his testimony by insinuating that it had been paid for by various levels of law enforcement. But Randall was equal to the challenge and showed himself to be something of a scholar of the legal system, based on his long experience of being in trouble with the law. Consequently, he handled Bloss with an ease that was amusing. But Bloss did succeed in establishing that Randall would lie to the police at the drop of a hat. On one occasion, Randall was stopped while driving in Ohio (in violation of his probation agreement), and cocaine was found in his vehicle. According to Randall, the female occupant of the car was responsible for the cocaine, and he didn't know that it was in the car. He did know "about the weed," but he denied it when asked by the patrolmen. The patrolmen had asked him why he was carrying so many baggies, and Randall had replied, "I'm shopping for diamonds." Bloss was his usual thorough self. "And were you *really* shopping for diamonds, Mr. Randall?" Bloss suddenly struck me as the kind of guy who used to teach catechism class when I was a youth. Now there was a torment I hadn't thought about in a long time.

In the Ohio case, Randall was told that if he pled guilty to the cocaine possession charge, he wouldn't have to go to jail. Randall pled guilty, and he got out of going to jail. During his testimony, it came across as an afterthought that he had also agreed to work with the FBI on the murder case of Nancy McCloskey. He was arrested again after the Ohio incident, and he agreed then to testify in court if necessary. Bloss repeatedly tried to establish that Randall did this only to knock a few years off his sentence. But Randall was vehement that he had already been sentenced, and he said that "you can't modify a sentence after the fact." Randall seemed to know what he was talking about. What a waste, I found myself thinking again, as Randall's testimony wound down. Here was a man who really could have amounted to something.

My judgments of people were getting more solid as time passed. The judge was vintage; I had figured that out during voir dire. I liked Dearington a great deal, too. He was the classic prosecutor with a good guy demeanor—irresistibly decent. Bloss had my respect, though there was that catechism thought that I couldn't quite banish. As much as I attempted to reserve judgment, I was becoming more certain that his client was guilty as sin. As for my fellow jurors, I had spoken to all of them on an individual basis. When we assembled for the first time every day, there were two waiting areas. One room was more or less frequented by the Yale professors and other professionals and the other by the regular workers. By habit, I went with the workers. (I had long since put Dante on the shelf.) The jury pool looked to be a good one. Only Thomas stood out as a major irritant.[5] He was a former legal aid lawyer, a city government attorney, and a local politician,

---

5. Thomas is a pseudonym. I have changed the names of all dissenting jurors.

who I later realized was my alderman. Now he ran a nonprofit agency that helped people with mental and substance abuse problems. He seemed to be harmlessly irritating, but he was irritating all the same. He had one of those noise tics, somewhere between nervously clearing his throat and making animal noises. The tone in court was always so hushed and serious, and Thomas's sudden interjections were not only irritating but also disruptive. Too bad it didn't come out during voir dire, I thought.

We had our jury clown, Dennis, and our earnest family man, Russ. Dennis was our youngest; he was probably in his midtwenties. When you asked Dennis what he did for a living, he would grin broadly before answering. "You know those embroidered decals that people wear on jackets? Regal Red? Chicago White Sox?" We did. "Well, I work for a company that makes them." Pause. "Someone has to." Russ worked at Yale; his department was listed as Machine Shops. He was a toolmaker who assisted students and professors in the designing and manufacturing of various parts and total assemblies that were required for their scientific experiments. Mostly, he worked for the Yale Chemistry Department. The only black juror, Doleen, was a bus driver. I wondered about the racial component of this trial. It seemed as if it should have mattered more than it actually did.[6]

Before the next key witness, we heard from Detective Lawrence Mazzola, who was the identification officer at the scene of the crime. He was responsible for identifying and coding possible evidence. Two of the objects that were numbered in the photograph were Cinder Block B and Cinder Block C. Mazzola testified that he had seized Cinder Block C from the murder scene because when he had moved it, he had exposed a bed of fresh leaves underneath it, as opposed to the caked dirt he had found under Cinder Block B. Because this was an abandoned lot and it was December, there was a deep layer of unraked leaves covering the yard. The medical reports had already

6. Jeffrey Rosen claims that "the conventional wisdom about race and juries turns out to be wrong. The . . . ordinary American jury is experiencing a crisis of a very different sort. Over the past two decades, the most dramatic trend in jury trials has been a significant increase in hung juries" ("One Angry Woman: Why Are Hung Juries on the Rise?" 55). See also Rosen, "After 'One Angry Woman,'" 180–95.

established the potential importance of a heavy object, such as a cinder block.

Bloss's questioning of Mazzola had to do with Mazzola's failure to photograph what was underneath Cinder Block C. This made us punchy. (Mazzola, get with the program, why didn't you take a picture of the dirt?) Bloss led Mazzola through an excruciatingly dull accounting of every single itemized object visible in the photograph. Bloss asked Mazzola where he sent the crucial evidence. "The Connecticut State Police Forensic Laboratory." That's Dr. Henry Lee's lab? "Yes." (Uh, oh. Here we go.) I take it, sir, that Dr. Lee and the Connecticut State Police encourage you to send anything that may be of evidentiary value to the state lab for testing? "Right." Bloss persisted, "They don't say, 'Hey, we've got enough. We don't care about cases in New Haven.'" Looked at in a certain way, this wasn't dull material at all. It had just taken me some time to discover Bloss's comic side. Mazzola was made to repeat that he didn't think he took a picture of the leaves that were underneath the cinder block. "No, you didn't, did you, sir?" Bloss asked. "Because you just went through the hundred or so photographs that you took before you came up here and testified this afternoon, right?" Mazzola answered affirmatively. "And you went through it pretty carefully, right?" "Yes." "Because you know this a murder case, right?" "Yes." "You know this is an important case?" "Yes." "And you wanted to make sure your testimony was accurate, right?" "Yes." This kind of exchange took us through the day.

Next to testify was Joseph Young, the jailhouse snitch, from Chester Correctional Institution, who eventually became the make-or-break witness for the jury. He was currently serving eighteen years in protective custody for first-degree assault and first-degree robbery. He claimed that he did not commit "the Milford robbery," but he admitted that he did do "the New Haven one." The State's Attorney's office reportedly had evidence to convict him of both crimes. Therefore, he had "pled an Alford," which seemed to mean that he accepted a guilty sentence without acknowledging guilt, since the police said that they had enough evidence to convict him. Why would he do such a thing? Young referred to a trumped-up charge against his wife. In return for the police dropping the charge against her, he had pled guilty to the

Milford robbery and had taken the eighteen years. He didn't want his wife to go to jail; he had two kids at home. I didn't believe or disbelieve any of this; his just looked like another life lost. And that Alford thing sure sounded like a strange admixture of police work and law.

Young was in some kind of holding cell at Walker, a correctional institute in Suffield, Connecticut, on December 11, 1998, when Anthony Bazier was brought into the same place. That was a Friday, so they were together until Monday. Young recognized Bazier from the streets, though they had never spoken before that weekend. During those days in the cell together, Bazier reportedly told Young that he had murdered someone, a white woman, with whom he had been smoking crack and running (this was another new term: *running* is defined as going back and forth for more cocaine). He said she wouldn't have sex with him, and he hit her in the head with a cinder block. He also allegedly told Young that the police didn't have any evidence, that the clothes they had taken from him were not the clothes he had been wearing on the night of the murder. Dearington asked if he knew what Bazier had done with the clothes he had on, or where he had changed. "It was behind a red building," Young replied. "It was a red building with some kind of temporary service." This was the first of several pieces of information that stuck out awkwardly to me, for the combination of its high specificity and extraneous nature. (It was not that the information itself was extraneous, but it was strange in that it was provided by Young, who would have had no conceivable reason to make up such details.) Young told us that Bazier was homeless at the time and had a girlfriend, with whom he had had a child. She was staying at a motel, the Three Judges Motor Lodge, on the first of December. The motel is eerily named for those who condemned King Charles I to death during the Puritan Revolution in 1649. After the Restoration brought Charles II to the English throne, the three judges fled to New Haven and supposedly hid in a cave in West Rock, which towered over the motel. Bazier said he was supposed to go pick her up, and a grandfather or uncle was supposed to be there.

Young's recollection was picked up by Bloss because Bazier was said to have mentioned that he went back to the motel after the murder to check out—and nobody checks out after nine o'clock. This was a typical scenario during the trial. It had happened during Johnnie Washington's testimony, and now it was happening during Young's. The defense appeared to have trapped Young into agreeing to something he didn't really mean, based on his own prior testimony. Bloss asked Young if Bazier told him "that after the incident he went back to the motel?" Young replied, "Went to the motel, yeah." "After the incident," Bloss filled in. "I—I didn't say after no murder," Young maintained. "Okay," Bloss continued, "I'm not asking you what you said. Did Mr. Bazier say to you that after the incident he went back to the motel?" "I guess," Young responded, "yeah." "Mr. Young, did he say that or did he not say that?" Young answered, "I'm telling you what he—what I told you that he said. He said that he went back to the motel. I didn't say after the incident or no murder or nothing like that." "Sir, do you remember giving a statement to Mr. Kelly. . . ." Bloss would win these encounters every time—to questionable effect, because Bazier's words may well have been imprecise. Bloss asked if Bazier had said anything about "throwing the woman out of the window" or "stomping on her." "No," Young said, "he had just said that he hit her over the head with a cinder block."

Young acknowledged that he was angry that Bazier was apparently getting away with murder, while he was in jail for eighteen years for a robbery he did not commit. He testified that he thought about telling somebody, and he asked his friend Anthony Davis ("another Christian brother") what to do if someone confessed to a murder in front of you. Davis reportedly said, "leave it alone." Young left it alone. Through some course of events that was not made clear to the jury, Inspector Kelly, who had been seated next to the state's attorney throughout the trial, heard about Young's conversation with Davis. Inspector Kelly then arranged to interview Young. Eventually, Young agreed to give him the statement about Bazier.

Dearington asked Young about his subsequent encounters with Bazier in the prison system. Young testified that they were transported to court on the same bus. "He didn't want to talk to me when he seen me," Young testified, "and I asked him why, and he say, 'You know why,' and he started saying that I lied to—I lied on my statement that I made against him, and at that time there was a lot of people on the bus, and being in prison if you tell something that somebody

told you—especially being a cell mate . . . Then we went to New Haven
and they put me in the bull pen with him. There's about thirty people
in—this one holding area [in the Whalley Avenue jail]. . . . He showed
the statement that I made to the inspector [Kelly] about what he confessed to me about. To confirm that I did snitch on him. And then he
told me to tell his lawyer that I did not make the—that the statement
that I made against him was a lie, and then to talk to his lawyer. At
that time I was scared, you know, cause it was more than just me and
him in the holding cell, and I told him, yeah, I would do that." An
ominous scene developed in the holding area in which other prisoners
threatened to spread this word through "kites." Bazier apparently intervened before any physical harm could be done to Young. Young
explained that if anything had happened to him, it would have made
Bazier look bad. So nothing did. Dearington asked Young what happens to snitches in jail. "Well, they get hurt or killed, all beat up,
know what I'm saying? Labeled, nobody trust them, know what I'm
saying?"

On cross-examination, Bloss insinuated that Young had found out
all the information that he had supplied from a police report. (Since
that insinuation was picked up and clung to by one juror, it should
have been confronted by the prosecution. Were the specific items in
Young's testimony consistent with material in the police report? If so,
it would have made a difference to the jury.) As for knowing Bazier
from the neighborhood, Young didn't even know Bazier's name,
Bloss claimed, initiating a long exchange. Young said, "I didn't know
him as Anthony, I knew him as Tony." Bloss persisted, "And that's
what you told Inspector Kelly, you thought the guy's name might have
been Tony?" Young replied, "I know the man's Tony." "Well," Bloss
said, "that's not what you told Inspector." "Well," Young said, "but
that's what I'm saying. I knew him as Tony. I didn't know him as
Anthony." It didn't end there, lacking as we were the tight script of
Perry Mason. Bloss asked again about where Bazier was said to have
changed clothes. "And that was near a park with a passway and a red
building with a temporary job service?" Young confirmed that that
was what Bazier had said.

Young did not get any time off for testifying in the prior case. Thus
he claimed throughout this trial that he had nothing to gain from

testifying against Bazier, though he had something to lose, as his testimony about what had happened to him on the bus had made clear. He, too, showed moral outrage in regard to the McCloskey murder. Bloss concentrated on Young's plea under the Alford doctrine, and he focused on the unlikely scenario that Young was an innocent man who had received bad advice from his lawyers. I sure didn't believe that Young was an innocent man who had received bad advice from his lawyers. But I did believe his account of Bazier's confession. That confession and its veracity would be the major point of contention among jurors. On redirect by Dearington, Young concluded by saying, "I don't think it's right for somebody to brag about something, and say they gonna get away with it. That's wrong to me. You know what I'm saying? And I'm not lying about what he said to me. He said it to me."

The final witness for the state was Dr. Maxwell, a criminalist working for the Department of Public Safety in the State's Attorney's office. She had cosigned the report written by her supervisor (Kiti Settachatgul) regarding the results of forensic tests on the clothing, in which hairs and fibers were analyzed and compared. We were told that there are three racial classifications for hair: Caucasian, Negro, and Mongoloid. The contrast hairs that the department had available belonged to the accused Anthony Bazier and the victim's boyfriend, Daryl Allen. The only Negro hair found on the victim's clothing was similar to Daryl Allen's hair, not Anthony Bazier's. On Bazier's clothing, the department found Negro hair similar to Daryl Allen's. Dr. Maxwell went through a long explanation to show how a "double transfer" of hairs could take place, that is, how a hair from Daryl Allen could get on Nancy McCloskey and then be transferred onto the clothing of Anthony Bazier. The concept was clear, but the science remained inexact. All anyone could say about the hair was that it was similar to that of Daryl Allen, but that it was not necessarily Daryl Allen's. Another revelation was that "gold" and "white" and "brown" clothing fibers were on some piece of Nancy's clothing. Cruz's description of Bazier's pants came to mind. Yet that was it, in terms of physical evidence. Clearly, Nancy McCloskey was in no condition to resist her attacker, which explained the lack of trace evidence. But the murderer was extraordinarily lucky.

The Defense

Before we heard from Octible Jones, who was to be the last major witness, the defense put New Haven's version of the Keystone Cops on the stand. First was Detective Ingraham, another identification officer; he arrived first on the scene the next morning, the second of December. He wrote in his report that Cinder Block B had been removed to the police station. I thought to myself that someone had B and C mixed up. But that wasn't the worst of it. Ingraham then took us through the soon-to-become infamous experiment that was devised by him and conducted at the New Haven Police Department. In this experiment, the police dropped the cinder block that they suspected was the murder weapon onto a piece of vinyl. The block was dropped from a height of a few feet, with the intention of ascertaining whether it made marks on the vinyl that were consistent with the marks on McCloskey's leather coat. Nothing happened, so they retried the experiment. On the second attempt, their evidence smashed into pieces. Bloss asked if it had occurred to them to send the cinder block to the lab for testing. "No." Then he asked if they had preserved the vinyl for testing. "No, we threw it away."

Next on the stand was Sergeant Anastasio. He was the officer who had accompanied Cruz to the park where Cruz had thought that he had spotted Bazier. Cruz had testified that he knew he'd been wrong after he heard Chapman speak, but Anastasio testified that Chapman never spoke. Further, Anastasio claimed that as he and Cruz approached Chapman, Cruz said "I don't think that's the guy," as if there were some uncertainty. Anastasio reported that Chapman was taken in for questioning. Bloss seized this opportunity to impugn the police again. Two more police officers followed in succession, both of whom allegedly had information about Chapman. Detective Adger told us about a one-inch cut that Chapman had on his hand that was still fresh when he had been taken in for questioning. But the jury were suddenly dismissed, and we were held in the deliberation room for at least an hour. We presumed that testimony was being taken—we could hear voices—but that it had been ruled inadmissible, because when we returned to the courtroom, the Keystone Cops were gone, and there sat Octible Jones.

Jones was the most difficult witness to hear and to understand, and he pushed every alarm button in my body. I've tried ever since to understand why, because it's not as if his companions or Bazier's arresting officers had presented such flawless self-presentations. But Jones was in his own league. His voice was strangely like Randall's, his friend "for all of [his] twenty-six years." Bloss asked Jones if he had ever seen the defendant before. "No." Bloss led him through the story of a "car ride," in which Jones, Randall, and Williamson (now dead) were present. Randall did not remember the incident. Jones said that they were talking about the murder and looking at a newspaper that had a picture of Anthony Bazier in it. Jones said that his comment was "that isn't the guy." And, according to Jones, Randall said at that point "I don't know. The police forced me. . . . I'm scared." (This statement sounded like something that Jones would say more than it sounded like something Randall would say.) Jones was asked if he were pressured and rushed. "They tried to," he answered.

Jones's version of the scene on December 1, 1998, differed from the previous renditions in that he claimed to have seen Randall grab hold of the much bigger man, and Jones denied that the man was Anthony Bazier. Jones reported that he was surprised at what he was watching that night: Randall was doing all the "tussling," with a guy who was much bigger than he was and who was sweating a lot. Jones swore that the man was a light-skinned black man; Bazier is dark skinned. Could the sweat have affected his perception? "No." Jones said that when Randall told him to hold the guy, he responded, "no." Randall said, "Okay, then watch him." The guy ran off as soon as Randall left them.

Dearington asked Jones if he knew how many felonies he had. "No. What's a felony? Is that like murder and assault?" Jones asked him. It turned out that Jones had five or six felonies on his record, for narcotics, failure to appear, and assaulting a police office. "I was trying to break up a fight," Jones insisted. Dearington started to ask Jones about a statement he had made earlier when Jones interrupted him to say that he did not trust that what was on the paper actually related to what he had said. Jones went on to claim that people "took stuff out" and "stuck stuff in" that wasn't supposed to be there. "They cut out the part about the tussling," Jones noted. His conspiracy theories abounded. Dearington led him to the part of the statement that Jones said was tampered with, and the court was dismissed for the day.

The next day, each juror was presented with a typed version of the part of Jones's statement that he claimed had been tampered with. The judge instructed us that the taped transcript was the evidence, not the written version, but without the written transcription, we would have understood almost nothing of it. At the point in the tape where Jones claimed that someone had cut out his testimony, we did hear a noise; perhaps the tape being shut off and turned on again? That possibility was not pursued because suddenly Jones called off the conspiracy and claimed that the part that was supposedly omitted was actually there—in the line "Randall was up on him." Jones explained that that meant they were fighting.

Dearington came back to the car scene again and again. Jones testified that a short time after the murder, he thought he saw the guy walk in front of his car and go into a homeless shelter. "He look-ed like the guy," Jones repeated, pronouncing the word as if it rhymed with *crooked*. He testified that he had told the police to look for the guy in the shelter. "Did you want the police to find him?" Dearington asked. "Yeah, I wanted them to find him. He seen me."

Jones was driving Dearington to distraction with his answers, as he alternated between the world of checkable fact and the presumed reality in which the police forced testimony and doctored the evidence. From what we had already heard, such premeditated police malice was to assume way too much competence on the part of the police. Dearington and Jones kept circling around a couple of issues. First, there was the statement taken by Inspector Kelly at the State's Attorney's office about two weeks after the murder. Jones reported that he gave the statement because he was being hounded by the State's Attorney's office. "My office was hounding you?" Jones replied affirmatively. "To do what?" Dearington asked. "To tell you what is not true." Dearington was incredulous. "We wanted you to lie to us?" Jones answered, "Yes, just like you do now." Dearington asked him why he had come forward at all. "My mother made me." Dearington asked Jones if he recognized the guy who had been sitting next to him the day before, as the one who had interviewed Jones about three years ago; Inspector Kelly was not then present in the courtroom. "I don't remember," Jones said with irritation. "It was three and a half years ago." Dearington persisted, "But you remember for certain that the accused is not the guy you saw, and you remember for certain that the guy who walked in front of your car looked like the guy, so you seem to have a very good memory." Jones replied, "Yeah, I guess so."

Second, Dearington spent a lot of time questioning Jones about an interview from November 2001. The interview had been transcribed and was placed in front of Jones. Jones swore that it was the exact statement that he had made earlier. Do you know what a snitch is? Dearington asked Jones. "What's a snitch?" Jones replied. I wasn't sure for a moment whether Jones was being intentionally hostile. Dearington proceeded as if Jones were on the level, which, apparently, he was. "Do you know what a rat is?" Jones just stared at him. Dearington continued, "Did you ever hear of prisoners in jail testifying against other prisoners in order to get their sentences lightened?" Jones answered, "Oh, yeah, I heard of that." Dearington asked, "What do you call that?" Jones replied, "A tattletale." Dearington didn't laugh. Neither did we, but only because of the courtroom hush. "A *tattletale?* That's the term used by incarcerated men?" Jones responded, "I don't know what they say. I don't get involved with incarcerated men." Dearington explained that he, Jones, was incarcerated. "By definition you do: you are in jail." Jones said, "I keep to myself and worry about my self." Jones then added that he hadn't wanted to testify before and he didn't want to testify today. He didn't want anything to do with the whole thing. He wouldn't look at Bazier. Once, he grinned. Bloss's reference to his reluctance to come forward to testify at an earlier hearing brought such a wide smile to Jones's face that Bloss smiled, too. But Dearington objected, and we never heard about the lengths he had gone to in order to avoid testifying. I'm sure it was good, but it didn't change my assessment of his character: he specialized in disappearing. Instead of ethical principles, there was a blank, and a tendency to assume the conspiratorial worst.

The defense rested, and we heard closing arguments. Dearington surveyed the now familiar territory and reiterated that Washington, Cruz, and Randall had all identified the photograph of Anthony Bazier. In the case of Washington and Randall, they had done so twice, on different occasions and with different photographs. He reviewed the sightings that placed Bazier at the scene, beginning at the alley next to Washington's house and ending with his flight up Norton Street. Dearington anticipated the defense attack on the discrepancies in the clothing descriptions. You have seen the court reporter here every day, Dearington remarked. "So how many of you could say what she was wearing yesterday? And yet you would not have any trouble recognizing her face." Bloss did concentrate on the conflicting accounts given about the appearance of Bazier and, most of all, of his clothing. He responded to Dearington's thought experiment by asking the jurors, "If you were meeting someone in Grand Central that you didn't know, wouldn't you tell them what you were wearing, as the means to identify you?" In reviewing his case, Bloss sometimes appealed to the police as authoritative and sometimes as the ones who botched the investigation. Dearington responded to Bloss's arguments by saying that yes, clothes are great markers when you arrange beforehand for them to be so. But that wasn't the case here. The trial was over. "Each side's story is always being a little spoiled by the law."[7]

Next, the judge gave the jury their instructions. He told us that we were responsible for finding the facts, and he read the official injunction. Our decision had to be unanimous. We could take into account the fact that certain witnesses had been convicted of felonies, for example, but we were not to presume anything by the fact that the defendant had not taken the stand. Our first business was to elect a foreperson. The foreperson would keep track of the exhibits and was to be the only person to correspond with the court, through the marshal or clerk, by a knock on the door. We were amazed to hear nothing more. There was no further guidance about the election of the foreperson. It seemed quite strange suddenly to be electing a leader when up until that point, we had not been permitted to speak to each other about the case. Still, it was pretty clear that the job was Johnny's if he wanted it. But at a break in the closing arguments earlier that morning, Johnny had quietly approached me and said that he wanted to nominate me. We had rarely spoken before this exchange. I was

7. Janet Malcolm describes the way that the law protects "plaintiff and defendant alike from the narratives that tell their opponent's story too persuasively" ("The Side-Bar Conference," in Peter Brooks and Paul Gewirtz, eds., *Law's Stories: Narrative and Rhetoric in the Law*, 108–9).

surprised and pleased and told him so. He said that I had been very responsible, that every time we fell into talking about the case, I was always the one to redirect the conversation. "You have kept us honest."

No, that would come later.

We returned to the courtroom.

Finally, it was time to begin deliberations. The alternates were dismissed, and Kristen left her quarter. Little did I know then that I would soon be pleading for her return. We waited awkwardly as the exhibits were brought in. Various jurors filled the silence with nervous talk about procedure. Then David began the nominations, putting forth the names of Johnny and Thomas. I began seriously to doubt David's judgment; *anybody* but Thomas, I thought. There were more comments about procedure, and then Johnny nominated me. "No offense, Thomas," Johnny explained. "But you strike me as being a voluble person, who will always say what you want to. Norma is judicious, and I think we need that trait." A few others jurors, including Jen, strongly seconded the nomination. And so in a split second, I became (in my words) foreman. The judge never called me anything but "foreperson." Either way, the title came with virtually no job description.

III

Deliberation

You will see the miserable people,
those who have lost the good of the intellect

DANTE, *Inferno III*

The Apprenticeship of Freedom

Our first act was to take a secret vote to see where we stood. To my dismay, the result was seven guilty votes, two not guilty votes, and three unsure votes. Our impromptu discussions were emotional and disordered. Eventually we agreed to go around the table again, to declare our votes publicly, and to say anything we wished about the way we had voted. Thomas showed himself to be the voluble one that Johnny had predicted. His initial theory was that the accused "had not been proven guilty" (later he would say that Bazier "probably was guilty," but he himself was a lawyer and was going to hold the other lawyers to his own standards); he had voted unsure. What he wanted to say was that he was angry, angry with both the prosecution and the defense for not giving us a better case. He was close to tears. He had seen court cases before, he said, and he had watched TV, but this wasn't like that. His unending refrain throughout the deliberation process was about the difficulty of matching photographs to faces.

No surprise there: Thomas had already related to us a formative story from his past. He said that he had been stabbed in the chest, had stared his assailant in the face—and had subsequently picked out the wrong man from a photographic lineup. Somehow the police had arrested the right man. If that story were true, and Thomas was a politician, I certainly wouldn't go around admitting it in public. Show us your scar, I thought wickedly. Much later, in a confrontation with Thomas, I asked him accusingly if he had told anyone during voir dire about the stabbing incident. My point was that suffering such a crime and making such an error might well have disqualified him from this particular case, as dependent as it was on photographic identification. He looked at me blankly, and he said, "The what?"[1]

David also voted unsure, though he seemed to have switched to guilty before the afternoon was out. Old habits from his tenure as dean? For the amiable sort that he was, the retired dean did our side no favors with his long-winded and tepid formulations. Where's the "but," I would find myself thinking, as he began a discourse with long acknowledgment of the virtues of the opposite side. Johnny considered him an absolute peril.

Another vote of unsure came from Louise. "I don't know," she said, "you know, I just need to be convinced more; it's just, I don't know . . ."—and her voice trailed off.[2] Her voice did a lot of trailing off. Louise had a master's degree in English from Brown and the reproving look of a schoolmarm, so her continuous, indistinct murmurings were unexpected. In fact, she was a paralegal who specialized in corporate and complex litigation in one of the big New Haven law firms, where she must have had to express herself with precision. But in the deliberation room, she was the mutterer, always piggybacking on someone else's comment when making her own. I noticed this about her because I was trying assiduously to call on people to speak in the order in which they had raised their hands, the system to which

1. I did not trust Thomas from the start, but I did not suspect that he would actually try to subvert our deliberation process. Nor did I have any idea at the time that this had become a recognizable phenomenon. According to Jeffrey Rosen, Eric Holder, the United States attorney for the District of Columbia, "says that the preeminent challenge for prosecutors today is to identify what he calls the 'unreachable' jurors and to strike them from the jury pools." "But frequently these people simply lie," Holder claims. "They get on juries and essentially sabotage the system" ("One Angry Woman," 55–56).

2. Louise is a pseudonym. I have changed the names of all dissenting jurors.

we had all agreed. We could interrupt each other, for short and urgent contributions, but no unrecognized conversations were permitted.

It was the Liberty Fund way. It amused me to be utilizing the methods of an organization that most academics viewed with horror, as a group of fanatics hopelessly fixated on the great books, who gathered at places such as Jackson Hole or Colorado Springs to drink brandy and discuss the pre-Socratics for four days at a time. (This characterization is mostly true. My next scheduled conference was on a dude ranch in Montana, to discuss *The History* of Herodotus.) When participants don't play by the conversational rules, they don't get invited back. Louise would have been a onetimer. For all of the motion of her lips, she never actually said anything. Johnny, who didn't miss much, instantly declared her to be passive-aggressive.

Meanwhile, Doleen opined that there had to be more assailants, for surely no one man could have caused the victim such massive physical injury. There was something they weren't telling us. This claim passed without further comment. It was my fervent hope that it would stay that way. That annoying current expression "don't go there" popped into my head. No one did. Gene and Fred were the two not guilty votes, and neither of them chose to elaborate. Things looked very, very bleak.

The one positive notion to come out of that first afternoon was that we needed to be able to express the facts on which there was agreement. Well, I was a Yale professor who taught rhetoric, and if we lacked a chalkboard, that was no problem because charts were my thing. We could improvise, and this group was crying out for some direction. I vowed to use every teaching trick in the book to persuade all of the jurors of what I fervently believed: Bazier was guilty as charged. I wasn't a fool. I knew the vote count and the unlikelihood of changing minds.[3] We were like a Kafka story in the making, where all the action is in the opening sentence. But I also had spent years studying Aristotle, and I had come to believe that he was right about something: "The true and the just are stronger by nature than their opposites."[4] That strength might manifest itself gradually, withstanding test after test. Could we be that patient?

3. "With very few exceptions the first ballot decides the outcome of the verdict. And if this is true, then the real decision is often made before the deliberation begins" (Harry Kalven Jr. and Hans Zeisel, *The American Jury,* 488).

4. Aristotle, *On Rhetoric: A Theory of Civic Discourse* 1355a21–23.

My strategy was classic. Examine the facts from all conceivable points of view, and, eventually, all decent people will acknowledge the truth. Such an approach is neither as blindly optimistic nor as resistant to other points of view as it first appears. It invites debate. "*Why* is a true proposition more likely to be interesting than a false one?" Burns asks. "Because truth is more complex and subtle than the lazy abstractions through which we usually understand human reality. And so understanding a dense bit of human reality actualizes more of our (usually anesthetized) cognitive powers. Again, the often-described experience of 'elevation' of faculties experienced by jurors has its roots here." I felt that the longer our deliberations lasted, the better my side would be served, for the core story held together.[5]

Before we were sent home that day, Judge Fracasse reiterated that everything he had said during the trial carried over into deliberations. For as long as the case lasted, there was to be no discussion of what went on in the deliberation room, not with each other and, certainly, not in public or with the media or with anyone else. Thankfully, there was no media interest in this case, so that was one dimension we were spared. I had no interest in a public forum at that point, but my private life was quite another matter. In this regard I had not obeyed the judge's instructions during the trial, and I wasn't going to start now that I was foreman. Who was going to tell me that I could not talk to my husband? In fact, the only reason I started taking exhaustive notes at the beginning of the trial was that I realized in my nightly reports to him that the story was getting very complicated. So, during lunch hours, I began writing down what I remembered from the morning sessions, and, in the evenings, I wrote down what I recalled from the afternoon proceedings. I tried to be Herodotean, listening for conflicting testimony and memorable formulations, always aware that it was impossible to know for sure what would turn out to be significant.

5. Burns, *Theory of the Trial,* 199n36. Later, Thomas wrote to me about his frustrations with the way we deliberated: "You insisted with great strength that we should limit ourselves to talking about the evidence and not draw on our outside experiences. You knew that there were four holdouts against conviction. Did you really think that talking in this limited and stilted way would change our minds?" The answer to his question is yes. I really did think that it would change the minds of the dissenting jurors.

One other juror, Russ, also reported that he had taken notes. On some strange jury scale, I suppose, such actions were unfair. Yet my notes left me far more informed than I would have been otherwise. Discussions with my husband about the jury's deliberations were of a wholly different order, however, than they had been during the trial portion of the case. For the period of nine days that our deliberations lasted, my conversations with Charlie allowed me, simply, to get a grip, for jury duty had become a serious strain.

The presentation of evidence during the trial had fascinated me because it illustrated beautifully an issue with which the greatest writers in the West were obsessed at the turn of the twentieth century: fragmented narrative. I found the court analog compelling. Jurors were repeatedly challenged to sift through conflicting accounts; we were prohibited access to all sorts of information; and the witnesses were sometimes partial, untrustworthy, flawed. Out of this amalgamation, we outsiders looking in were supposed to reconstruct events and judge a murder case that had occurred years earlier. Burns wrote that the jury "is an institution, perhaps the institution, where we moderns can do what we need to do: pass judgment on our practices not from a single authoritative perspective 'above' those practices but rather from the resources that exist within the multiplicity of those practices."[6] Could we rise to the occasion?

I was not particularly surprised that the highbrow literature I taught at Yale applied to the nitty-gritty life of New Haven, Connecticut. My prejudice was to find my liberal studies to be relevant everywhere. After all, Faulkner and Stein and Freud and Kafka and all the authors that constitute my course the Intellectual Making of the Modern World were representing what they understood to be the new reality—no mere imaginative construct or fantasy. We human beings see the world through partial fragments, which we reconstruct into a

6. Burns, *Theory of the Trial,* 184. I am in good company in finding Burns persuasive on the forms of practical intelligence realized in the institution of the American jury. David J. Smigelskis praises Burns for seeing "the impossibility of talking about correct results *in these types of situations* except by a concrete participation with others in a particular trial, for which any reconstruction, however richly imaginative, cannot be a substitute" ("Realizing the Practical Intelligence of American Juries," 1021). A symposium in honor of Burns's book was sponsored by *Law and Social Inquiry* and published in spring 2003.

unitary vision of the world, with our biases affecting the result. At the turn of the century, this notion was a commonplace in genres as distinct as literature, painting, and relativity theory. Nonetheless, it was extraordinarily gripping to me to be placed in the middle of this same reality, with people's lives in the balance and our own integrity as jurors at issue. The mere storytelling of the case was electrifying, and I knew at once that it would become my next book project. With the onset of deliberation, however, that project was transformed, and now with distance, I can say that it was for the good. I modified the focus from how one puts a compelling narrative together out of deficient memories, to the more insistently ethical question of how one makes room for judgment in a relativist world. What really mattered in *The State of Connecticut v. Bazier* was that jurors eschewed judgment. From their point of view, they were making some kind of a moral appeal, as if the proper response to a knotty issue was not to presume to take a stand.

The court provided us with large sheets of white poster board, magic markers, and scotch tape, by request of the foreman. I was not identified as such, and since my communications with court representatives were conducted without any face-to-face contact, it was at least conceivable that they didn't know who the foreman was. On the second or third day of deliberation, I asked Charlie if he thought they had identified me. "They knew it was you before *you* knew it was you" was his response. He had a point. The attorneys spent a lot of time studying juries, and we were just pups, continuously stunned by our presence in this strange world. (After the ordeal was over, the prosecutor complimented me on not insisting on taking Seat #1 for myself. "Most foremen insist on their preeminence," he observed. I just nodded, wondering how I had overlooked the numbered seats.) Every time we walked by the lawyers, the defendant, and the judge, we felt their eyes on us. "Do you ever notice how the defendant always stares at us when we go through?" Kathryn asked one day. "He never looks at me," Doleen, the sole black juror, responded. *That* got our attention.

Occasionally we had light moments. I asked Johnny if he realized how much we could mess with their heads by changing our facial expressions. "Why don't you try winking at the judge this morning when you walk by?" he suggested. This was before I had read John Grisham's *Runaway Jury,* and I can say that in our imaginations, at least, we were equal to anything he devised. The courtroom inspired delicious humor. I have become much more attentive to the comedy of Kafka's *The Trial.*

The second day of deliberation was as exhilarating as the first had been depressing. I assumed my most self-effacing posture and proposed, "if it was all right with everybody," to tabulate the facts of the case as we could agree to them—one full poster for each of the important witnesses. The witnesses would be scrutinized according to the same series of concerns, and we spent considerable time discussing what those categories of evidence would be.

True confession: this plan of action was no spontaneous performance on my part. The evening before, Charlie and I had talked at length about how best to organize these topics, and I had lain awake much of the night reviewing and reworking my strategy. By the time our deliberations began the next morning, there were rings under my eyes, but I knew exactly which five categories we would end up with: Identification, Corroboration, Credibility, Descriptive Ability, Unique Observations.[7] I made the other jurors say what I wanted said, but who knew? Only Johnny. Every teacher knows the thrill of executing this maneuver. Without even discussing it, Johnny and I both understood that however distant our political orientations may have been (and we are practically parodies to each other), we were as one in that jury room.

Filling out our answers to those categories for Washington, Cruz, Randall, Young, and Jones took the entire day. It was an excellent antidote for the two minefields that I worried about most. The first was the problem of bad recall, both in terms of gaps in our memories and in terms of conflicting accounts given by the jurors. Of course, we could always ask to rehear testimony, and Thomas proposed this several times a day, with Louise muttering backup. If the rest of us had humored them, we would have reheard the entire case. I, too, might

7. Our methods served as validation for some theoretical work in psychology of which I had not been aware. See, for example, Reid Hastie and Nancy Pennington, "Explaining the Evidence: Tests of the Story Model for Juror Decision Making," 189–91.

have preferred that to present company—all of us longed for the quietude of the trial—but sooner or later, we were going to have to judge this case. Thomas was not one to stay with the evidence that we had heard during the trial or the evidence that we reheard in the deliberation room. The rehearing of testimony was merely an excuse for him to take flight.

The second minefield was the too easy dismissal of all of the evidence because of the shaky nature of some of the evidence. Gene adopted this posture. "What do we really have here? Just the photographic identifications, and they are flawed." I was convinced that even the category Identification wasn't as simple as all that, and I wanted everyone to be reminded of this, physically. Bazier had been seen, and he had been heard. He had been recognized, too, a separate matter that we labeled Convinced Recognition, that is, identified by personal conviction. This label allowed us to differentiate between, for example, Johnnie Washington observing Bazier hanging out on the corner at the end of her street, her recognizing him at 8:30 p.m. without seeing his face, and her photo identification of him. The scientist among us was not impressed. I persevered, hoping to expose his position as unscientific, due to its impenetrability to persuasive reason.

We proceeded in our divisions. When we talked about Corroboration, we also talked about Lack of Corroboration. Cruz was given credit on the first count for his story of the interrupted drug sale, and he was debited for the amount of drugs he claimed to have purchased, a point on which we believed Randall instead. Randall exuded the clear-sightedness of a businessman, which, I suppose, he was. We did not mistrust Cruz so much as recognize his fallibility. Kathryn reminded us to keep weighing the two sides against each other and to note the disproportions. Did it really matter that Cruz had left out the supposed raccoon noises? For Credibility, we mentioned Randall's act of flagging down the police; on Lack of Credibility, we noted his history of breaking agreements with law enforcement authorities. The most heated debate was about Young's Credibility and his supply of Unique Observations. We knew that we would be returning to that topic soon enough. The same was true of the photographic identifications. By working our way through each question together, no one juror dominated and no one hung back. There is nothing like democracy tempered by some quiet authoritarianism.

On the elevator after a break, I found myself alone with Gene. I had tried to be friendly throughout the trial and to be civil during deliberations, but amiability went against the grain, seemingly for both of us. Now that our views were on the table, there wasn't much hope. Charlie always says that you aren't a serious person if you don't have enemies, an assertion that has consoled me through many a semester in the political science department. I felt myself getting more serious all the time. Now the bicycling professor with the supercilious expression could be added to my list of enemies. I intend no slur against bicycles; they are wonderful contraptions. Perhaps it was the helmet that offended? I pegged him as a Berkeley or Palo Alto type, with his unearned sense of moral superiority. He was probably a vegan who drank Fair Trade coffee. (I have since investigated: his PhD is from Berkeley.) No doubt he sniffed out my conservative credentials a mile away. Up yours, I thought, in the silence of the elevator ride; I *walk* to the courthouse every day. I should pull out my NRA membership card or a copy of the *Weekly Standard*. I looked at the sneer on his face and admitted to myself that there was no way he was going to come over to my side. He finally broke the silence. "Norma," he said, "you're doing a great job."

That day we all left the courthouse with a sense of contented accomplishment. Dearington said to me later that from the court's point of view, our jury was "always" smiling. "A lot of juries start showing signs of hostility toward each other; certain people won't sit next to others, but your jury wasn't like that. You can tell." We had our days, but this was a good one. Our collective memory was impressive; this was one alert group. Now we had our own permanent record that we could tape to the walls every day, for future reference. It was one of the mysteries of the court that we were obliged to go through the re-taping procedure every day. In late afternoon, we would take down our artwork from the walls and hand it over to the marshal. The next morning, it was returned, and we hung it back up. This became Dennis's job. He liked to sit with his back to the beautiful city view and gaze at the charts.

I walked home with Russ. His car was parked on Science Hill, past my street. He was my candidate for the *spoudaios* man, Aristotle's serious or earnest man, whose conduct serves as a measure for others. Russ rarely spoke, but when he did the room became earnest, too. Leaving the courthouse, we talked about how much the case was taking over our lives. It wasn't the actual hours in the courthouse that wore us down, but the nonstop preoccupation afterward with what went on there. The tape never stopped rolling.

The next day, the jury confronted the most contentious issues, the status of the photographic identifications and Young's credibility as a witness. On the latter, there was a marked reluctance at the start to credit Young, the jailhouse snitch, with much significance at all. No one mentioned the infamous case of Leslie White of a dozen years earlier, but it was on our minds. White was the longtime informant for the Los Angeles District Attorney's office who had demonstrated how easily he could research the case of a fellow inmate in order to gain enough detail to fabricate a jailhouse confession. From inside prison, he gleaned sufficient information on the circumstances of the crime to deceive prosecutors, twelve times, into believing that he had been on the receiving end of an unprompted confession. White was particularly brazen in targeting these so-called confessions from inmates he had never met.[8] Similar horror stories were readily available in the popular media, as in *The Thin Blue Line.* There was a shared recognition among us that Americans had been burned by this kind of thing before. However, there did seem to be a difference between our case and others that might be recalled in respect to motive. We were told repeatedly that Young received nothing for his testimony, that he had no prospect of a reduced sentence. But did he *think* he did? We went back and forth on this.

There was a general demand to see the eight-packs again, the collection of mug shots from which Washington, Cruz, and Randall had identified Bazier. There were three distinct sets of photographs. The first eight-pack was the one shown to Randall before the police had made an arrest. Randall surprised the jury when he said that he knew four of the eight men in the packet; they either were related to him or

---

8. For a full description, see Jana Winograde, "Jailhouse Informants and the Need for Judicial Use Immunity in Habeas Corpus Proceedings," 755–56.

were friends of his from the neighborhood. Of all the eight-packs, this one had the fewest men in it who looked anything like Bazier. No surprise there, at least for most of us, since he had not been identified yet. Another eight-pack was assembled after Bazier had been arrested, and these eight men more closely resembled each other. A third eight-pack was put together at a later date, with a different photograph of Bazier (and a different photograph of Darryl Belton, the man who Johnnie Washington thought closely resembled Bazier).

A few jurors suspected police malfeasance in regard to the assembling of these photographic packets; the suspicion was that the police had stacked the deck. This proposition stunned me into silence. Two charges were made. First, Bazier was the biggest, blackest individual, so witnesses would, of course, select him (and the police would, of course, know that Randall was acquainted with four of the first eight individuals), and second, the other mug shots didn't look anything like Bazier's physical type. These assertions provoked a surprisingly frank discussion on the ability of a person of one race to distinguish respectively between the physical characteristics of a person of his or her own race and a person of another race. But it went in the opposite direction of the claim that everybody could see how distinctive Bazier was from the others.

Then there was Thomas, insisting that "we shouldn't assume that any person can ever make a positive identification."[9] I felt the conversation deteriorating and hung back, dejected. How could this happen so quickly? I knew my limits, and sarcasm would not help. There was no delicate way of saying that the New Haven Police were too incompetent for the scenarios being circulated here to be true. Perhaps that

9. The history of eyewitness and photographic identification is troubled. Michael L. Radelet, Hugo Adam Bedau, and Constance E. Putnam determined that the most common causes for erroneous convictions are "perjury by prosecution witnesses and mistaken eyewitness testimony" (*In Spite of Innocence: Erroneous Convictions in Capital Cases,* 18). Nevertheless, it is an unwarranted leap to refuse to consider the validity of any such identification. Radelet, Bedau, and Putnam note, for example, that about 90 percent of the cases they discuss concern "official judgments of error," which underlines the critical need to educate (not abandon) judgment (18). In "Identification from Photographic Evidence," Frank Bates puts forth a series of standards for photo-identification procedures that the police do seem to have followed in our case (95–96).

is too strong, but there was no question that the cinder block test hung heavily over our proceedings, putting all of us on the lookout for dubious police practices. Most disturbing to me was that on this topic of identification, the more suspicious jurors intimated things that went way beyond anything suggested by the lawyers in cross-examination. As for the claim that no human being can identify people through photographs, that was another of Thomas's contributions that was beyond discussion. I listened, gratefully, as Johnny and Kathryn took the lead in the debate.

Although I appreciated Kathryn's reinforcement, I could see that she was off-putting to my fellow jurors and that her comments sometimes rankled. She worked in the UConn Health Center in Clinical Trials (she, too, had once been affiliated with Yale) and had several degrees that were unfamiliar to me listed next to her name: RDS, MS, CCRR. She was what Charlie and I call "one of the big ladies," that is, someone whose comportment entitled her to a better seat, a better view, and better service. But the deliberation room was a great equalizer, and her demeanor did not translate well. Strangely, among an apparently well-to-do jury, this vague class indicator seemed to be more detrimental to our chances at accord than any race issues, amid what was potentially a racially charged case.[10] Once Kathryn complained to me that jurors had to use a parking lot two blocks north of the courthouse. "It's not a great neighborhood," she sniffed. I lived there, though, and thought differently. (Not far away are the clay courts at the New Haven Lawn Club: world-class and perfectly safe.)

It turned out that Johnny, too, soon reached his limit. When Thomas observed one more time that photographic identification was extremely unreliable, Johnny suddenly roared back at him: "What's your point, Thomas? You have said that twenty times already. What's your point? Tell us what your point is." I tried not to laugh. This was what Aristotle meant by catharsis! Thomas was shaken and indignant. His voice quavered, and he said, "I don't like the way you're talking to me." I like it, I like it, I said to myself, and I noticed more than a few smirks around the table. "You don't have to raise your voice,"

---

10. This correlates with Rosen's research: "Although race is often discussed during ordinary jury deliberations in the District, most jurors there seem able to transcend their racially fraught experiences and to cast their votes on the basis of a scrupulous evaluation of the facts" ("One Angry Woman," 55).

Thomas continued. "I have listened to you, and now I want you to listen to me. There are a lot of cases I can tell you about in which people
have been shown to have picked the wrong man."

Johnny lowered his voice, making it truly scary. "Thomas," he said,
"I'm not here to be your friend." Of this, there was little danger. He
continued, "We'll listen to whatever you say, but stick to the evidence
in *this* case. We don't want to hear any more stories about what you
saw once in court or on TV." Early in our deliberations, the question
had arisen whether any one person could lift a nearly fifty-pound cinder block and use it as a weapon. Johnny had intervened with one of
those (impermissible) appeals to experience that no one would be
able to forget: "I once lifted a seventy-five pound ottoman over my
head and stopped myself just before hurling it down." Really, Johnny?
And what was that about? No one pursued it, and no one doubted
the ability of one man to lift that much weight. Now the dean cleared
his throat nervously and spoke soothing words, and the moment
passed. I roused myself enough to say that I would try to keep us all
on track, focused on the facts. Even if I obviously had views of the
case, I could be impartial on our procedure. Johnny winked. Good
cop, bad cop.

The magic markers kept running out. It became a standard line, to
have to ask for a new magic marker every day. We weren't writing that
much. It was just that they were not giving us fresh markers. I suppose we cleaned out the supply of magic markers for the entire New
Haven County Courthouse. As deliberations stretched out, my fellow
jurors started to slip me gifts in the form of pens and markers of all
varieties. This gesture crossed all factions. Fred the tire man and I
were definitely on opposite sides. He had alluded to some serious issues that he had had with the police, and it appeared that he had
brought enough baggage along to be siding with the defendant out of
solidarity. (We, the guilties, never doubted that we would bring Fred
over to our side, if we could deal with Gene and Thomas. I was prepared to resume smoking again to get some one-on-one time with him
during his cigarette breaks.[11]) One morning Fred approached me

11. Is this the "intimidation factor" that Kalven and Zeisel wrote about in
their classic book on the jury? According to Abramson, their findings suggest
that "intimidation, not rational discussion, was the tactic through which the initial majority almost always prevailed in a small group situation." But I would

shyly. "I want you to have these. They are much better quality than the others." He actually blushed as he handed me two magic markers. Those went into my memento pile, along with Kristen's quarter.

Johnny and I went out to lunch for the first and last time during the trial. It didn't seem to be a good idea for any of the jurors to be seen together, with the prohibition on discussing the case. It was a sign of desperation. We walked the short distance down Wall Street to Naples Pizza. "We've got to get one of the two of them," Johnny said. I agreed; we had two obstacles, not four. "I think that we can shame Gene," I responded. "We have to make clear to him that we are on to his elitism. He is assuming a holier-than-thou position every time he shakes his head and says 'I just don't buy it'—as if we have to sell something to him. It's like he is above it all and the evidence doesn't have any claim on him. We've got to make him engage with the facts of the case." Johnny looked at me doubtfully. I wasn't exactly bursting with confidence, admitting "anyway, Thomas is absolutely hopeless." He nodded. I brought up Louise's name, and Johnny snorted. "It's one consolation that after jury duty is over, we'll never have to see some of these people again for the rest of our lives." True enough, I thought, except that at the first holiday party of the season I attended after the trial ended, I ran smack into Thomas. Not to worry, I told Charlie, after pointing him out as the villain, "there is no way he will be able to recognize my face."

Johnny and I ordered our sandwiches and warned each other to keep our voices down. Then in walked Judge Fracasse. "He eats here every day," Johnny remarked. I looked down at my soggy tuna melt and thought that the judge surely knew something that I didn't. He was remarkably without pretension to have made this his hangout. What, was he a Yalie? Johnny didn't think so, but he knew that Judge Fracasse was a fellow at Calhoun College. I filed this information away, because I was really looking forward to speaking to the judge when this was all over (but he politely declined to be interviewed). "Did you read the excerpt from the jury book in the *New Republic*?"

---

argue that Kalven and Zeisel's conception is a peculiar image of "rational discussion." The point was to make a human connection, not a logical one, and only then to "talk sense" (Jeffrey Abramson, *We the Jury: The Jury System and the Ideal of Democracy,* 197).

Johnny asked me. I had; it had certainly piqued my interest. This became the book *Trial by Jury* by Graham Burnett. After our trial ended, I read the entire book—after our trial ended I read a lot of jury books—and I was considerably less taken with it. He wanted to hang the jury, for God's sake, to make someone else decide. Another shining example of intellectuals at work. I did, however, enjoy seeing him use one of my new vocabulary words. Someone had peazies in his case, too.

Johnny and I talked about our spouses, our families, our career paths, and our work. He wanted to know whether I was going to write a book about this trial. "Definitely. Are you?" No, he said wistfully. At first he had planned to, but now he had decided that it would take him too far from his current project. "Well, I don't know that I'm going to like the ending of the book I write, but I'm going to write it all the same." We returned to strategy, with the judge safely in the back room. "Do you think that I lose my effectiveness when I become obviously partisan?" This was tormenting me. As foreman, should I remain detached, above the fray? Johnny didn't think so. "You should talk more," he advised. "The foreman is allowed to have an opinion. Just continue to be fair about procedure." I never stopped worrying about this, but there seemed to be no sense in holding back, the way that things were going.

I tried to move forward in the next session by inviting suggestions on other informational charts that we might want to make. "The magic markers are at the disposal of the entire jury," I announced. Thomas leapt to his feet, waved his arms wildly and said, "I want them! I want them!" After our previous ordeal, everybody laughed, and the comic relief was welcome. I relinquished my position, and Thomas stood at the head of the table and announced, "If you will just bear with me for twenty minutes, I want to give you my theory of the case."

Someone let out a high-pitched scream; I'd have to guess it was me. "No, Thomas! No theories! No theories! We are not here to devise theories! We are fact finders, and we have to interpret the facts. Keep your theories at home! You can say anything you want about the case but not another word about anything outside of this courtroom." So much for the good cop. I was shaking and furious, one of the furies from the deep, dark past. I was becoming Allecto, in Virgil's *Aeneid,* an avenger of justice with serpents coming from her head instead of hair. But no, that image wasn't quite right. Allecto is the one who instills the poison of irrational rage into her victims, and I was the one feeling the poison here. Kathryn, more composed, managed to redirect attention to Thomas. "You are incorrigible! Do you hear yourself?" We had been through this issue so many times already. Interpretation or conjecture, yes; external theories or mere intuition, no.[12] Everybody understood the difference, even if we had to remind ourselves of it from time to time. No special knowledge, arrived at apart from the evidence, was permissible. But Thomas was attached to his theories by a bungee cord, and he kept bouncing back again and again and again.

Louise took the occasion to piggyback, muttering "you only want to hear one side." I was next to her, and for once, I heard her clearly. I exploded. "Do you want to talk, Louise? Talk then! Talk so everyone can hear you! You say that we only want to hear our side; well, here is your chance, speak up! Let's hear what you want to say!" The room went still. "Uh, well, I don't know, I don't have anything to say right now," she stuttered, "but you won't let me talk when I do." This was too much. I am an even-tempered soul, but my powers of self-rule were finite, and now they appeared to be wholly depleted. "I won't let you talk? You talk all the time! You never stop talking! You just always do it while someone else is speaking. Would I love to hear you talk, all by yourself! Try me. If you'd raise your hand, you'd be the first to be called on!"

This screaming scene that unfolded with cinematic clarity was one of several that I would recommend to social science researchers studying juries, those who seek to specify a cognitive theory of decision making in the form of computer program simulation models. A certain something may be lost.[13] Even the dean was beside himself at

12. "Many critics refer to conjecture and intuition as if they were interchangeable," Robert Dale Parker wrote on the subject of Faulkner's *Absalom, Absalom!* "But conjecture describes a reasonable surmise from actual yet insufficient evidence, whereas intuition refers to something quite different, to interior knowledge reached independently of evidence" (*Absalom, Absalom! The Questioning of Fictions,* 135).

13. Academic researchers who rely on mock juries should strive either to re-create this human element or to confront more readily the distance of the mock jury from the real experience (see Norman J. Finkel, *Commonsense Justice: Jurors'*

this moment. The rancor was palpable, and the foreman had lost it. David begged everyone to calm down, to take a breath. I was calm. I was thinking calmly to myself that I was showing signs of severe sleep deprivation. Then again, it was very satisfying to scream insanely at a passive-aggressive person. Thomas was already killing the deliberation process. Still, I apologized for raising my voice, and I vowed to myself to take a time-out. (I maintained my composure for two more full days.) Louise spent the rest of the afternoon circling the room like a catamount, and she ceased her under-the-breath commentary, at least for that day. I then experienced one of my periodic "jury duty is like *x*" thoughts: jury duty is like belonging to a secret society at Yale. Someone will say things to your face about your deportment that no one in polite society would ever say, and neither of you can just walk away. Then again, the delegates in a secret society like each other for the experience.

Gene thought it was time to tell Judge Fracasse that we were hopelessly deadlocked. He said that he personally had not changed his position at all since we had begun deliberation. Oh, and have you begun deliberation, I queried silently. Some of the more reserved jurors spoke up, to object. Dennis said that he had learned a great deal already, that we had put together a rich account of events out of the scattered pieces from the trial. Others agreed. Jen said it would be terrible to interrupt the progress we were making. I didn't say anything, since I had so much invested in the question, but I grew to feel very strongly about this phenomenon of the majority's conviction growing with time. Jurors were constantly adding sensible remarks in response to challenges, and this had a cumulative impact, no matter how small the examples. A question had come up in regard to the street lighting on Norton. Was it even bright enough for the witnesses to have made solid identifications? Certain police officers had testified that the nearest streetlight was out, and that the bar across the

---

Notions of the Law, 58–62). When jurors speak of the intensity of their experiences, they are reflecting their personal investment in the case, which is far from the "behind the veil" situation imagined by John Rawls or others who focus on the individual calculating actor. Marianne Constable has some penetrating observations about the presuppositions of such research "that a jury informed by the truths of social science is preferable to a jury informed by 'common sense'" ("What Books about Juries Reveal about Social Science and Law," 368).

street was darkened and apparently closed. "A bar in that neighborhood closed at nine o'clock on a weekend night?" Doleen asked incredulously. She was our Virgil guiding us to another path. "Don't you think they might have closed early on account of the murder?" Oh yeah, good point. The bar wouldn't be staying open for the benefit of the New Haven Police.

Another question revolved around the lack of physical evidence on the body of the victim. Why hadn't any hair been found? "Do you ever notice how, when your hair is greasy, it gets all matted down?" Kathryn asked us. "It's only when you wash it every day that it's flyaway." Everyone had to be remembering the peazies. "Do you suppose people who are homeless wash their hair every day?" she added, unnecessarily. The consensus was that we should keep plodding through the deliberation.

Johnny remarked that we had all better be thinking about clearing our calendars for the next week. The jury moaned in response. This prospect had been unthinkable, and now it was all but certain. Doleen said that there was no way that she was going to be able to spend another week on jury duty. Others mentioned unbreakable commitments that were imminent. I knew that Johnny had a trip to California planned for an important research project. For my own part, I was supposed to visit María in Paris, to eat sublimely for four days and possibly see some sights. We had planned it ages ago, to take full advantage of her leave. I stated the obvious, "If we can't all be here, then we will break until we can. Judge Fracasse has honored every single one of our requests to leave early for work commitments." It was getting difficult to juggle all of our duties. Thank God for Charlie, who had started covering my freshmen sections of Directed Studies. I had taught my senior seminar that week, but it was one of the most taxing efforts in the classroom that I have ever had to make. My students wanted details. "Maybe next week," I had responded, without conviction.

Our moods shifted, up and down. We can do it, no we can't. The next morning I arrived in the ninth floor waiting area to find Johnny and David already seated at a table. With my copy of Aristotle's *On Rhetoric* in hand, I cornered them. I pointed at the book with uncontained glee. "Look! Look what Aristotle says about the usefulness of rhetoric." I gestured toward the text, but neither of them moved quickly enough for me. I read the passage aloud, culminating in "the true and the just are by nature stronger than their opposites." Johnny and David eyed each other uncertainly. "Wait," I said, "I don't mean it's going to work now. It's a reference to future unfoldings," but it was too late; they clearly thought that I had taken leave of my senses again. Now other jurors were arriving, and I had to put the text away. I was going to have to give further thought to this passage on my own time.

By popular demand, the jury returned to a discussion of the reliability of Young's testimony. Gene, in his inimitable manner, declared that he didn't buy any of it. Why would Bazier be so stupid as to tell a total stranger that he had committed a murder? In a rare moment, Gene revealed himself. Johnny turned squarely to face him and went in for the kill. "Young wasn't a total stranger to Bazier. Young testified that he knew 'Tony' from the streets." Johnny had that right, for we had been through the tortuous exchange between Bloss and Young on this topic. To my memory, that exchange had lasted deep into the afternoon; where had Gene been? Johnny continued, "And there are compelling psychological reasons why someone would feel the need to talk about a crime he has committed, particularly a violent murder."

Gene held a faint smile, as if he were dealing with a child. I don't expect that he has read much Dostoevsky. Or that he had encountered Josef K. That was when I had the idea to nickname him Josef K. in this account. True, Josef K. was a banker, but there were similarities between him and the scientist. Neither one of them seemed to understand the need we have to extend ourselves imaginatively into the lives of others, how we are all implicated in the human condition and burdened with the requirement of self-questioning. After reading Kafka's *The Trial* for the second time, I came to agree that Josef K. is guilty, guilty of having unlearned the knowledge of good and evil. As Martin Greenberg wrote, Josef K.'s role is to act "the sleeping innocent who refuses to take responsibility for who he is."[14] In the end, though, I decided it wasn't right to reuse the name of an actual literary character as if he didn't exist already.

14. Martin Greenberg, *The Terror of Art: Kafka and Modern Literature,* 136, 164.

Some jurors prodded Johnny to give a psychological account that would explain a confession. And Johnny did, better than I can re-create here. With his eyes fixed on Gene's, Johnny held the room spellbound as he supplied motive and cause and tied together every piece of evidence from Young's testimony. He began by taking us back to the first week of December 1998. The murder was on December 1, 1998, and from that day forward, Bazier would have been in a state of extreme alert and panic and frantic activity. It was unlikely that he had had much sympathetic human contact during this interim, from December 1 until his arrest on December 6.

Then the interrogations began. When Bazier was not being questioned, he was alone in a cell. He had to know that there were three witnesses at the murder scene who might have identified him. These three individuals—Randall, Cruz, and Jones—had seen him up close. Were there others, possibly from the neighborhood? But days passed, and his lawyer must have told him that no physical evidence had been found: no prints, no conclusive hair or fibers, no semen. Perhaps he told Bazier that juries wouldn't convict without physical evidence. Imagine Bazier's relief, but imagine also the seesaw effect: they've got me, they don't have me.

Then suddenly Bazier was transferred to another cell. In his new cell, he was not alone; he had a cell mate, someone he recognized from the street. They started to talk about religion, according to Young—life and death matters. They played cards, mindlessly. They had a lot of time on their hands, and Young said that they just talked and talked. One hour of exercise a day, then back to the cell, for more talking. Bazier relaxed, and it just came out, after ten days of being alone with his thoughts, alone with the knowledge of what he had done. He said it casually. "I murdered someone. A white woman." Young didn't react, didn't judge. This was a sympathetic listener, it seemed, someone who was not law enforcement, someone who was also in trouble. It had been such a close call. Bazier kept talking. "I hit her over the head with a cinder block. She wouldn't have sex. Bitch." In fact, Young was scandalized. He was facing eighteen years for robbery, for God's sake. He had a wife. Two kids. His daughter was doing bad things to herself, he had revealed. Young did a slow burn as his cell mate unburdened himself.

The psychological state that Johnny was describing had to do with being cut off or having cut oneself off from human contact, on account of a hideous, inhumane act. But how often does the murderer fail to come back? Whether it is to atone for the deed, or whether it is self-aggrandizement, the instinct to see oneself as integrated again in the stream of normal life seems irrepressible. So, against all reason, criminals return to the scene of the crime, and murderers confess (of course, they don't always confess, and they don't always confess in ways that will get them incarcerated). Johnny convinced me that something like that was true, or close enough. "The point is not that the story is true—or that storytelling leads us to 'the truth'—but that it is faithful to the reality of what happened, and so conveys its meaning. What is at issue is simply whether one can recognize the experience of the story."[15]

It was a clarifying moment for others as well, though I am acutely conscious here of not fully capturing the persuasive quality of Johnny's intervention. Jen said afterward that until Johnny's elaboration, she hadn't taken Young seriously as a witness. He seemed to have so much to gain from his testimony (or, more accurately again, he might have thought he did). Johnny convinced her that Young was a credible witness. Dennis reported the same transformative experience. Gene shrugged, and he said again, "I just don't buy it." There were alternative explanations, he said. Young could have learned all of these details from newspapers or from a police report brought into the cell. I restated my position. Bazier may well have thought that he killed Nancy with a blow to her head. From the autopsy report, we had heard about her massive injuries. It was dark behind the house, that was for sure. The official cause of death was not the head injury, so Young could not have gotten his misinformation from an official transcript. And why would Young have put in all the extraneous details, such as the reference to the red temporary labor building, behind which Bazier was alleged to have discarded the clothes he was wearing on the night of the murder? Why all the detail about the hotel pick up, by the uncle or grandfather? His account was a jumbled

15. Melvyn A. Hill, ed., *Hannah Arendt: The Recovery of the Public World,* 297.

assemblage of odd observations that we had not heard from anyone else and that did not seem to add anything substantive. The details were seemingly too minor to have been reported publicly.

In Dearington's office almost a year later, I told him that it was a continuing torment for me to pass that red temporary labor building on the way to tennis every week. He looked at me incredulously. "You know where that building is? The police don't know where that building is. They never found it!" We walked through the hallway to an oversized map, where I pointed to its exact location. The building was directly on Bazier's alleged route. The building was not just red; it was an extremely striking colonial red, next to the park, just as Young related. Temporary Labor Service was in big, block letters. Good grief! Where exactly had the police *look-ed?*

Unlike Gene, Thomas was "totally convinced" by Johnny's rendition of Bazier's emotional state. "There is only one part of the story that doesn't fit," he argued. "Young said that Bazier boasted of the murder, that he bragged about it. If your rendition is correct, it doesn't make sense that Bazier would have acted in that way. Except for that, I would be behind your account one hundred percent." I wasn't at all sure how that followed, but it was the end of the day, and Thomas had the last word. It so happened, though, that we had requested to re-hear the testimony of Young, and our request was granted first thing the following morning. Rehearing testimony is an awesome experience, since jurors have so much more at stake during deliberation. As hard as any juror was straining that morning, no one heard the slightest mention in Young's testimony of Bazier bragging or boasting about the murder. It was one of those moments that must have jolted the court. The majority of jurors broke out in wide smiles as we anticipated Thomas's retraction. Don't gloat, I said, grinning at Johnny as we headed back to our room. But back in the deliberation room, Thomas did not retract. Our smiles disappeared. Thomas decided that the boasting wasn't the issue anymore.[16] He had discovered new grounds for complaint on this new day. "In his heart," he said, he still wasn't sure about Young.

16. Thomas turned out to be right about the boasting: Young had said that in earlier testimony, as I confirmed when I checked the transcript. But none of us knew that at the time. The bottom line was that Thomas continually shifted his standard of evidence according to the conclusion he wanted.

The exchange between Johnny and Gene, or lack of exchange, epitomized the different challenges that our main holdouts represented for the majority. Typically, we could not get Gene to interpret testimony. He held himself aloof. Was this related to his training as a scientist and his predilection for dealing with certainties? He told us that he was open to changing his mind, but he didn't know where the "revelation" was going to come from to accomplish that. Another time he asked where the rabbit was going to come from, so it seems that we were in need of a magician to bring him over to our side. I kept thinking that there was some block there to which we were not privy. Kathryn suggested more than once that Gene's standards were misplaced. Johnny agreed; he himself was a historian and accustomed to knotty issues of interpretation. Meanwhile, Thomas was more than happy to interpret and to suggest alternative possibilities and, generally, to keep conversation going, but the problem was that none of it meant anything to him. He wanted us to like him. His weakness was to lose touch with the evidence we had, in favor of bringing in what we did not. In a pinch, he would appeal to his higher, sentimental authority.

Russ hadn't spoken in days, and when he motioned to me, I recognized him at once. It was clear that he had been working himself up to give a small speech. "You know, when I found out that I was on a jury with a bunch of Yale professors and a lawyer, I was really worried," he began. Good opening line, I thought. He was nervous, he didn't quite know how to say this, he didn't want people to take this the wrong way. "People who are smart like that are often, you know, well, not too practical, they just don't have any common sense." Here was a man who probably had some war stories from the workplace. Russ said that for the most part, he had been so pleasantly surprised, so happy, when he found us to be sensible after all, but—and here he turned to look directly at Gene—it was time to get back to the bottom line again, time to ask what made basic common sense. I smiled my support, grateful to have found one of those interludes that was making this all worthwhile. He continued. "This case is really difficult for everybody. It is the hardest thing that I have ever had to do in my whole life. I'm not sleeping well. My family is worried about me. I can't even eat. And we're all getting sick." Indeed, we were now sneezing and coughing as a team. Russ finished, "But I know what I have to do, and that is to vote Bazier guilty as charged. And I ask all of you who haven't come to that decision to get back to common sense and to face all of the facts of this case." I told Russ later as we walked home that he was a hero to me. He studied me carefully. Praise was a problem for the *spoudaios* man; it had to come from the right person. "Really?" Really. He was not the slightest bit fearful about speaking plainly to those who controlled the weapons of words.

Our charts provided their own forward momentum. In truth what we were seeking to define as we proceeded with our deliberation was the nature of reasonable doubt. If Thomas and Gene had very different methods of argumentation, they joined in the strategy of claiming that they had reasonable doubt about Bazier's guilt, whereas the rest of us did not. Reasonable doubt was causing them to hesitate.[17] We should simply agree to disagree. This had to be a challenge for any jury, and we had gone back to the judge multiple times seeking clarification. We asked for a written copy of the definition of reasonable doubt. The court denied our request. Judge Fracasse did, however, reread the definition to us: "The meaning of reasonable doubt can be arrived at by emphasizing the word *reasonable.*" Was that an auspicious opening, for a definition? I wouldn't let my students get away with a tautology like that. He continued with a list of negatives, sometimes doubling up: "It is not a surmise, a guess, or mere conjecture. It is not a doubt suggested by counsel which is not warranted by the evidence. It is such a doubt as, in serious affairs that concern you, you would heed; that is, such a doubt as would cause reasonable men and

17. Years later, I experienced shivers of recognition when I read an article written by Judge Stephen J. Fortunato Jr. in which he insisted that reasonable doubt should be viewed as a subjective state of mind. "It is not a cause, but rather an effect, a result, and a consequence of the impartial examination of the evidence presented at trial. After receiving the evidence, and discussing it with one's fellow jurors, a juror's internal disposition will be either one of belief to a 'subjective state of near certitude' that the defendant is guilty as alleged by the state or it will not. . . . Reasonable doubt is not an objective standard of measurement existing apart from and capable of observation by a factfinder" ("Instructing on Reasonable Doubt after *Victor v. Nebraska*: A Trial Judge's Certain Thoughts on Certainty," 417). His formulations address the dissatisfaction I felt every time my fellow jurors spoke of "having reasonable doubt" as a kind of objective possession that caused them to behave as they did. At the time, it seemed to me that they used reasonable doubt as a screen to hide behind—the ultimate unanswerable appeal.

women to hesitate to act on it in matters of importance. It is not hesitation springing from any feeling of pity or sympathy for the accused or any other persons who might be affected by your decision. It is, in other words, a real doubt, an honest doubt, a doubt that has its foundation in the evidence or lack of evidence. It is doubt that is honestly entertained and is reasonable in light of the evidence after a fair comparison and careful examination of the entire evidence. Proof beyond a reasonable doubt does not mean proof beyond all doubt; the law does not require absolute certainty on the part of the jury before it returns a verdict of guilty. The law requires that, after hearing all the evidence, if there is something in the evidence or lack of evidence that leaves in the minds of the jurors, as reasonable men and women, a reasonable doubt as to the guilt of the accused, then the accused must be given the benefit of that doubt and acquitted. Proof beyond a reasonable doubt is proof that precludes every reasonable hypothesis except guilt and is inconsistent with any other rational conclusion."[18]

Some of us rolled our eyes after hearing that and got down to business. Occasionally we felt that we were the adults who had to take charge of the situation. (With some relief afterward, I discovered a large amount of literature on reasonable doubt instruction. It is no secret, to the legal community anyway, that the instruction contains a baffling heap of terms.[19]) From this mess of a definition, or from what we could retain of it after several oral readings, we tried to construe the meaning of reasonable doubt that began at "very certain conviction" but that was this side of "absolute knowledge." The redundancies,

18. State of Connecticut Judicial Branch, "§2.8 Reasonable Doubt," http://www.jud.state.ct.us/CriminalJury/2–8.html.
19. According to Donald A. Dripps, reasonable doubt instruction is a "Delphic pronouncement"; to Larry Laudan, it is "obscure, incoherent, and muddled" (Dripps, "Reasonable Doubt: Uncertainty about 'Moral Certainty' Continues," 84; Laudan, "Is Reasonable Doubt Reasonable?" 295). In a column on the subject, Judge Lawrence V. Johnston III rips apart the definition of reasonable doubt sentence by sentence. And his analog of going to a doctor's office to ask if you are having a heart attack is not to be missed: "A heart attack is not a broken bone, a rash, hypochondria, or chest pain. Such symptoms must not influence you to return a diagnosis of no heart attack if you have an abiding conviction that it is a heart attack" ("Criminal Law: The Instruction on Reasonable Doubt: 200 Years of Sophistry Is Enough," 61).

missing steps, and non sequiturs in the definition could be bypassed, so long as we all understood how high the standards were to declare someone guilty beyond a reasonable doubt. We resigned ourselves to what was given and attempted to rely on our own wits. It turns out that according to some legal scholars, that outcome is precisely the one hoped for.[20]

Johnny had an example ready to test us, showing instinctively the practical bent of a working historian. "Let's say there have been a rash of thefts from garages in your neighborhood, and you have just become the latest victim," he posited. He squared off against Gene again. "One of your neighbors calls to tell you that she noticed a white male around twenty-five years old coming out of your garage early that same morning." Johnny went on to describe three separate sightings of the same individual, each by an impeccable source (the concerned and trusted neighbor), with varying accounts of the clothing of the suspect but with general agreement as to his physical makeup. I observed silently that he had just cleaned up our case: gone was any mention of murder, drugs, prostitutes, police malfeasance, or racial stereotyping. "Would you be able to convince yourself in this case, beyond a reasonable doubt, that the suspect. . . ." But Gene interrupted; he was no dummy, he saw where this was going. "How about if we posit that one of your witnesses was identifying a physical type rather than the distinct features of a specific individual?"

Fair enough—that was Gene's theory about Johnnie Washington, the neighbor and reluctant witness. I thought Johnny had scored a point here, merely in bringing to the surface Gene's dismissive treatment of Johnnie Washington as a witness. Gene sounded patronizing, sort of how one might expect a Yale professor to sound, and, more to

---

20. The argument is made in "Reasonable Doubt: An Argument against Definition" that courts should leave reasonable doubt undefined in order to "imbue the trial process with the collective wisdom of the community" (1972). I'm not inclined to argue with that position in a book that seeks to champion the practical judgment of the ordinary person. But I don't see the point of throwing obstacles in the way of jurors either. The incantatory nature of the instruction as it stands seems to encourage jurors to speak of their reasonable doubt as if it were a mystical power that controls their actions. Rosen notes that most holdout jurors "say they have reasonable doubts about the defendant's guilt, even when their doubts appear, to many, to be unreasonable" ("One Angry Woman," 55).

the point, his reading was not generally shared. The concerned and trusted neighbor, peering through her window at the suspect or actually walking by the suspect on the sidewalk, is going to see (and hear) a physical type? Sure. Many of us have had neighbors who were, shall we say, more watchful than that. Gene's tone seemed to make Thomas uncomfortable, for one, and I relished the idea of making the space between them more visible. Anyway, this whole thought experiment was useful (not to Thomas, though, who accused me of playing favorites by allowing Johnny to spin theories). It made us confront how difficult our position really was. Moving back from the analogy to our real case, we had to marvel that despite all of the weak elements in the case, most of us were still firmly convinced that the defendant was guilty. This had to do with the cumulative impact of the evidence that struck us as true and that had held up in our debates. We struggled to put this into the right words. In one of these intense moments, Thomas looked up suddenly and announced, "You people terrify me."

When I got home that night, I asked Charlie when lawyers had gotten so squishy. I had always believed that legal training was rigorously logical, that by disposition lawyers would insist on sticking to the facts. I've watched loved ones go through law school. I've flipped through their casebooks, their outlines, their notes. It was incomprehensible to me that the lawyer in our group should be the one so brazenly consulting his heart for signs of evidence. In response to my question, I expected Charlie to say that the beginning of the end was in the 1960s—an answer that could be predicted safely for most questions put to him on the topic of decline. But he answered gravely, "It all started with Oliver Wendell Holmes Jr." This completely startled me, not because I knew anything in particular about Oliver Wendell Holmes Jr., but because I had been breathing the academic atmosphere for years in which his name was always uttered with reverence. "Give me the short version," I requested. "Justice Holmes lived to be ninety-four," Charlie summarized, "so he had lots of time to succeed in destroying every possible foundation in the law, beginning with the natural law tradition." That was enough: the scales suddenly fell. I teach this stuff; I should have known better (a quick survey of my bookshelf turns up relevant titles, admittedly unread at the time, such as Richard Posner's *Overcoming Law*). A little research could go a long way. "Law had an identity crisis when Oliver Wendell Holmes . . . suggested in 1881 that law was not certain after all but depended on how the judge and jury saw the facts."[21] Or, in the words of the justice himself: "I see no reason for attributing to a man a significance different in kind from that which belongs to a baboon or to a grain of sand."[22] Oliver Wendell Holmes Jr. may not have accepted pragmatism as a theory, but his practice was another matter altogether. The legal profession had never attracted me in the slightest, but now I was galvanized. Was it too late for law school?

From my teaching I also knew that in an age without foundations, the infallible strategy for refuting one's opponents is to call them *absolutists*. Those of us who were prepared to vote guilty beyond a reasonable doubt were tagged with that charge ("It would be *nice* to be so sure of oneself"). But none of us was suggesting that the case was uncomplicated or airtight or denying that human beings err. None of us was trying to play God. I lost track of how many times jurors uttered the phrase "this is the hardest thing that I have ever had to do in my life." In the background of all of our reconstructions was the nagging question "but what if?" We all read the papers and watched the news. Everyone was familiar with the terrible errors that have been made in courts of law, many of them racially motivated, errors that came to light because of DNA testing. We didn't want to make a mistake that would destroy an innocent person's life. We wished we had some incontrovertible physical evidence that would have relieved us of the responsibility of making a decision. But if this had been an easy case, this jury would not have been formed in the first place. Thomas found us frightening, but I found us worthy of praise, trying desperately to do the right thing and worrying incessantly that we were inadequate to the task. One thing was for sure: ducking the call to judgment was not an honorable option. For the victim, we were it.

21. Philip K. Howard, *The Death of Common Sense: How Law Is Suffocating America*, 23.
22. Albert W. Alschuler, *Law without Values: The Life, Work, and Legacy of Justice Holmes*, 23. In a review of this book, Morris B. Hoffman wrote that "Alschuler makes a powerful and elegant case that Holmes, more than anyone, is responsible for the current sorry state of jurisprudential affairs: a choice between the valueless deconstructionist nonsense that is 'critical legal studies' and its valueless cousin, law and economics" (598).

In the course of trying to hammer out a workable definition of reasonable doubt, we came in sight of the negative, the territory labeled here as the unreasonable. In my mind, I had already titled my future book *Unreasonable Doubt,* in reference to my opponents' ways of appealing to a ground that was literally not subject to debate. ("People cannot be identified through photographs"—end of story.[23]) They were unreasonable but not evil, malicious, or even particularly exceptional. Far from it: they were evidently upstanding members of the community, living decent lives and attached to worthy causes. Still, there is something of larger cultural significance at work here in our inability to find common ground in the midst of the most democratic of institutions. Dialogue shut down along familiar lines. Thomas and Gene mapped easily enough onto subjectivism and scientism. The inner compass that Thomas used to situate the evidence was his heart of hearts. Gene rejected out of hand any evidence that did not attain to scientific certainty. There was no *reasoning* with either of them. But the story is even older. According to Plato, the adversaries of Socrates were the poets, with their uncheckable inspiration, and the sophists, with their skepticism. They were the original enemies of the jury system.

As our deliberations stretched on, the prospect loomed of a third week at the courthouse. We had to make specific plans. Some jurors had commitments, and, anyway, it was helpful to know beforehand if we were meeting only for half days. I had already told María that Paris was looking doubtful. It was growing increasingly impossible even to imagine such a diversion. We conducted one of our periodic checkups on each other. Johnny turned to Doleen and asked, "Are you going to be able to make it all right to the court next week?" She responded

23. In contrast, the courts have followed the only reasonable course of action on this matter, which is to devise rough guidelines. In general, they have found that "the longer the witness's opportunity to view the offender; the greater the attention to the offender at the time of the offense; the more detailed the initial description from the witness; the greater the certainty demonstrated by the witness; and the shorter the length of time between the crime and the viewing of the photographic array; the more reliable the identification" (Connie Mayer, "Due Process Challenges to Eyewitness Identification Based on Pretrial Photographic Arrays," 844). The most questionable item in this series pertains to witness confidence (857). For our case, the relevant witness is Cruz, who was the most confident and also the most detailed in his observations. Sometimes, perhaps, witness confidence correlates to a prior exposure.

affirmatively, "I'll be here." I was pretty sure I understood this new attitude. By the state's own reckoning, we had gone beyond ordinary service, and we were now being paid for our efforts to the tune of fifty dollars a day. Not that this was a great sum alone, but most of us were still carrying our full-time workload and our salaries. Doleen had always managed to complete her morning bus route easily enough, but with our early dismissals, she found that frequently she could finish her afternoon routes as well. Jury duty was a lucrative interval. When we walked away from the jury room battered and ashamed, we each had five hundred dollars to our credit.

Jury and Text and Tocqueville

I had been thinking, teaching, and writing about Tocqueville for years. In the quiet of the study, my reading of *Democracy in America* was effortless, if not wholly untroubled. Now, on a jury face-to-face with an accused murderer, and with a cacophony of moral, social, individual, and emotional concerns swirling about me, I realized that political theory was now being tested by life in the raw. There was nothing facile in Tocqueville's observations about the courage required to sit in judgment of another.

In *Democracy in America,* Tocqueville supports the perpetuation of those democratic institutions and conventions in America that counsel prudence. But for reasons that he elaborates, very few of those institutions or conventions seem to be up to the task any longer. One might say that with the exception of the jury, the text itself is the only thing left standing as a worthy example of teaching prudence to Americans, as the salutary religious, philosophical, historical, and political traditions touted by Tocqueville at the start of his reflections all steadily lose force.[24] Now that connection between the jury as an institution and the great text as an entity is highly suggestive, for the institution and the text both seem to impart an acceptance of our

24. For a discussion of how the historical and religious traditions recounted by Alexis de Tocqueville in *Democracy in America* increasingly succumb to the leveling forces of egalitarianism, see my *The Ship of State: Statecraft and Politics from Ancient Greece to Democratic America,* 123–36. In this work, I focus more narrowly on the political institutions that Tocqueville accentuated in his work.

epistemological situation. That teaching, which forces us to recognize our limited knowledge, is the crux of my claim about how useful the study of the humanities is in a court trial or how useful it is in any other scenario that requires political judgments to be made. The combination in the jury of free formation and commonsense reasoning seems resilient enough to help the individual withstand pressures to relinquish judgment. Burns wrote of trials as "a response to the modernist predicament of our needing our conventions while simultaneously knowing that we have created them and can criticize them."[25] This is an opening for a more optimistic rendering of Tocqueville's findings than he himself produced. But Tocqueville shows the way, in pinpointing the jury as responsible for giving Americans their "practical intelligence" and "good political sense."[26]

To understand the democratic conundrum in America, Tocqueville argues, one must first take note of the exceptional reach of democracy's "primary fact," equality of conditions. This fact remains pertinaciously apart from all others in its effect on the course of society. As Tocqueville details in his introduction, equality "gives a certain direction to public spirit, a certain turn to the laws, new maxims to those who govern, and particular habits to the governed." Equality of conditions cannot be contained: "It creates opinions, gives birth to sentiments, suggests usages, and modifies everything it does not produce." Tocqueville recounts that "I found it before me constantly as a central point at which all my observations came to an end." Accordingly, the practice of politics changes with the advent of democracy because democracy means a perpetual democratic revolution. "It cannot be said too often," as Harvey Mansfield and Delba Winthrop note, "that democracy, or modern democracy, is a democratic revolution." Tocqueville testifies to how the "love of equality" grows steadily with the equality of conditions, such that the sight of the smallest dissimilarity "becomes more intolerable as uniformity is more complete" (*Dem*, 3, xlix, 645). There is no stopping the extension of any idea, but this one, the dominant idea in the new democratic age, is particularly resilient.

25. Burns, *Theory of the Trial*, 183.
26. Tocqueville, *Democracy in America*, 262 (hereafter cited parenthetically as *Dem*).

Of the many distinctions that Tocqueville traces in *Democracy in America,* one of the most operative is that between the democratic taste for freedom and this "ardent, insatiable, eternal, invincible" passion for equality. They are "two distinct things," Tocqueville insists, and he fears that the former may well be sacrificed to the latter. "They want equality in freedom, and, if they cannot get it," he declares, "they still want it in slavery." That dramatic assessment should underscore what is often missed by Tocqueville's readers, that what he means by the American passion for equality is not some kind of project for seeking economic parity—a "new economic plan" for democracy. Instead, he stresses that it is a passion, and its object is any pretense to rank or privilege: "they will tolerate poverty, enslavement, barbarism, but they will not tolerate aristocracy." This passion for equality easily outpaces the taste for political freedom, for in satisfying the love of equality, Tocqueville states, "one develops it" (*Dem,* 480, 482, 645). Tocquevillian statecraft is a corrective to this overdevelopment and an attempt to shore up the more vulnerable side, the taste for political freedom.

In Tocqueville's rendering, this democratic passion for equality correlates with a steady concentration of power in the central government. Relinquishing power to a distant administration does not appear to inflame jealousies as much as relinquishing power to an equal does, someone who is irritatingly near at hand. "This immortal hatred, more and more afire, which animates democratic peoples against the slightest privileges, particularly favors the gradual concentration of all political rights in the hands of the sole representative of the state. The sovereign, being necessarily above all citizens and uncontested, does not excite the envy of any of them, and each believes he deprives his equals of all the prerogatives he concedes to it" (*Dem,* 645).

Throughout *Democracy in America,* Tocqueville notes that democrats are attracted to simple and general ideas. This observation holds with particular force in the case of the idea of a lone central power. "Men of our day are therefore much less divided than one imagines," Tocqueville concludes. "All conceive the government in the image of a lone, simple, providential, and creative power." From the lone central governing power follows an expectation for uniform legislation. "As each of them sees himself little different from his neighbors, he hardly understands why the rule that is applicable to one man should not be equally so to all others. The least privileges, therefore, are repugnant to his reason." The one fortifies the other, seemingly to the advantage of all. But Tocqueville repeatedly returns to the root problem: "uniformity spares [the central government] the examination of an infinity of details with which it would have to occupy itself if it were necessary to make a rule for men, instead of making all men pass indiscriminately under the same rule" (*Dem,* 642, 641, 645). Without a thought, as it were, the central government steadily accrues more power. What starts out looking like an unqualified good—the search for uniformity in laws—ends up pointing to a massive political problem: the ungainly growth of the sovereign.[27]

Tocqueville encourages the creation of artificial bodies of all sorts to remind democrats of the attractions of self-rule. Thus he isolates the admirable political institutions that serve to resist the untrammeled extension of the egalitarian idea. Tocqueville finds much to counteract the extremes of the egalitarian idea in the vigorous daily practices of American political life. These countervailing forces provide an education in prudence, that old Aristotelian virtue concerning things "whose fundamental principles are variable" and "not capable of demonstration"—but which is yet a "truth-attaining rational quality, concerned with action in relation to things that are good and bad for human beings."[28] Tocqueville observes that American political practices frequently serve as correctives to their more ungrounded ideas about how the world works. He names three institutions in particular that concur most to the maintenance of the democratic republic: the federal form, the township institutions, and judicial system, which includes the jury (*Dem,* 274). Each institution promotes variability, and each is critically important for the continuing health of American democracy.

One constant emerges in Tocqueville's work: the idea that space is preserved for American citizens or lawmakers or judges to use their

27. For other works that pick up this Tocquevillian narrative in our own time, see Eugene Bardach and Robert Kagan, *Going by the Book: The Problem of Regulatory Unreasonableness,* and Linda L. M. Bennett and Steven Earl Bennett, *Living with Leviathan: Americans Coming to Terms with Big Government.*

28. Aristotle *Nicomachean Ethics* 1140a34–1140b9.

common sense and to deliberate. "But no one deliberates about things that cannot vary, nor about things not within his power to do." That is Aristotle again (*NE* 1140a32–34), but it may as well have been Tocqueville, for whom the image of prudence is one that is "somehow dialogic in nature, as emerging out of and yet, at the same time, providing a certain critical purchase on a common sensibility."[29] Indeed, Tocqueville's account is relevant because he carefully delineates the various workings of the "common sensibility" that undergird the democratic republic. The common sense of the common man is acclaimed in the law of the land at the same time that it is distrusted.

On the subject of the federal system in America, Tocqueville characterizes the creation of the Constitution as "a double blessing." The Articles of Confederation were in effect for eight years before Americans realized that they were not a viable political solution. This was long enough for the revolutionary passions of the new American patriots to cool but not so long that the framers of the Articles were no longer among the living. The framers of the original articles, according to Tocqueville, "included the finest minds and noblest characters that had ever appeared in the New World." The silent contrast to events during the French Revolution is instructive. How likely was it that any group of people would be able to compose what amounted to a sacred document, on the second try? The brilliance of the Founding Fathers is in the way in which they struck a workable balance between the idiosyncratic features of local government and the more streamlined procedures necessary for the functioning of a national power. Tocqueville admires the ways in which the convoluted properties of the federal system mirror the unsystematic push-and-pull of politics. Tocqueville's language accentuates the "difficulties," the complex "object of justice," and the ineradicable tensions that are held in balance. "All the passions fatal to republics grow with the extent of the territory," he summarizes, "whereas the virtues that serve as their support do not increase in the same measure." Accordingly, the "sovereignty of the Union" must of necessity be "a work of art." The skills required to achieve this work of art seem to go against a basic impulse in human nature toward simplicity. "Among the vices inherent in

29. Peter J. Steinberger, *The Concept of Political Judgment,* 33.

every federal system the most visible of all is the complication of the means that it employs," Tocqueville wrote, and yet, "in general, only simple conceptions take hold of the minds of the people" (*Dem,* 107, 131, 151, 157, 155). It is America's great good fortune that the creators of the Constitution were talented and virtuous men who were able to persuade their fellow citizens to accede to a unique, and uniquely contrived, federal form.

Tocqueville also admires the model image of politics in the New England township, an image that is still appealing today. "The inhabitant of New England is attached to his township because it is strong and independent," Tocqueville observes, "he is interested in it because he cooperates in directing it; he loves it because he has nothing to complain of in his lot; he places his ambition and his future in it . . . in this restricted sphere that is within his reach he . . . understands the harmony of powers, and finally assembles clear and practical ideas on the nature of his duties as well as the extent of his rights." Tocqueville is not blind to the petty jealousies that infected that particular form of political community—"Freedom creates particular hatreds"—but there is another, overriding concern that "despotism gives birth to general indifference" (*Dem,* 65, 486). That indifference is the real danger, and Tocqueville, like Machiavelli, prefers the turmoil of politics to the quietude of despotism.

The apathy and the depoliticization that is visible in the modern despotic state is subsumed under Tocqueville's word *individualism.* This displacement of citizens is something akin to, but not the same as, *selfishness.* "Individualism is a reflective and peaceable sentiment that disposes each citizen to isolate himself from the mass of those like him and to withdraw to one side with his family and his friends, so that after having thus created a little society for his own use, he willingly abandons society at large to itself." The New England township institutions are the antithesis of that constricted world, as they promise a vibrant political life in which one's duties and rights are coterminous. Tocqueville knew as well as anyone that those townships were a thing of the past, but he believed that their vitality could be re-created for any age in associations. Associations are the artificial means for stimulating political virtue, for whenever human beings gather together in small units "sentiments and ideas renew themselves, the heart is enlarged . . . the human mind is developed only by the reciprocal action of men upon one another." To join an association of almost any kind is to become transformed in Tocqueville's view; one extends oneself and becomes capable of more activity, more vision, more disinterested politics. This is the best-case scenario for the jury. "In democratic countries," Tocqueville wrote, "the science of association is the mother science; the progress of all the others depend on the progress of that one" (*Dem,* 482, 491–92).

The third area that Tocqueville highlights as helping to maintain a democratic republic in America is found in the constitution of the judicial power, which is, perhaps, the model for exercising practical virtue. Only in America, Tocqueville claims, are all of the distinctive characteristics in judicial power preserved. The simplicity is breathtaking. First, "in order that there be a judge, there must be a case." Second, the judge "pronounce[s] on particular cases and not on general principles." Finally, judicial power acts "only when it is appealed to." The judge does not seek a generalized theory but "thinks case by case, focusing heavily on the particular facts of the case and abstracting only to the extent minimally necessary to render judgment in a way that respects the integrity of the law."[30] Behind judicial power in America stands the Constitution, and judges base their rulings on *that* rather than on the law. They have an opening to find laws unconstitutional, but that opening is not large. "An American constitution is not supposed to be immutable as in France; it cannot be modified by the ordinary powers of society as in England." In accordance with the will of the people, there are prescribed forms for changing the Constitution, and the Constitution itself represents the will of the people. "It is the origin of all powers," Tocqueville notes, and it can vary. It does not represent objective truth per se. Judges must take risks in reading the Constitution: How is the law to be applied? Is the law to be applied? "On the day when the judge refuses to apply a law in a case," Tocqueville asserts, "at that instant it loses a part of its moral force" (*Dem,* 94–96). The story is ongoing. Characters and plots come to the fore and drop away again, depending on their worth. Every element is time tested.

30. David Luban, *Legal Modernism,* 4.

Everything in this exercise of judicial power depends on the space for deliberation not being impinged upon by outside forces. In this, the judge's ruling is much like the example of the jury. In the same way that the judge is challenged by a case to place it into received law, without having an objectively true standard to prove that it is so, so the jury is challenged to decide between different versions of an event without having an appeal outside, as it were, where the objective truth might reside. Tocqueville notes that the jury "serves to give to the minds of all citizens a part of the habits of mind of the judge; and these habits are precisely those that best prepare the people to be free." Jurors have to decide, with limited information, conflicting testimony, and incommensurable views. A certain pride comes when they recognize that this can be done, after all, and in good conscience. "The jury teaches each man not to recoil before responsibility for his own acts—a virile disposition without which there is no political virtue" (*Dem,* 262). That gray area of decision making about human actions turns out to be entirely negotiable. If deliberating as an activity requires a certain amount of intellectual courage, it pays off with a corresponding sense of freedom.

A serious imbalance soon comes to light. It slowly emerges in Tocqueville's text that American practices cannot neutralize or even influence certain axioms of democratic theory. These axioms include principled demands by Americans for uniformity, simplicity, and generality. The hard lesson that Tocqueville teaches democratic legislators is that in the quest for more uniform rules and simple, generalized procedures, they risk legislating too far and eradicating the space for political virtues to develop. Democrats need to be able to make choices, for better or for worse, that affect their own governance. Once choice is removed—even with the best of motives—deliberation ceases and with it the training ground for self-rule. Thus where things have gone wrong most seriously in political institutions is just where Tocqueville found their original strength, in the creation of space for deliberation. By his own account, Tocqueville's efforts to shield good political practices from the relentless push of democratic theory are doomed to fail without strong countervailing forces, but every force that he names takes on more egalitarian features over time and looks less able to cope with democracy's homogenizing principle. Thus by the end of volume 2, Tocqueville has presented us with a conundrum. If the problem is one-dimensionality in democratic life, the solution must lie in preserving multiple dimensions in intellectual life. But the tendencies of the regime are toward more uniformity, simplicity, and equality.

Democracy in America was written in the 1830s, only forty years after the Constitution was ratified, but Tocqueville was already clear about the contemporary irrelevance of the ideas of the Founding Fathers. "The Federalists struggled against the irresistible inclination of their century and of their country. Whatever their goodness or vice, their theories were wrong in being inapplicable in their entirety to the society they wanted to rule." Just as artificial means once had to be created, so now they would also have to be aggressively sustained. His unanswered question was whether the American federal system could survive the Federalists, perhaps out of an American attachment to or respect for something decidedly their own. Much depended on whether succeeding generations of Americans would identify themselves with that collectivity. "[In] democratic nations," Tocqueville observed, "each new generation is a new people" (*Dem,* 168, 448). Jefferson worried openly about the antidemocratic quality of any founding, for clearly the Constitution would make claims on generations to follow, on people who had had no part in the original deliberations—hence his call for periodic revolutions. It seems that presentism must undermine the stability of even a twice-blessed event.

The associations that Tocqueville looks to for sustaining the vitality of the old township institutions seem also to be all too susceptible to the ills he diagnoses. "The task of the social power will . . . constantly increase," he predicted, "and its very efforts will make it vaster each day. The more it puts itself in place of associations, the more particular persons, losing the idea of associating with each other, will need to come to their aid: these are causes and effects that generate each other without rest." More and more, the citizenry looks for protection of its rights from the distant social power and loses sight of its duties to the local township. The cycle is difficult to break. Sure enough, over time, the alarming statistics on the decline in civic associations across America have been increasing. For example, one work that political scientists across subfields cite on this subject is Robert Putnam's *Bowling*

Alone. Putnam uses the concept of social capital to refer to "social networks and the norms of reciprocity and trust that arise from them,"[31] a concept that has resonance for readers of Tocqueville. Significantly, Putnam associates the decline of social capital with the rise of cultural ills such as teen suicide, early pregnancy, drugs, and crime; he uses the metaphor of dwindling bowling leagues to reiterate the fears that Tocqueville first expressed under the term *individualism.* "One cannot say it too often," Tocqueville wrote, "there is nothing harder than the apprenticeship of freedom" (*Dem,* 491, 229).

The reforming impulse toward uniformity in democracy is one that Tocqueville well understands, but he also sees that otherwise positive reforms may contribute to the erosion of areas for thoughtful deliberation. One contemporary example is chronicled in the book *Fear of Judging,* which traces how sentencing discretion has been taken away from judges since the passage of the Sentencing Reform Act of 1984. The authors find that sentence uniformity has not increased since the reform act was passed, but that the act has greatly impacted a judge's ability to deliberate. "Fed by a fear of the exercise of discretion—by a fear of judging—and by a technocratic faith in experts and central planning, the federal sentencing reforms of the 1980s sought to relocate authority from individual sentencing judges to a distant administrative tribunal of experts not influenced by the particulars of each case at hand."[32]

Tocqueville posits that for both judge and jury, the temptation to duck away from the need to exercise their prerogatives is real. Instead of taking on the judging role that Tocqueville finds so instructive, judges and jurors hold out for objective sources or hand over questions to resident experts. David Luban accounts for changes in this direction and the disconnect between legal theory and the meaning of legal events by noting "the modern substitution of a *scientific* ideal of understanding for a fundamentally *narrative* ideal."[33] According to Anthony Kronman, former dean of Yale Law School, the consequence

31. Robert D. Putnam, *Bowling Alone: The Collapse and Revival of American Community,* 19.
32. Kate Stith and José A. Cabranes, *Fear of Judging: Sentencing Guidelines in the Federal Courts,* 177.
33. Luban, *Legal Modernism,* 13.

for the American legal profession as a whole is that it "stands in danger of losing its soul" along with its loss of belief in the central virtue of the lawyer—prudence.[34] Lawyers, too, often feel palpable discomfort with the gray area.

If the jury as an institution is potentially exempt from these tendencies, that is because its members aim to agree on a story line; they must embrace "the narrative ideal," if they are to serve their function. It might happen (it *did* happen) that jurors get to a point where they decide no DNA, no crime. But that is an irrational position, quite beyond debate. For those who are willing to debate, it is important to stress that elevating the narrative ideal over the scientific one does not mean relinquishing all hard evidence for a soft postmodernism. It is simply to recognize the kind of material that is at hand. Aristotle reminds readers of his *Nicomachean Ethics* that in areas of human behavior, it is misguided to expect too much precision. "We must not look for equal exactness in all departments of study, but only such as belongs to the subject matter of each, and in such a degree as is appropriate to the particular line of enquiry" (*NE* 1098a26–29).

Aristotle's warning is worth revisiting. In his practical works, he suggests that the authorities that are relevant in the realm of ethics are exemplary historical or fictional characters. This most analytic of philosophers, then, uses Achilles, Pericles, or Socrates as his referents as he categorizes moral and intellectual virtues. Those figures, in turn, signify many possible stories or interpretations. For example, in depicting Achilles, Aristotle highlights as his ascendant feature not his warrior courage, as one might expect, but his friendship with Patroclus. This brings home how much ambiguity and looseness is at the heart of Aristotle's material, as he constructs the tightest of arguments. It must be said that there are not infinite uses of inherited stories or characters, and Aristotle is indeed doing something implausible with his traditions. But even for a less radical thinker, there is nothing predetermined about the meanings of exemplary figures. To endure as representative men, they have to be advocated as honorable and their virtues have to be established through argument.

34. Anthony T. Kronman, *The Lost Lawyer: Failing Ideals of the Legal Profession,* 1, 5.

Jury and text come together here. Granted, contemporary American jurors are not likely to allude to Achilles or Pericles as their benchmarks in deliberation, but no doubt they will have their own contemporary counterparts in mind as they go about synthesizing what they have heard and considering plausible constructions of the evidence. Analogies are constantly made: x is like y, this witness is like that one. Jurors forge a compelling account out of singular elements, with nothing foreordained about the result. This is not a task to be resolved by the scientific expert or the man of feeling. There may well be a dominant voice or two in the jury deliberation room, but that dominance is earned through persuasion, or it will be resisted. The product of the debate is then tested constantly in the deliberation room. Is such and such credible? Corroborated? Does it contravene common sense? Jurors put their own mark on the story. They have to. Their instructions are minimal, and no matter how many times they return to the original transcript, they have no other reasonable option than to decide on its meaning. Some jury results are better than others, some worse; in the best case, as with great texts, the more worthy narratives will survive debate, and the lesser ones will fall away. It is not far-fetched, then, to appeal to the experience of studying classic texts as ideal training for jury deliberation.[35]

To study the deepest texts of the Western canon is to be pulled into a verbal universe of someone else's making, with rules to discern that are likely not to be forthright or familiar. Often the close study of an earlier work will be of scant use in breaking the code of a later work

---

35. James Boyd White has devoted his life's work to advocating the importance of a literary education for practitioners in the law. In an example that is germane to this book, he analyzes Jane Austen's *Emma* to reveal the overlap between the character Emma and the reader. Both are in various stages of disorientation until they learn to read situations more carefully: "The analogy between Emma and the reader begins with the very act of reading, as we both try to observe things accurately and to understand what they mean. For as Emma must learn to 'read' her world if she is to judge and act and speak well within it, we must learn to read the text well if we are to understand what happens to us as readers. Like her, we are constantly trying to locate ourselves with respect to what we are told, to figure out what to expect and how to respond; like her, we are always asking what things mean, and we ask that question of the same things she does" (*When Words Lose Their Meaning: Constitutions and Reconstitutions of Language, Character, and Community,* 185).

in literature, history, or philosophy. Moving from the *Iliad* to the *Odyssey*, or from Herodotus to Thucydides, or from Plato to Aristotle is an exercise in tracking the untrodden path. Authors wish to avoid being overshadowed by their predecessors, and they brazenly chart new territory, in a version of Harold Bloom's "anxiety of influence." So readers of great books learn to slow down and really attend to the text, to interrogate it, to ask what are the cues and what are the demands of the language that need to be mastered, to uncover meaning. They learn to make judgments solely within the terms supplied.

When jurors put together the final narrative (even without unanimity), they become conscious of a certain gratifying kind of self-rule. It is an ennobling of the common sense of the common person. This is the experience of celebrating human freedom that the reading of great texts may replicate. "Just think of it," exclaims the character Yuri Zhivago to Lara in *Doctor Zhivago*, "the whole of Russia has had its roof torn off, and you and I and everyone else are out in the open! And there's nobody to spy on us. Freedom!"[36] When everyone is out in the open, the question is whether they can manage themselves, without succumbing to bad authorities. Conditions are set up for bad authorities when democrats become so jealous of distinctions among themselves that they will accept equality in despotism if they cannot have it in freedom. Tocqueville characterizes various instances in which Americans unthinkingly eliminate individual initiative from their political institutions, and he enjoins their democratic leaders to find the means to preserve some room for citizens to deliberate for themselves. The alternative is the growth of the steadily encroaching social power—the worst of authorities—that conceivably might relieve citizens of the responsibility to think for themselves.

In the Russian case cited above, the citizenry succumbed wholly to ruinous authorities. Pasternak conveys the untold horrors following the Bolshevik Revolution of 1917. The space was too large and too intimidating, and bad authorities moved in to fill every gap. How distant is this example from *Democracy in America*? Even if Bolshevism is not an American failing, after reading Tocqueville, it is best not to be too complacent about the visible and invisible authorities we rely

---

36. Boris Pasternak, *Doctor Zhivago*, 146 (hereafter cited parenthetically as *Zhivago*).

on in the shaping of our opinions. A default relativism might be as incapacitating to individual freedom as any other dogma. In *Doctor Zhivago,* Lara looks back over the ruins and comments, "The main misfortune, the root of all the evil to come, was the loss of confidence in the value of one's own opinion. People imagined that it was out of date to follow their own moral sense, that they must all sing in chorus, and live by other people's notions" (*Zhivago,* 404). The people who are valorized in *Doctor Zhivago* are those who see things as they are, and those who preserve their vision for the consideration of others. "The only freedom to be had is the freedom to observe, to give things their proper names, to achieve insight into . . . 'the mess and chaos' of existence, and to write these observations down for a later generation."[37] The point for Tocqueville—and for us—is that vision is a shareable good. We democrats can discern an exhilarating moment of prudential judgment, capture it, and treasure it, like a favored photograph that reveals our best features. Freedom!

Breakdown

Back in the deliberation room, Thomas called for evidence that we did not possess. "Why can't we ask for the transcript of the interview between Inspector Kelly and Davis?" he demanded. Davis was the friend in whom Young had confided about Bazier's confession. Why indeed? It was more exasperating every day to hear these requests, and we knew that if we gave into his preposterous wishes, he would just come up with some new reason for not changing his vote. "Why can't we ask if there was a police investigation of red buildings that house temporary labor service offices?" That one still smarts. "Why can't we have the transcript of the police interview of Bazier?" Why can't we sacrifice just one juror? I thought to myself. That week I taught Roberto Calasso's *The Ruin of Kasch* to my senior seminar. They were puzzled by his recurring theme of "the king must die." I explained that there is some human impulse to kill one for the sake of all. "Some massive community benefit accrues," I said, knowingly.

We returned to the photographs. Fred was making a concerted effort

37. Edith W. Clowes, ed., *Doctor Zhivago: A Critical Companion,* 39–40.

to persuade the rest of us that Randall was coached by the police into identifying Bazier. "But the police didn't know it was Bazier until Randall identified him in the first place," someone said, for the zillionth time. I got up to use the restroom. This was so tedious. Official conversation ceased, but as they were poring over the eight-packs, I heard Johnny say, "I know that guy. He's a homeless man who hangs around the corner of Sherman and Chapel." Thomas chimed in with "I know him, too!" Kathryn said something I couldn't hear, and the room exploded in laughter. I made her repeat her comment when I returned. "Oh, I just asked Thomas how he was able to recognize the man from a photograph." Touché! Everyone laughed again. Thomas protested, "It's much easier to identify a person in a photograph when you already know him." That seemed right, like Cruz recognizing Bazier because Bazier had cheated him on a drug deal.

But this was not a light matter, and Thomas's behavior pushed me over the edge one last time. It happened just before noon on a Friday; we were scheduled to be dismissed for the day at one o'clock. I accused Thomas of being intentionally obstructionist, and I swore that I would ask the judge to throw him off the jury. The other jurors looked up with interest. This was getting good. I knocked loudly on the door, signaling to the marshal that I had a request for the judge. The marshal came but looked stricken. Our action was unexpected because of the timing, and no one was around. "I don't even know where the judge went." I told him that we just needed a coffee break. To my fellow jurors I said that I needed fifteen minutes to compose a letter to Judge Fracasse. This was our first requested break, and the marshal couldn't see why our request should not be granted. "Just don't leave the building," he warned.

We headed to the ninth floor, where there wasn't any coffee, either. The attendants mostly dozed. Willoughby's French roast beckoned from across the street. "I'm going out to get some coffee," Kathryn announced. Others assented. This was a small rebellion in the making. I wondered what would happen if the jury ran into Judge Fracasse out on Church Street. Would our coffee break be cause for a mistrial? It was all the same to me: we were headed there anyway. Beyond Willoughby's was Anna Liffey's, an Irish pub. Maybe the jury would just keep walking? I'd have to write a second note to the judge to tell him that I'd misplaced my jury. But at the last moment, a bored day juror was found to fetch the goods. As everyone dispersed to await the coffee, the jury divided into sections, right down party lines. This hadn't happened before. It was the beginning of the end. I sought out a corner to be by myself.

To Judge Fracasse, from Norma Thompson, Foreman.

> As foreman, I have come to the conclusion that, should legal procedures permit it, consideration be given to dismissing Thomas from the jury. His repeatedly stated position in jury deliberations is that no witness under any circumstances or conditions can ever accurately identify another human being. Thus although he may find a witness credible, his stated belief is as a matter of principle or conviction that no eyewitness or photographic identification can be given legal credence. Consequently Thomas by his own self-description is unable to give rational consideration to evidence pertaining to identification. I stand ready to meet with you to discuss this matter if you wish.

After I'd composed the note, I returned to the jury room and read it aloud to everyone. Thomas told me that Judge Fracasse would laugh me out of the courtroom, and, anyway, he didn't agree with my description of him. "I am sure the judge will hear both sides," I answered, and knocked again. The marshal took the note, and as the last minutes ticked away before we were dismissed, it was an effort for me to keep from being physically sick. My action seemed colossally important at the time. When we were assembled in the courtroom, Judge Fracasse said that he had received the note, and that he would respond to it on Monday morning. This note was the only one that he failed to read aloud to the court.

Did I really do that on my own volition? I asked Charlie later that evening. I mean, where did I get the presumption? Did you perhaps plant the suggestion in me that it was legitimate for the foreman to write a note to the judge? *Is* that within the power of the foreman?[38]

---

38. For the record, the answer is a qualified yes. The judge must ensure that the defendant's constitutional rights are not infringed at the same time that the prosecution must be assured a fair trial. Above all, the court must not, according to Judge José Cabranes, "remove a juror because of a different yet honest view of the evidence" (David C. Brody, "Facing Allegations of Non-Deliberating Jurors," 241).

Who told me I could do that? What possessed me? I was pretty sure I couldn't have done that on my own, but Charlie assured me that I had come up with the idea all by myself. And he was confident that the judge wouldn't laugh. Lordy love us, I've done it now. Charlie returned to his book, and as I registered his selection, *Law without Values,* I broke into hysterical laughter. Perfect! "It's Thomas, Mr. Law without values!" I declared maniacally. I didn't even need to read the book.[39] So much for a relaxing weekend. I couldn't stop imagining the possibilities that Monday would bring. Would Judge Fracasse interview all the jurors? I would have to remember to tell him Thomas's stabbing story. (For that matter, Gene would reveal a similarly troubling story on the final day of deliberation.) Maybe I'll ask the judge about the propriety of an alderman sitting on a jury? Thomas is a public figure after all. Maybe he is legitimately terrified of becoming a target if we came out with a guilty verdict. Judge Fracasse might relieve both Thomas and me of jury duty. That outcome would be wholly acceptable. Then Kristen could come back and save the day! I yearned for Kristen. Alternate jurors could be brought up to speed in a flash, for there were all those blessed charts. No doubt the jury would have to start all over from the beginning, but they would be on much firmer footing than we had been on day one.[40] I wondered what

39. I did eventually read the aforementioned work, in which Alschuler cites one of Oliver Wendell Holmes Jr.'s most famous pronouncements from *Path of the Law:* "If you want to know the law and nothing else, you must look at it as a bad man, who cares only for the material consequences which such knowledge enables him to predict, not as a good one, who finds his reasons for conduct, whether inside the law or outside it, in the vaguer sanctions of conscience" (*Law without Values,* 133). Ah ha! Oliver Wendell Holmes Jr. was the enemy. I didn't want him on my jury either.

40. It is preposterous for courts to demand that jurors who are forced to restart the deliberative process testify that they can "[erase] from their minds any opinions which they might have already formed," as if they had not been affected by the reasoning process (Lynne A. Sitarski, "Criminal Procedure," 999n57). Or even worse, to take away the charts! Why diminish our ordinary reasoning capacities in this way? As a group we could have led a discussion that would have brought an alternate juror up to speed in a flash and without prejudice. This is another example of people underestimating the substantive gains made in the free exchange of opinion. If my jury had been permitted to start again with an alternate juror, for example, no one would have ventured any conspiracy theories; we would have zeroed in, right away, on the murder weapon, the jailhouse confession, and the photographic identifications. And we would have been able to explain to the alternate why we were concentrating on this evidence.

would happen to the group dynamic now that I had made my move against Thomas. To help time pass, I watched movies. *To Kill a Mockingbird. Witness for the Prosecution. Twelve Angry Men.*

Monday morning arrived, and the jurors were giddy. Something new and remarkable was sure to happen. The judge opened the proceedings with unusual gravity. Then he reread the juror's oath to us. "As a juror, you may draw any and all inferences that you find reasonable and logical from the evidence you hear. . . . You must follow this instruction as to the law, whether or not you agree with it. As jurors you must put aside your personal opinions as to what the law is or should be; you must apply the law as the court instructs." With that, he sent us back to the deliberation room. That was a fat lot of help; was this judge humor?[41]

It seemed a slight reprimand of a nullifying juror. Whatever it meant, we were on our own again. Surprisingly, a new camaraderie was in evidence. Thomas was the first to speak, and he addressed me directly. "I've been thinking about what you said all weekend," he began, "and I've decided that you were right. I shouldn't have introduced the kind of external matters that I did." This concession was followed by the deepest silence. How could he say this? Could he *mean* it? I stared, disbelieving. "Thank you, Thomas" was all I could muster in my state of shock. Kathryn was seated next to me. "I wonder how long *this* will last," she said under her breath. She was right. Before the day was over, Thomas had reverted to his usual ways. It was like fighting with a shadow.

All of our wrangling about reasonable dcubt led me to propose a new chart that would chronicle our grounds of agreement and disagreement. This was an old tactic. When philosophic debate fails, take a vote. This became my favorite chart. It was wonderfully fact filled, and it immersed us in the case again. I was ready to stick with it

41. Abramson mirrors my frustration from the other side of the courtroom: "Rarely are jurors even provided with written copies of the instructions; little attempt is made to translate jargon into common language. Most annoying of all, juror questions about the instructions are usually rebuffed with verbatim readings of the same instructions" (*We the Jury,* 91). But Peter Tiersma points out that there is a good reason for judges to behave in this way: fear of reversal. "Judges who bravely try to explain a concept in their own words . . . risk having the verdict overturned" ("The Rocky Road to Legal Reform: Improving the Language of Jury Instructions," 1087).

until the cows came home. Longer! Forget Paris; this was justice. My suggestion caused Johnny to blanch. I think it actually made him lose his nerve. He was not interested in devoting the remainder of his life to this case. But Russ was with me. "I won't back down," we promised each other. Ever.

That evening, I was expected at a dinner hosted by the Whitney Humanities Center, in the unreal environs of the Union League Café. I thought of that great Kafka line: "What is it that makes you all behave as though you were real?"[42] Everything outside of the deliberation room seemed unreal, but this experience was especially unreal. The Union League was New Haven's finest French restaurant. It was also New Haven's only French restaurant—the Elm City defines itself as Italian, through and through—but there was no denying that it was good, very good, New York quality. The center was honoring the new director of the Sterling Library, Alice Prochaska, and the new director of the Beinecke Library, Barbara Shailor. It was too bad María couldn't attend; these three powerful and energetic women were a triumvirate in the making. Each was in charge of a big-time Yale institution, with full moral and financial support from the administration. I have never felt more inadequate as a stand-in than I did on that night. María added sparks to any room she entered, whereas I worked the room with only one topic. I was a jury bore, worse than I was on the topic of tennis or the political science department. Now nothing was as important as the jury. But, apparently, I was not the only one with loose lips. At dinner, Elizabeth Dillon, an assistant professor of literature, seated on my right, said to me, "Oh, you are on the same jury that Thomas is on; he is my next-door neighbor. His wife is a novelist. She has published fiction in the *New Yorker.*" Really, I said; she should try her hand at nonfiction. Elizabeth continued, "I think of them both as kind of aging hippies, so interested and involved. Thomas has lots to say about your case. He went to Harvard Law School. Isn't he wonderful?" I allowed that he was something special.

I turned to my left, to speak to Dudley Andrew, professor of comparative literature and film studies, whom I had not met before. "Oh, you're on the jury that Johnny Faragher is on," he remarked. "It

---

42. Franz Kafka, quoted in Greenberg, *Terror of Art,* 33.

sounds so fascinating." Dudley told me that he himself had just been called for jury duty. What did I think? I think it's an experience. "Don't expect to have a life while it goes on. But it's great for losing weight." I dug guiltlessly into my crêpes suzette, knowing full well that they would not be any match for the acid churning in my stomach. I detected the faint flavor of orange rind through the richness. It was tantalizing. Dudley's dessert plate sat untouched. "Are you going to eat that?" I asked him.

The next day we returned to our new three-part chart. The first part was a nice statement of the prosecution's case. Category one included physical evidence—hairs or fibers—that potentially could put the accused at the scene. The secondary physical evidence was the cinder block. (Dearington said later, "We were amazed at how you zoomed in on the cinder block. That was amazing.") Category two included eyewitness testimony—from Cruz and Randall—that placed the accused in an immediate time frame or location of the crime—a matter of seconds or feet. Category three included eyewitness testimony—from Johnnie Washington—that placed the accused in a more distant time frame or location of the crime—a matter of days or more than one hundred feet away. Category four was evidence of a confession, and category five was photographic identification.

The second part of the chart represented the defense's case. This was tricky, considering that the defendant never took the stand, and that we could not hold it against him. I was treading a fine line, attempting to show where the defense had answered the prosecution, and where it had not. There were attempts to impugn the testimony of the witnesses, particularly because of conflicting descriptions of clothing. There was Jones's insistence that Bazier was not the guy. There was all the independent junk, as I labeled it in my partisan way: Chapman's cut, Randall's drop of blood, DNA tests not done, Dr. Lee not being consulted. I wanted to argue that if there wasn't anything in the defense's case to refute the evidence presented by the prosecution, we could take note of that without violating the stricture about the defendant's right not to testify. But no one went for it, and this section was ignored. The law, apparently, was the law.

The action was in the third part: the Juror and Reasonable Doubt. What could we agree on, as reasonable? Our questions were organized by the prosecution categories on the first part of the chart, and they were prompted by the kinds of interjections the minority side had been making over the course of our deliberations.[43] As Aristotle says (but I did not), "it would be strange if an inability to defend oneself by means of the body is shameful, while there is no shame in an inability to use speech."[44] For our first question, the vote was unanimous: Is it reasonable to discount Anthony Bazier as the murderer because none of his hair or semen was found on Nancy McCloskey? The answer was no, 12–0. We arrived at this only after sustained discussion with Fred, and it was one of the reasons that many in the majority felt sure that if it came to it, we would get him to our side. He just needed coaching. Fred was troubled by the lack of physical evidence. We had to go over this issue a few times before he agreed that physical evidence or not, we still had a murder; therefore the lack of physical evidence did not discount anyone as a suspect. Unanimity was a good habit. Our second question was redundant. "Is it reasonable to assume that no hair from the murderer was found on Nancy McCloskey?" Yes, 12–0. On the next question, we took a baby step forward. "Is it reasonable to assume that the hair found on Nancy McCloskey is accounted for by her boyfriend Daryl Allen?" Yes, 12–0. We were slowly making our way through category one. "Is it reasonable to assume that the fiber evidence is inconclusive?" Yes, 12–0. This was a concession on my part. It was not that I thought the fibers proved anything, but I did think that we should note that fibers not belonging to Nancy's clothing were found on her clothing, and that those fibers were the same color as the fibers in Bazier's pants, as noted by Cruz, our man with the descriptive eye. At least I got the fibers on the table for discussion.

Not a bad day's work. We anticipated an early dismissal that day because Kathryn had an important meeting in Hartford which she could not miss. During that morning's session, she had had to inter-

---

43. Steve Sheppard argues that there is an undue burden put on jurors who argue against the state to justify their reasonable doubts, but none of our dissenting jurors seemed to think so. If a jury is trying to come to agreement, isn't it reasonable to expect that everyone on that jury can justify his or her opinion? ("The Metamorphoses of Reasonable Doubt: How Changes in the Burden of Proof Have Weakened the Presumption of Innocence," 1240).

44. Aristotle *On Rhetoric* 1355b1–3.

rupt proceedings to take calls on her cell phone, and we were acutely aware of her situation. Judge Fracasse had never delayed us when we had a prearranged early dismissal. He would err the other way. But it was 2:30, and there had been no summons. Jurors started to look at me expectantly. "Shouldn't you knock, to remind the judge that we are waiting?" I hesitated; forgetfulness was not the problem here, and everyone knew it. I was about to speak—now it was 2:35—when someone hissed, "They're talking!" We froze, and sure enough, we could hear Dearington, then Bloss, then Dearington. Their voices were recognizable if not exactly audible, back and forth, back and forth. The idea took hold among us that Bazier had decided to plead. It was 2:40. How we came to this conclusion I cannot explain, but we were suddenly, ecstatically sure that the case would be over imminently, and that we would be sent home. We could hardly restrain our glee as the minutes ticked by. Kathryn's meeting was forgotten as even she was ready to jump out of her skin from the excitement. All was forgiven in an instant, and we were a unified body. Johnny recalled later that at that moment, Thomas had said, "I hope he *does* plead; then we'll know he's really guilty." The knock finally came at 2:45. In an instant, normalcy was restored, and our hopes were somewhat dashed. We were dismissed in the ordinary manner. Still, we left convinced that the next day would bring the wished-for ending. Inspector Kelly had suddenly reappeared, and it was clear that something was up.

The next morning revealed that nothing was up, at least as far as we knew. We returned to our work. Question five was the stickler. Is it reasonable to assume that the cinder block was involved in the attack on Nancy McCloskey? The initial vote was an unacceptable yes, 8–4. I was not deterred. "Let's write down on the chart all of the reasons why that is *not* a reasonable assumption," I proposed, "and let's identify which jurors put forth which objections. Then we'll have clear matters for discussion."[45]

45. Thomas V. Mulrine traveled the world, as it were, looking for the most satisfactory way to instruct jurors on reasonable doubt, and he came up with something vaguely similar to the procedure we adopted. The British Columbian Court of Appeals, he recounts, proposed that the instructions given to jurors should be centered "around the concept that 'if you ask yourself why do I doubt?—you can assign a logical reason by way of an answer' . . . [jurors] need

Even Gene couldn't argue with a plan like that. I took down their objections as they dictated, lettering each in turn: (A) there was not enough trace evidence (the cinder block dust) found on Nancy's clothing to be convincing; (B) from the photographs that we had of the cinder blocks, it didn't look as if they had been moved (This was particularly delicious coming from Thomas. All this, discernible from a photograph? The others went along with him); (C) Detective Mazzola's testimony was not reliable. He was the identification officer who placed the stanchions around the crime scene, dusted for prints, and took photographs; (D) former detective Ingraham's testimony was not reliable. He was the identification officer who initiated the infamous cinder block test; (E) there were alternative hypotheses that were just as convincing (I looked forward to the public airing of these); and (F) the cinder block would have made a different mark on the body of Nancy McCloskey than it apparently did. (What? I just wrote it down.) Louise and Thomas put their names to all but the last. Gene accepted all but D, and Fred accepted them all.

We debated these six propositions for several hours, for each one of these objections could be profitably discussed. This appeared to be a routine activity of truth seeking: assert, question, defend—or drop. "The justice system's rules and procedures should, and to some degree do, mirror how individuals attempt to determine truth," Chambers wrote. "The system's reliance on various procedures and rules is a recognition that society believes those procedures and rules are or have been reliable aids to truth-seeking."[46] Right, or at least society had better believe in those procedures if the jury is to retain its critical role in our democracy. Take the police testimony, for example. Gene discerned something suspicious there and wanted to dispense with the whole of it. Well, he was right; there was something fishy about the way the police officers testified. Sometimes it was wooden, sometimes rehearsed, and sometimes incoherent; however, it was never wholly valueless. It was clear that the officers were trying to form their

---

to be able to articulate to themselves the reason behind their doubt that the defendant committed the crime" ("Reasonable Doubt: How in the World Is It Defined?" 224).

46. Henry L. Chambers Jr., "Reasonable Certainty and Reasonable Doubt," 677–78.

testimony around legal stipulations. The cynicism that is engendered in that relationship was troubling even to first-time observers, and it was quite possibly the most corrosive element of the legal process that we encountered.[47]

It had been a long time since we had heard the autopsy report, and we were having difficulty remembering the exact description of the marks left by the cinder block on Nancy McCloskey's body. We submitted a request to rehear the report. The court complied immediately. Several of us were stunned when we returned to the deliberation room. We kept coming back to a single phrase that none of us had recalled from the earlier testimony. The doctor described the marks as "circular punctates in a rectangular form." "How many kinds of objects have circular punctates in rectangular form?" I mused. "It is practically a definition of a cinder block. How many times is the word *punctates* even used?" Gene scoffed, "I use it all the time." Dennis stepped forward to make his most stirring speech of the trial. Before that, Dennis had interjected mostly one-liners. He was the funny guy, not the speech maker. But he suddenly became eloquent. After rehearing the report, he was convinced that the cinder block was the murder weapon, that it was not merely the favorite thesis of the police, as Gene had it. Jen concurred. She said that she had had the exact same experience that Dennis had just described; she was absolutely certain that the cinder block was the murder weapon. That alliance was most gratifying. Thomas objected, saying it didn't sound to him as if the doctor was drawing the conclusion that Nancy McCloskey was hit by the cinder block. The quiet jurors responded again, with effect. "*He* is not supposed to draw conclusions, Thomas, *we* are." The jury became so caught up in reactions to the phrase

---

47. Morgan Cloud details the scope of police perjury in her disturbing essay "The Dirty Little Secret." She describes perjury as "a uniquely corrupt lie, because it is offered by government officials who are sworn to enforce and uphold the law" (1311). William Pizzi makes another forceful argument that the whole Miranda line of cases has had the insidious result of making the trial system dishonest and cynical, "as police officers shade or sometimes distort their testimony to avoid the suppression of incriminating statements. . . . [and] a certain amount of dishonesty comes to be expected and tolerated of everyone—even police officers and judges" (*Trials without Truth: Why Our System of Criminal Trials Has Become an Expensive Failure and What We Need to Do about It,* 68).

"circular punctates in a rectangular form" that we submitted a request to have it read to us for a third time. That was placed on the next day's agenda. We posed our own question five again before departing for the evening. Is it reasonable to assume that the cinder block was involved in the attack on Nancy McCloskey? The revised vote was yes, 12–0. It was our finest hour, I thought. We had succeeded in shaming them.

That day, I was able to make it to the tail end of my last Directed Studies section of the year. As I headed into Harkness Hall, my shoes clicked in the empty corridors. I felt like an interloper. Had I really taught in this building just three weeks ago? There was that feeling of unreality again. I stood at the classroom door unobserved for a few moments. Charlie was teaching Aquinas, and the students were engrossed in his lecture; all eyes were focused on the blackboard and his complicated rendition of the interrelations of Aquinas's categories of law. He paused, and then announced, "the foreman has arrived." My students gaped. What kind of appearance had I made? It was a distressingly emotional moment for me. As soon as Charlie left, our frivolity started; there would be no more learning about eternal law today. They asked all the questions that I was not permitted to answer. I had to be circumspect. The majority jurors have two adversaries, I told them. "One is a poet, and one is a sophist. Each is accomplished in sabotaging our deliberation." I told them that it was an ordeal, in the courthouse and out. "I get up at 2 a.m. and watch stupid movies until dawn." I felt as if I was the one who was eighteen and seeking counsel. "What did you watch last night?" *Clueless,* I answered. They all burst into laughter, but I didn't get it. When we assembled one last time for the final examination review, they brought a present for me: my own copy of *Bridget Jones's Diary.* "You'll sleep better," they promised.

I attended my first Directed Studies function in weeks. It was the final colloquium of the semester, and the featured speaker was Stanford's former president Gerhard Caspar. His speech was on Aristotle and citizenship. President Levin was in attendance, and there was a celebratory dinner directly after the event at his house. I hadn't seen my colleagues in weeks. Now I was a celebrity juror. The two presidents turned their chairs around to face me before the event began and quizzed me about the case. Each had his own story of being called to jury duty while sitting as university president. President Levin related that the judge had said to him, "I'm sure you have better things to do," and had sent him home. He had already served on a jury before, when he was an assistant professor at Yale. He was the lone holdout against conviction, until his fellow jurors persuaded him that his doubt was not reasonable. When it was all over, he recounted, the judge congratulated them all on their courage—and then shared the devastating priors of the defendant that they had not been permitted to hear. Gerhard Caspar said of his jury experience in Palo Alto that he was snapped at, told to sit down and wait his turn like everyone else. As he waited, he heard three prospective jurors get dismissed by saying "I hate lawyers." President Caspar then took the stage and told Stanford-Yale jokes. Eventually he got serious. "I'm going to talk to you about Aristotle and jury duty," he began.

Back in the courthouse the next day we reheard parts of the autopsy report, as requested. Then we returned to the deliberation room expecting to move on to question six: is it reasonable to assume that the accused would not have been aware of what the coroner determined to be the official cause of death? I was champing at the bit: another day like yesterday and we would be on our way. But no. It was back to the cinder block imprint, for Gene and Thomas had retreated and wanted a new vote. On the third hearing, they had observed that "the doctor said the imprint was *almost* in rectangular form. The mark wasn't a perfect rectangle." The rest of the jurors were aghast. I suddenly developed an excessively high voice. "You were expecting an imprint of a *perfect rectangle,* on the human body, through a leather jacket, sweater, and shirt?" Gene repeated those awful words, "He said almost."

Just like that, we had gone from our highest high to our lowest low. The search for the perfect rectangle. They were serious. The jury broke down. Johnny suggested it first: it was time to write that note. I resisted, in disbelief. We went around the table again and heard everybody out. Most of what we said to each other from that point on just caused pain. "He's getting away with murder; he will do it again." Fred had tears in his eyes as he listened to comments like the following: "I hope you can live with yourself. I have a daughter, and now

I'm going to be afraid for her sake every time she goes outside." Doleen interrupted, "He is not going to *your* neighborhood; he's coming to *mine*." No one disagreed. To the last, race as an issue was nowhere in this case, and everywhere. Now it was over. At one point, I had vowed to myself that I would never write the note to Judge Fracasse saying that we were deadlocked. If it came to it, I would ask to be taken off the jury because nothing was going to make me give in. But I changed my mind; I belonged with the majority.[48] The majority had decided that it was impossible to proceed, and we surrendered.

Before the judge would accept our surrender, however, he read us the Chip Smith instruction. The minority party was told that they should show due regard and deference to the majority, that "they ought seriously to ask themselves whether they ought not to doubt their own conclusions." Whoever Chip Smith was, he sure had the lawyer's knack for peculiar locutions. Louise said that she had tried thinking that way, "but I always end up with a reasonable doubt." Gene took the occasion to tell us about the time he overheard a man on a bus talking about a murder he had committed. Gene had turned to get a look at the speaker. Leaving the bus, he went straight to the police. "I was flabbergasted," he related. "I couldn't distinguish the people in the mug book from my recollection." I was flabbergasted that he had waited so long to reveal this. Here it is, I thought, the block, the thing that made him unreachable, that prevented him from deliberating. No one could make a positive identification if he could not. Why was he on this jury?[49] Thomas was next. He said that he had given himself the Chip Smith charge all the way through. Kathryn retorted rudely, "You did not. You called for things, you got them, and you went on holding your view." It was like fighting with shadows.

48. I was somewhat consoled later to be reminded that I had not actually betrayed my Aristotelian roots. "Aristotle nowhere explicitly says that the aim of rhetoric is to persuade. As near as we have been able to determine, the aim of rhetoric is to practice judgment (to enact *krisis*) where certain sorts of problematic materials are concerned" (Thomas B. Farrell, *Norms of Rhetorical Culture,* 94).

49. Eric Holder, the U.S. attorney for the District of Columbia, is quoted by Rosen on the topic of certain unreachable jurors "who are *beyond help* . . . These are the people who get into the jury rooms and then simply don't deliberate" ("One Angry Woman," 60).

We couldn't refute with no one to answer. The last notes I jotted down were from Thomas, appropriately emotional: "I remember feeling there wasn't any distinction between the different witnesses." It was a little late for Chip Smith.

Judge Fracasse came to our room to discharge us. There was no question that we had given it our best. Fred was in the bathroom, and someone asked the judge if he could wait for him to rejoin us. It appeared that we were still an entity. I froze in my place and couldn't say a word; the lump in my throat was prohibitive. The judge attempted small talk. The view was beautiful, it was a nice day, warm for so late in the season. I was aware of my ludicrous position—speak, foreman, speak!—but it was no use. I was so ashamed for us, so sorry for Nancy and for everyone in her unhappy family. I felt that we had betrayed many good and responsible people, from the prosecutor to the school kids, implausibly sitting through our trial. I thought of Suzanne. The judge's kind words were only going to release a torrent of tears if I let down my guard. I remained mute throughout his dismissal. In that same state, I managed the last elevator ride up to the ninth floor, deserted but for us. Half of the group was milling around when I got there. Jen came toward me like a torpedo and embraced me fiercely. "I want to tell you," she said, "that I respect you more than any woman I have ever met, for what you did in there." That did it. The trickle of tears had begun and wouldn't stop for days. Johnny came over and gave me a hug that was just short of crushing my bones. When he released his bear hold, he said, "I'm sorry I let you down." I told him that he didn't let me down, and I hope he knew: I *meant* it. My devotion to the cause had gone over the top. It is one of my best features to recognize my lunacy, and others', when it surfaces. We all went home. It was a nice day, warm for so late in the season. There was nothing to do but to go to Paris after all. Forget justice.

IV

My Literary Jurors

The book, if you would see anything in it, requires to be read in the clear, brown, twilight atmosphere in which it was written; if opened in the sunshine, it is apt to look exceedingly like a volume of blank pages.

—NATHANIEL HAWTHORNE, *Twice-Told Tales*

Escape to Paris

Too late. Paris is an enchanting city, but it will match you, mood for mood. By my request, we visited the cemeteries. My companions and I (not Charlie—"Been there," he'd said) strolled through Montparnasse: Man Ray, Baudelaire, Samuel Beckett, Simone de Beauvoir, Jean-Paul Sartre. This trip was very cool, very Paris, but I was still distressed, out of sorts. We pushed on to Père Lachaise. María led the tour, rehearsing and reliving the Jim Morrison saga as her twelve-year-old daughter, Margaux, clambered over the stones. Then she delivered an improvised lecture on Héloise and Abelard. We scouted out the markers for Proust, Apollinaire, Balzac, Maria Callas, and Talleyrand. But where were Gertrude Stein and Alice B. Toklas?

I told Margaux that Gertrude Stein was a famous literary figure who gave invaluable advice to aspiring writers. "She's the one who said 'It is inexcusable to remark that you had lunch and not to say just what you ate.'" Margaux responded that her favorite poet was Percy Bysshe Shelley. "'Zeinab and Kathema' shows the power of love," she explained, "and the cruelty and guiltiness of humankind." Oh. Well, I was a groupie in search of Gertrude Stein. In earlier years, my well-meaning academic friends had tried to dissuade me from including a chapter on Stein in my otherwise highbrow *Ship of State*. You will risk your academic reputation, they warned. But I held firm. "She's way funnier than Aristotle," I protested, but I did not manage a single convert. No matter; Gertrude could take care of herself. Soon we located the gravesite of Stein and Toklas. "There's one thing you can say for dead writers," I remarked to María. "They're never the first ones to cut off the conversation." And that was my ah ha! moment in Père Lachaise. I would round off my jury story with the help of the dead.

Why not summon a full complement of alternate jurors? I could steal a page from *The Devil and Daniel Webster* by Stephen Vincent Benét. In this work, I recalled, the Devil formed his jury by combing through the pages of American history to find the most odious characters imaginable. The reverse tactic might serve me well, to help me sort through the large themes of crime and punishment, theory and reality, and knowledge and uncertainty that were still preoccupying me. Whereas the Devil included on his jury the cruel Governor Dale, who broke men on the wheel, and Teach, the bloody pirate, with his black beard curling on his breast (Benedict Arnold was previously engaged), I would select the likes of Plato, Jane Austen, Faulkner, and Aeschylus. After all, from the start of my ruminations, I had enlisted the help of serious thinkers of the past. The nascent jury was already at least half formed. To reach their full potential, my literary jurors just required one further step of recognition.

In María's apartment during my final evening in Paris, Margaux wanted to hear everything about the jury experience. She devoured the notes I had taken during both the trial and the deliberations, and she pestered me with questions, about the jurors I liked and the jurors I hated. What's a stop sign hat, she asked. What's cousin to Mother's? She was attached to Cruz and his flair for description. I told her Randall was "the man." Margaux and I had private jokes—María was saving herself for the book—that involved quoting lines back and forth. The jokes weren't funny ("What's that noise?" "Raccoons."), but I began to laugh again. Had it really come to that? Later I learned that Johnny never made it to California. Some undiagnosed illness laid him low for several weeks. David, too, became seriously ill right after the case ended. But I had suddenly regained my footing. By the following afternoon, after having snuck into the atelier at 27 rue de Fleurus and eaten lunch at Chez Renée (coq au vin with the house wine, followed by two servings of crème caramel), I was ready to return to New Haven to convene my new and preferred jury.

My juror one, Herodotus, needs a little explaining. I refer not to the old saw about him being both "Father of History" and "Father of Lies" but to the rather odd fact that in this text, he has come up only once before. (Another foreman neglecting to take his seat?) That single mention is revealing, however, for in it I acknowledge my hope of being Herodotean in my trial observations.[1] I mean this literally. As Hannah Arendt wrote, "no human world destined to outlast the short life span of mortals within it will ever be able to survive without men willing to do what Herodotus was the first to undertake consciously— namely, *legein ta eonta,* to say what is. No permanence, no perseverance in existence, can even be conceived without men willing to testify to what is and appears to them because it is."[2] My identification with Herodotus is complete, and to explain *that* requires a slight detour, from Maine to Chicago to the Committee on Social Thought.

Juror two is Plato, almost as dominant in these proceedings as Herodotus. Plato is highly relevant not only for his searing indictments of poet and sophist—the old enemies of the jury—but also for his account of the most famous trial in the Western world in *The Apology of Socrates.* From Plato, two more modern jurors follow neatly, in theme and in my classroom teaching. Jane Austen speaks to the Platonic quarrel between philosophy and poetry in *Emma,* and William Faulkner addresses the ever-present threat of sophistry in *Absalom, Absalom!* Jurors five and six are Aristotle and Tocqueville, who have made their presence known throughout. Five quiet jurors are assembled for crucial backup: Dante, Thoreau, Longfellow, Gertrude Stein, and Wallace Stevens. For the final juror (last and first, as Aristotle might say), I turn in my last chapter to the archetypal author

1. For more on the historian's double appellations, see my *Herodotus and the Origins of the Political Community: Arion's Leap,* 1–6.
2. Hannah Arendt, *Between Past and Future: Eight Exercises in Political Thought,* 229.

on unavenged murder, Aeschylus. Thus assembled, my literary jurors have the last word on an ordinary murder in New Haven.

From Learning Process to Judicial Process

I went to Bowdoin College in 1977 because I had heard that it was a good place to study literature. Then I didn't study literature. Unfocused, I turned to history, which I was good at, except for the names and the dates. The requirements for a degree in history were few and far between. To be a history major, you had to take eight courses, including one non-Western sequence. I must have specialized in something. This was the era of the decline in survey classes and periodizations. As a result, for years I confused the Renaissance and the Enlightenment. These seemed to be just different names for the same thing, the claim that from now on people would be reasonable. The closest I came to taking a science course was Probability in the mathematics department, which I thought might help my gambling skills. Actually, it established gambling as an irrational activity, sort of in line with my early selection of courses.

As that uneducated student Allan Bloom would write about in *The Closing of the American Mind,* I knew Hawthorne and Longfellow (connected by a hyphen) only as the namesakes of the library. When I began to fill in the gaps in my education, I was gratified to discover that they had more in common than the mere accident of matriculating at the same time at Bowdoin College. Longfellow reviewed Hawthorne's *Twice-Told Tales:* "These flowers and green leaves of poetry have not the dust of the highway upon them. . . . for [to the poet Hawthorne] external form is but the representation of internal being, all things having a life, an end and aim."[3] A life, an end, an aim? At eighteen, nineteen, twenty, one longs to fill in those blanks. Overspecialized courses in college do not do the trick. Students who are adrift are liable to be duped.

At Bowdoin I started to gravitate toward courses in which the texts addressed good and evil: Professor Geohegan (whose nickname on campus was God) on Kierkegaard and Hegel, Professor Karl on Nazi

3. Longfellow, review of *Twice-Told Tales,* by Nathaniel Hawthorne, 59–73.

Germany. For my junior semester, I went abroad to the London School of Economics and took a tutorial with Philip Windsor on Marx and Alienation. This pedagogical situation was eye-opening. He'd assign me eight or ten books, with instructions to come back with one page of comments to read aloud. There was no slumping in the back row; I was on all the time. I lost fifteen pounds studying *The Economic and Philosophic Manuscripts of 1844,* while my roommates took tea at Harrods and roamed the city. One day Windsor shouted, "you've got it!" and I understood more than the early Marx: thinking about books could be the most exciting activity in the world. I returned to Brunswick, Maine, a committed Marxist.

As I completed my degree in history, I took many more courses on nineteenth- and twentieth-century authors: Tocqueville, Dostoevsky, Nietzsche, the Frankfurt School. I gravitated toward political theory courses offered by the government department. I especially liked Joan Tronto's classes. At the time, she was the only female in the department. She was young, smart, and outspoken, and she was finishing her dissertation at Princeton. In addition to teaching courses from Plato through NATO, she formed a feminist group for the Brunswick-Bath area. I became a Marxist feminist. Our meetings were held in a church basement downtown. We sat in a circle, so that no one's voice would be dominant. The excruciatingly banal chatter was only relieved when Joan would resume speaking. So my first lesson was that leaderless groups are an irritant and a bore. We had a bake sale, to send someone to Chicago to support the ERA amendment. It was May 1980, and eighty-five thousand or so of us turned out to march by the lake. My second lesson was that masses of people aren't so great either. The city of Chicago, however, definitely caught my eye. When I returned to Maine, Joan suggested that I write my senior essay on Hannah Arendt's *Origins of Totalitarianism* as a way of bringing together political philosophy and history. It was an inspired idea. Mary Dietz, a scholar of Arendt, had joined the Bowdoin faculty that year, so it was settled. If all of this was a bit fortuitous, I had, by the end, become open to the power of books. In the course of my senior year, my mind became set on graduate study at the University of Chicago. This didn't go over very well with my college professors. I expect they foresaw the end of my allegiance to the People. "Watch out for the Straussians," they warned, and I just nodded; for all I knew, they might as well have said, "watch out for the Martians."

Like Athena, the University of Chicago sprang full-blown from the brow of Zeus—in this case John D. Rockefeller, who brought (bought) William Rainey Harper, a Hebraist from Yale, to the Midway and enabled him to gather (steal) the greatest array of professors in the land. Then in the 1930s, Robert Maynard Hutchins, the boy-wonder dean of Yale Law School, took over. He abolished Chicago's Big Ten winning football team and created the most intellectually intense blast furnace in the world.

Drawn by that reputation, I went to Chicago. My dissertation adviser James Redfield, the classicist, wrote in an open letter to the faculty and students,

> The University of Chicago lives on its morale. It is located in an unpleasant city, in a nasty climate, a thousand miles from anywhere; most members of this faculty could immediately increase their salaries by going to other universities. They are here rather than elsewhere because they value their colleagues and their students. If the web of those relations is torn, the University will fall in on itself.

At the University of Chicago, it was said, you either thrive on intellectual ferocity or you don't. When I arrived on campus, one of the perennially popular best sellers of the time was *Zen and the Art of Motorcycle Maintenance*. Phaedrus arrives at the University of Chicago as a graduate student in the Committee on Analysis of Ideas and Methods, where he finds himself in a battle with a philosophy professor. Phaedrus immerses himself in Plato in order to challenge the professor but the effort causes him to suffer a mental breakdown. It wasn't quite like that for me. I was busy filling in the gaps in my education and wasn't going to be challenging professors anytime soon, especially these professors, who wore their learning casually but unmercifully. Still, Phaedrus got the atmosphere about right, and all around me people folded in and dropped out.

The Committee on Analysis of Ideas and Methods sounded a whole lot like the Committee on Social Thought, to which I had, to my amazement, been accepted as a PhD candidate. The Committee

on Social Thought was created after World War II to be, in effect, the
"Chicago of Chicago," a pantheon of scholars especially selected for
their relentless intellectual curiosity and profundity, liberated from
tiresome departmental requirements and the restrictive methodology
of a single discipline. My principal advisor was David Grene, a great
classicist and a translator of Greek drama, then in the midst of his
Herodotus translation.

Whenever people write or talk about David Grene, they almost always do so in conjunction with some awesome literary personage
whom he knew intimately, such as Clytemnestra or Hedda Gabler. A
reporter for the *Chicago Tribune* was instructed by David on both accounts: "For heaven's sake, dearie, Hedda kills herself because it is
the only way she sees meaning anywhere. She is a woman with a
yearning to be somebody who really matters." And later in the same
interview, he said, "Aeschylus, you see, was concerned with how any
human carries the weight of their past into the present time. Clytemnestra becomes an agent of all the awful things that happen in the
house. And she has the mind of a man, you know."[4]

Saul Bellow, David's colleague on the committee, has been widely
quoted as suggesting that Grene "was on a first-name basis with
Sophocles and Aristophanes."[5] No doubt fifty-plus years of students
at the University of Chicago would add many more names to that list,
including Homer, Aeschylus, Shakespeare, James Joyce, and Yeats.
My own connection to David was made through Enobarbus, of *Antony
and Cleopatra,* three years into my coursework. After I wrote a paper
on how to direct the character Enobarbus, I existed in David's world;
before that, I did not. Existence is more meaningful when earned,
and David inspired a new kind of life. "Can you learn more from a
person or from a book?" That was my question a decade later to select Yale College seniors, aspirants to a secret society, on tap night at
Mory's where my husband and I joined the elders to usher in the new
delegation. Invariably, students answered, "a person" (a person can
change as you change and offer new guidance). Wrong! Charlie and I

4. Toni Schlesinger, "Zeus of the Classics," *Chicago Tribune,* December 7, 1986.
5. Douglas Martin, "David Grene, Colorful Expert on the Classics, Is Dead at
89," *New York Times,* September 17, 2002.

remained silent in our correction, but they were wrong. The book comes first, and David Grene proved it. People unshaped by books are usually shapeless, I concluded. People of the book are aware that life is both real and earnest. Later, my experience on a jury would compel me to revise that assessment.

Some people had a hard time fathoming how David Grene could be a full-time academic and a full-time farmer. It was simple, really: he did not split his days (at least when I knew him) but his year. From April until the start of September, David was in Ireland on the farm, and then he wintered in Chicago, where the university followed the intense quarter system. Steffi Nelson, my fellow student on the Committee of Social Thought and David's companion, traveled with him back and forth, studying Greek one month and milking cows the next. She assured us that the farmers in County Cavan had just as hard a time imagining David teaching classics to university students as we did picturing him on his dairy farm. Of course, there were some points of overlap. He could scarcely forget his Hesiod during planting season, Ireland or no, and for a long time, David also owned a farm outside of Chicago. He would come to his evening classes with the manure still on his boots to prove it.

Grene's students didn't care what he brought to class on his boots. To be in his presence was not exactly entertainment, on account of the demands put on the audience, but it certainly was captivating, as he plunged into the minds of his subjects and his authors. My first class with him was on the *Odyssey*. This class met once a week for English readers and twice a week for those students who read Greek. On Wednesday evenings, then—for I had not taken Greek, and to be truthful, I had not studied Homer in English before this—we worked through two books of the *Odyssey*. David would start off by talking for fifteen minutes or so, giving us his thoughts on certain passages, then he would end his lecture abruptly and turn to (on) someone he respected and demand a response. This is exactly what he did to me some years later at my inaugural address, the public event celebrating the completion of my dissertation on Herodotus. His question was fifteen minutes long.

For several weeks, I sat through David's class in stark terror before I realized that he would never waste his time on someone like me who always had that deer-caught-in-the-headlights look on my face. That moment of recognition was followed by furious preparation to become the first person called on. (And since one could not be really serious unless one read Greek, I duly enrolled for the intensive language course over the summer.) David would make the most arresting comments in class. About Telemachus, he announced early on, "I never liked that boy." I remember looking around the classroom furtively. Could you *say* things like that? I didn't care much for Telemachus, either, and in David's class, it was a perfectly respectable observation that would be backed up by detailed readings of the petulant exchanges between Telemachus and Penelope. David was insightful on the family relations and the personalities of the servants—the savage Eurykleia in this story, Kent in *King Lear,* and Enobarbus in *Antony and Cleopatra*—but his real genius was in apprehending the world of the lovers. He did a mean Cleopatra.

David Grene was a man who did not mince his words and who did not care about his status. On those ubiquitous forms that academics have to fill out, he left blank the sections on academic honors and citations. This is the man whose *Complete Greek Tragedies* (coauthored by Richmond Lattimore) sold over a million copies. For memberships in learned societies, he should have listed Jimmy's, the run-down joint to which he repaired for lunch every day, and where after his evening seminars, his conversations with his students continued. A typical lunch consisted of two martinis and one hamburger, loaded with salt. In the evenings, I never saw anyone eat anything.

Other professors routinely sat in on his classes. One of them later recalled that David kept calling on him in a Greek class. Finally, he took Grene aside to remind him that "I'm a *professor* here." Grene responded, "All right; I'll give you the hard parts." All that mattered to David was great literature, deep thinking, and people with ideas. This had predictable consequences. Very early in his life David had begun accommodating the two worlds of the seminar and the farm, just in case he should get fired from his day job. He did. As the story goes, he got fired twice in the same day, once by the chair of classics department and once by the chair of the English department. But instead of retiring wholly to his farm, David picked up a new job, when the president of the University of Chicago appointed him to the Committee on Social Thought. Robert Maynard Hutchins had anticipated this moment, putting a note in Grene's file that read, "This man is not to be fired without my permission."[6]

When I spoke at David Grene's memorial service in November 2002, I confessed that I liked to think that David was ultimately responsible for all the trouble I'd gotten myself into at Yale in the decade past. (Once I announced at a senior political science faculty meeting that the result of our attending so single-mindedly to quantitative matters in our hiring practices was that a certain kind of aggressive work dominated the department—scientific, tightly focused, abstract, and removed from values or principles or history or, especially, politics. They stared blankly. "And it's antifemale," I added, which it was. But I never could explain. They wore me down with their hard evidence. "Count the women! Count them! Count them!") Robert Pippin, chair of the Committee on Social Thought, declared Grene to be "the conscience of the Committee." More than my career, my temperament was formed by one of David Grene's dearest subjects, one that also became mine, Herodotus. "I don't only want to write about Herodotus," I acknowledged to myself. "I want to *become* him."

Grene's Friday afternoon seminars drew me inexorably to the study of Herodotean historiography. Herodotus established that there is an art to recognizing what is worthy of historical memory. He began his *History* with the acknowledgment that human beings can never know for certain what will turn out to be significant: "I will go forward in my account, covering alike the small and great cities of mankind. For of those that were great in earlier times most have now become small, and those that were great in my time were small in the time before."[7] His conclusion was that if there is to be any hope for grounded evaluations, the investigator must stick closely to what is said. This did not imply that the historian needs to be gullible about the accounts he takes in ("I must tell what is said, but I am not at all bound to believe it" [*Hist* 7.152]). It meant, rather, that he orients himself in the midst of multiple stories and self-descriptions. From his example we infer

6. Ibid.
7. Herodotus *The History* 1.5 (hereafter cited parenthetically as *Hist*).

that human beings cannot remind themselves too often that their views are partial and their understanding limited. Grene described the importance of single facts for Herodotus as really beginning only when they were thought and voiced and took on a new supervening shape, so that what was important was not the original isolated historical act, "but rather what was released by the act into the world of thought and feeling and continued thereafter." Herodotus listened for primary stories in which "the archetypes of joy and sorrow, truth and falsehood, strength and feebleness . . . [lived] in narrative form" (*Hist* 6, 13).

Only at Chicago. I began emulating an ancient Greek historian as an observer of the human condition. I am a believer still. He may be largely invisible in this work, but his imprint is everywhere. When Herodotus invented historical inquiry, he nailed it the first time through. If he passed himself off as a charming storyteller, these were stories with an edge, stories that carved out compelling truths in the conflict he traced between liberty and tyranny. My shorthand for his discovery is the fighting story: some things just have to be told, retold, and preserved.[8] He saw that certain accounts battle their way into common discourse and persist in that discourse, linking knowledge and life. These stories of Herodotus have many striking features. The winding excursus: how far afield can you take the reader? (As far as it takes.) The ear for language that distinguishes human beings. The belief that the complexity of history is best accommodated by building on the concrete and visualizable detail. The attention, but not slavish attention, to information that may be verified. The capacity and the willingness to judge. The recognition of the limits of human knowledge. All of these characteristics of Herodotus' *History* can be tried on for size—in the workplace, in the narrative, and, not least of all, in the courtroom. Herodotus was a phenomenal listener, and that skill above all else is the one I aim to cultivate.

Judging Socrates: The Poet in Plato's *Apology*

Like Herodotus, Plato has served a useful if understated role as literary juror throughout this book. Whereas Herodotus inspired the

8. See my *Herodotus,* 28–31.

methodology, Plato provided the unifying appellations *poet* and *sophist* that enabled me to recognize my adversaries in the deliberation room. If those terms strike the modern ear as archaic, the specific poets and sophists who appear as characters in Platonic dialogues display traits from emotionalism to relativism that are concrete and alarmingly familiar. Plato's main character and obsession is Socrates, whose infamous courtroom appearance qualifies him as the patron saint of lost causes. My own efforts in the deliberation room had been thwarted; I was unable to convince my fellow jurors that Bazier was guilty. But I decided that I might as well keep good company by seeking to lose my case with honor.[9] At issue in the battle is the kind of verbal authority that is to prevail in the courtroom.

In Plato's account, Socrates never has a prayer for acquittal after the capital charges of impiety and corrupting the young are leveled against him. The only unknown is what sense will accrue to the event. What is the lasting significance of the court case? The great imaginative flourish of the *Apology* is when Socrates transfigures Meletus, the insignificant but present accuser, into Aristophanes, the significant but absent poet. Socrates thereby connects the comic poet to the attack on his philosophic activity, and he stresses the obliviousness of Meletus to the whole matter. (Need it be said? Thomas is Meletus.) The poet and the philosopher appear to be locked in an age-old struggle over the issue of rational justification. In the *Gorgias,* a dialogue that only jests about a philosopher being executed by his city, an analogous transfiguration of sophists occurs, this one devolving from Gorgias to Polus to Callicles (and Gene is Gorgias). In this instance of dramatic reconfiguration, as in the case of Meletus-Aristophanes, Socrates enlarges the scope of the verdict against him to one of the city against the philosopher. Socrates impugns the authorities who are persuasive in the city of Athens as speakers interested only in the *command* of language and who dismiss its unstable forms. Poet and sophist are put in their rightful place.

Socrates is the sole speaker in Plato's *Apology,* except for a few lines reluctantly delivered by Meletus (and an interjection by Plato, reported secondhand). Concerned as he is to undercut the truth-telling value of long speeches, Socrates finds ways to import one-on-

9. James Redfield, "A Lecture on Plato's *Apology,*" 104.

one exchanges, fashioning in his imagination the interlocutors he needs and addressing his jury in singular terms. However, the serious peril for Socrates is not really the length of his speech (never has an individual been so well fortified in any rhetorical setting, so long as *logos* [argument] is respected) but the shortness of time. He is put on the defensive; the clock is ticking while he seeks to explain how it is that at the age of seventy he has been indicted for a capital crime. During this time the audience needs to be cajoled out of its theatric mode, or at least into recognizing it: "Socrates struggles to make conspicuous the court's implied demand that an accused *play* at his innocence . . . as an actor rehearsing a social script; one must pretend to be innocent, even if one really *is* innocent."[10] If the Athenians had had a law "like other human beings, not to judge anyone in a matter of death in one day alone, but over many," then, Socrates predicts, he would have been able to succeed in persuasion.[11] But he could not succeed in Athens, not on these terms. "For there is no human being who will preserve his life if he genuinely opposes either you or any other multitude and prevents many unjust and unlawful things from happening in the city" (*Apol* 31e).

What is worth saying, when time is short and persuasion unlikely? The Socratic response is to demonstrate that the threat to justice comes not from the philosopher but from the poet, particularly the unthinking kind of poet, such as Meletus. For if the court system is to call its citizens to account, it must uphold as its measure self-examination, the paradigmatic activity of the philosopher. Socrates will explain. He begins by focusing on the nature of performance and the way performers sweep their audience into an uncritical assent. In his opening lines in the *Apology,* Socrates associates the ability of his accusers to persuade with a kind of enchantment (such that he nearly forgets himself listening to them) and with a kind of deception: "And yet they have said, so to speak, nothing true" (*Apol* 17a). People who have a magnetic presence work most powerfully in public settings in which

10. Jay Farness, *Missing Socrates: Problems of Plato's Writing,* 41. Farness notes that the impersonality of the verb *apologeteon* (to make a defense) "marks the self-denial, the third-personing, of the merely persuasive or winning self-presentation, according to which the performer inhabits or impersonates the mentality of spectators" (41).

11. Plato *Apology* 37a (hereafter cited parenthetically as *Apol*).

they can declaim without interruption and at length. (To state the obvious, in our age we have entertainers aplenty who fit the bill. Poets can be found in the movies, on the playing field, making rap music, or delivering college lectures.) Although Socrates is being forced to put on a show of his own, his watchword is truth and not persuasion. Speaking plainly is his métier, and Socrates' plain assessment is that the judge, if he is worthy of the name, must venerate truth.[12]

Socrates introduces two sets of players during his defense, his old and new accusers. By his account, the old accusers predate the new ones by a generation, and they are more dangerous for having brainwashed many members of the jury when the jurors were just children. His old accusers are difficult to identify, "unless a certain one happens to be a comic poet" (*Apol* 18d). That would be Aristophanes, who is in fact the one who counts. In Aristophanes' comedy *The Clouds,* Socrates is caricatured mercilessly as a busybody who investigates the things in the heavens and under the earth and who makes the weaker argument the stronger. The theme of that portrait is that Socrates is a sophist living outside the concerns of the city and, indeed, threatening its conventions through his relentless disputations. By 399 BC, the sophists were vaguely associated with troubled times in Athens, when religious beliefs had begun to break down, traditional respect for authority was diminishing, and a new covetousness was taking hold. The conservative elements of the city were ready to lash out at anyone associated with these sophistic innovations.[13]

Without a doubt, Aristophanes left his mark on Socrates, and the

12. Is this mere platitude, or is it the key to what ails the American court system today? In his examination of American criminal trials, William Pizzi concludes that it is the latter. Pizzi strikes a Socratic note when he charges that our court system has placed too low a priority on truth. "A trial system that does not place a high priority on truth," he argues, "ultimately loses confidence in itself and becomes tentative and even apologetic." Pizzi observes that this system "encourages trial lawyers to think of themselves as actors on a stage as well as advocates" (*Trials without Truth,* 86, 129).

13. Aside from the sophists, Socrates had other connections that loomed as large to suspicious Athenian minds. Less than five years before Socrates' trial, the so-called Thirty Tyrants had ousted the democrats and ruled savagely until they themselves were overthrown. Among the leaders were at least two young men affiliated with Socrates, Critias and Charmides. The most notorious Athenian figure during the Peloponnesian War was surely Alcibiades, another Socratic figure. Thus Socrates' influence on the young was no light matter.

Athenians absorbed the caricature without attending too closely to the source; such is the power of the real poet, the unacknowledged legislator. Confronting this accusation later, Socrates reports, was like "fighting with shadows and refuting with no one to answer." It was up to the philosopher to point out that he was being prosecuted for charges in 399 BC that exactly befitted the protagonist of *The Clouds,* which was produced in 423 BC. In the play, the young man put under Socrates' care, Pheidippides, emerges sullen and disrespectful toward the old traditions. He is full of new enthusiasm for the clouds that the academic philosophers gaze upon: "great goddesses for idle men, who provide us with notions and dialectic and mind."[14] A generation later, Meletus accuses Socrates of doing "injustice by corrupting the young, and by not believing in the gods in whom the city believes, but in other *daimonia* [divinities] that are novel" (*Apol* 18d, 24c). Meletus does not seem to recognize that he is plagiarizing from Aristophanes. Yet he knows what he knows.

Perhaps, though, Aristophanes was correct in his judgment of Socrates? No reader of Plato's *Apology of Socrates* should discount this possibility out of hand. On stage as in life, Socrates appears to be adept at winning the point without affecting anyone's resolve. Frequently, Socrates seems actively to court the disfavor of his listeners, in carrying out his famous *elenchus* (refutation through cross-examination). Socratic elenchus has been defined as "a search for moral truth by question-and-answer adversary argument in which a thesis is debated only if asserted as the answerer's own belief and is regarded as refuted only if its negation is deduced from his own beliefs."[15] Correct, but these abstract terms in the definition soften the sting: in argument, Socrates can be such a pain. Of all times to display his hairsplitting techniques, he chooses to do so at this trial, arguing with Meletus not about whether the charge of impiety is valid, but about whether Meletus is consistent in the way he frames the charge. "Is there anyone who does not believe in horses, but believes in horse-matters?" Socrates seeks to ascertain. "Or anyone who does not believe in flute-players, but believes in flute-matters?" Again, when Socrates takes up

14. Aristophanes, *The Clouds,* 315–17.
15. Gregory Vlastos, *Socratic Studies,* ed. Myles Burnyeat, 4.

the charge that he is responsible for corrupting the young, he immediately lures Meletus into an untenable verbal maneuver. Either the claim is that Socrates corrupts students unintentionally, or it is that he does not corrupt them at all—but "in both cases what you say is false" (*Apol* 27b, 26a). No further mention is made of the shocking acknowledgment that Socrates may corrupt his followers unintentionally. Socrates' method of questioning clearly antagonizes the jury, for on several occasions he draws attention to the commotion being made in the courtroom. What possible constructive purpose could this approach have served? Socrates' defense of the philosophic life is underwhelming.

Nor does Socrates deny that, ultimately, he listens to a different drummer. He credits a certain divinity, a god designed solely for him. Since childhood, he reports, "something divine and daimonic comes to me . . . a sort of voice comes, and whenever it comes, it always turns me away from whatever I am about to do, but never turns me forward" (*Apol* 31d). Brann takes note of this inhibiting, negative character ("The *daimonion* is Socrates' *negative* enthusiasm, a permanently implanted restraining power . . . [his] ability to avoid wrong, his negative excellence") and puts it in the context of Socrates' philosophic activity as a whole: "Here, then, the philosophic activity is presented as an entirely negative effort, without an end or a substance"[16] The eccentric philosopher is himself a cause for wonder. According to Howland, "Socrates' total devotion to the quest for wisdom seems exceedingly odd in the light of the apparent fruitlessness of his inquiries."[17] The god has sent this man to awaken Athens through his ethical questioning, like the gadfly that goads the slumbering horse. He protests that this activity keeps him fully occupied but toward what end? The slumbering horse is roused, perhaps, but also mightily cross.

Socrates sees himself as caring for the souls of the Athenians, then, without any obvious way of avoiding the offense that he gives. Many powerful images from other Platonic dialogues reinforce this scenario.

16. Brann, *Music of the Republic,* 59, 61.
17. Jacob Howland, *The Paradox of Political Philosophy: Socrates' Philosophic Trial,* 34.

In the *Gorgias,* Socrates predicts memorably that he "will be tried as a doctor accused by a cook would be tried among children."[18] Another compelling one is the cave image from the *Republic.* In that work, Socrates imagines a dimly lighted cave in which prisoners are bound so that they can only see the back wall. They have been there since childhood, he says, "so that they are fixed, seeing only in front of them, unable because of the bond to turn their heads all the way around."[19] A fire from far behind them provides a source of light, and in between the fire and the prisoners is a road. Along the road is a wall, "built like the partitions puppet-handlers set in front of the human beings and over which they show the puppets." That wall is where the action is, for upon it walk "human beings carrying all sorts of artifacts, which project above the wall, and statues of men and other animals wrought from stone, wood, and every kind of material; as is to be expected, some of the carriers utter sounds while others are silent" (*Rep* 514c–515a). Those figures who project the images on the wall must include poets and sophists, and as they are the ones who manipulate what the prisoners see, they presumably have a great deal of power. They are the show makers, who are as delighted with their captive audience as their captive audience is with them.

In a nice touch, Socrates relates that the prisoners are so accustomed to their situation that they will resist if anyone attempts to free them from their bonds. Somehow, though, a single individual is able to release himself, make the painful turn, and eventually affect the ascent. This is the philosopher who escapes the confines of the everyday world to gaze upon eternal verities. Catching sight, finally, of the sun itself, he is blinded—and enlightened. But it will be a fine trick to persuade the others of their real circumstances once he returns to the cave from the brightness above. "Do you suppose it is anything surprising," Socrates asks, "if a man, come from acts of divine contemplation to the human evils, is graceless and looks quite ridiculous when—with his sight still dim and before he has gotten sufficiently accustomed to the surrounding darkness—he is compelled in courts or elsewhere to contest about the shadows of the just?" (*Rep* 517d).

---

18. Plato *The Gorgias* 521e (hereafter cited parenthetically as *Gor*).
19. Plato *The Republic* 514a–b (hereafter cited parenthetically as *Rep*).

In the *Apology* where Socrates actively must contest with the shadows of the just, he relates an analogous story to further his defense, a story hitherto unknown and, presumably, enraging to his audience. He relates that his associate Chaerephon took it upon himself to visit the Delphic oracle in order to ask if anyone were wiser than Socrates. The Pythia was alleged to have answered that no one was wiser. Socrates takes this response as a riddle to be solved: "for a long time I was at a loss about what ever [the god] was saying." Finally he resolves to refute the divination by uncovering someone wiser than he. So begin the labors of Socrates, recalling (in mischief) the labors of Heracles. He approaches, in turn, the politicians, the poets, and the manual artisans as people with the greatest claims to knowledge, seeking to test their wisdom. This is the genesis of the deep animosity that grew up against Socrates, for he reports that every time he questioned someone reputed to be wise, it would turn out that the wisdom inhered in that individual's eyes alone. For his part, Socrates, at least, can claim to apprehend his limits: "For probably neither of us knows anything noble and good, but he supposes he knows something when he does not know, while I, just as I do not know, do not even suppose that I do" (*Apol* 20e–21d). Socratic wisdom is outlandish and reserved at the same time.

Typically, Socrates reports, it was the people with the greatest reputations who were the most deficient in articulating their insights. About the poets in particular, Socrates comments that almost anyone could "have spoken better than [they] did about the poetry that they themselves had made" (*Apol* 22a–b).[20] It was not only the specific targets of this activity who took amiss the results of these examinations. Many of those who witnessed the cross-examinations felt the puncture vicariously, since they were not confident that they would have held up any better under Socratic questioning. Worse yet for Socrates' reputation, the young people who gathered around him enjoyed the exploits so much that they began to imitate him.

In seeking to refute the god, then, Socrates (accidentally) honors

---

20. Here as elsewhere one might feel compelled to stand up in defense of the poet, in favor of the poetry and not the exegesis. Yet if Socrates' standards are misplaced in judging the poets, so are the poets' in judging him.

him, but not before making himself exceedingly unpopular in the process. He portrays his elenchic activity as a service to the city, in line with his former patriotic deeds during the Peloponnesian War fighting in the battles of Potidaea, Amphipolis, and Delium. Is it unkind to observe that Socrates' service to the state consists largely of retreating well in the course of Athenian defeats? Strauss notes that "courage consisted less in remaining or staying than in honorably withdrawing or fleeing."[21] True, courage is a virtue regardless of the outcome of battle, but this retreating business is not the preferred mode of the warrior. It will take some work for Socrates to sell himself as the paradigm of courage—but that is exactly where he is going in this anecdote, which culminates, finally, in "the unexamined life is not worth living for a human being." Goldman investigates the philological background of the word *exetastos* (examination), and he discovers that it "is found quite infrequently in Plato, derives primarily from the language of fifth- and fourth-century military activity and service and from the notion of a review, examination, or mustering of troops and . . . it continues to carry this meaning and performative weight in that work."[22] Socrates appropriates the term en route to defining a new form of manliness. "Whenever someone stations himself," he insists, "holding that it is best, or wherever he is stationed by a ruler, there he must stay and run the risk, as it seems to me, and not take into account death or anything else compared to what is shameful" (*Apol* 38a, 28d). Taking his orders from the ruler or from the god, Socrates stands his ground. Since the god has stationed him in Athens, "ordering [him] to live philosophizing and examining [himself] and others," that is where he will remain, never to abandon his post for fear of death.

Funnily enough, Socrates is not joking, and no one in the courtroom is under any illusion that his philosophizing is somehow an inconsequential activity. He underscores his threatening role by gratuitously announcing that even if he were released from his current predicament, he would not cease to live the way he always has: "I,

---

21. Leo Strauss, *Studies in Platonic Political Philosophy,* 44.
22. Harvey S. Goldman, "Reexamining the 'Examined Life' in Plato's *Apology of Socrates,*" 3.

men of Athens, salute you and love you, but I will obey the god rather than you; and as long as I breathe and am able to, I will certainly not stop philosophizing" (*Apol* 29d). Socrates was initiating a culture war, and the Athenians were perceptive enough to apprehend it. If his view were to hold sway (and it did), it would signify a victory for rational justification as a gauge for truth. Reason counters poetic inspiration as the reigning authority in the city and in future courtrooms. Nietzsche, who favored the poet, finds much to censure in the moment: "Hence the image of the *dying Socrates,* as the human being whom knowledge and reasons have liberated from the fear of death, is the emblem that, above the entrance gate of science, reminds all of its mission—namely, to make existence appear comprehensible and thus justified; and if reasons do not suffice, *myth* has to come to their aid in the end."[23] Thus Nietzsche locates a pivotal moment in Western philosophy in the articulated stance of resistance by Socrates.

It is true as Nietzsche claims that Socrates brings myth to his aid in the service of logos. Homer is brought under his purview as he proposes an analog to his own elenchus. Socrates finds a parallel for himself in Achilles (identifying him obliquely as the son of Thetis), whose motive in rejoining the fray during the Trojan War is alleged to have been his fear of "[living] as a bad man and not [avenging] his friends" (*Apol* 28d). In this revisionist version, both Socrates and Achilles despise danger because they fear doing anything shameful. Homer has been left some distance behind. As West observes, "Homer's Achilles chooses to avenge Patroclus out of grief and anger. . . . Further, in Homer the death of Patroclus is for Achilles the private loss of his dearest friend, while Socrates transforms it into a crime that deserves punishment."[24] It is not a small difference, and the glaring incongruities lie right on the surface. The new account is particularly intriguing, according to Strauss, in that the comparison to Achilles suggests "that Socrates' way of life was not imposed on him by any command but originated entirely in his thinking."[25] We suspected as much.

23. Friedrich Nietzsche, *"The Birth of Tragedy" and "The Case of Wagner,"* 96.
24. Plato and Aristophanes, *Four Texts on Socrates: Plato's Euthyphro, Apology, and Crito and Aristophanes' Clouds,* 79n50.
25. Strauss, *Studies,* 44.

Socrates need not persuade anyone of his law-and-order Achilles in order to make the point that conventional Greek opinion is thoroughly formed by Homer and other poets. The philosophic alternative will not easily replace the conventional pieties that they have established. Whereas Nietzsche wholly condemns the "audacious reasonableness"[26] of Socrates, Plato keeps the focus on the parallelism: poet and philosopher each generate stories from an inscrutable source to explain man's place in the cosmos, and each possesses an uncommon knowledge. They are worthy combatants. When Socrates moves onto the poet's turf, his heavy-handedness is easy to criticize, for old warriors such as Achilles are not so easy to accommodate in the philosophic realm. Even so, Socratic storytelling remains self-reflexive and therefore amusing in its flights of fancy. Above all, he retains perspective. In one of the most moving moments of the *Apology,* Socrates addresses the judges who voted to acquit him and pleads with them to remain a little: "while the officials are occupied and I do not yet go to the place where, when I do go, I must die. Please stay with me, men, for this much time; nothing prevents our telling tales to one another as long as it is possible" (*Apol* 39e). To the last, Socrates just wants to talk—not to perform, not to assert metaphysical truths, not to rest easy with what he knows. Why rank his philosophic method among the great achievements of humanity? Vlastos asks. "Because it makes moral inquiry a common human enterprise, open to every man. Its practice calls for no adherence to a philosophical system, or mastery of a specialized technique, or acquisition of technical vocabulary. It calls for common sense and common speech."[27]

The vote to condemn Socrates was surprisingly close, surprising because Socrates hardly contested the point that philosophic authority is fundamentally at odds with poetic authority. Readers of Plato's *Apology of Socrates* have long concurred that the verdict was unjust. More than a generation later, when Aristotle chose to flee the city of Athens purportedly before it was allowed "to sin twice" against philosophy, no one had to ask about the original sin. Yet given the am-

---

26. Nietzsche, *Birth of Tragedy,* 84.
27. Gregory Vlastos, ed., *The Philosophy of Socrates: A Collection of Critical Essays,* 20.

bivalent nature of Socrates' defense, and the frequent supposition by readers that technically he was guilty as charged, it is perhaps worth pausing over the verdict. In my mind, this is a prime example of a trial in which the accused should have been acquitted by jury nullification because of the way the accused, Socrates, transformed the case into one of individual conscience. "Socrates does not answer the charge," Redfield concludes. "He makes it disappear."[28] The appropriate judgment, therefore, was nullification. Socrates recognized in his jurors who voted to acquit a certain prudential nature. As Abramson wrote, "we cherish trial by jury precisely because we expect ordinary citizens to repudiate laws, or instances of law enforcement, that are repugnant to their consciences."[29] Socrates paid tribute both to the consciences and to the reasoning powers of the common citizen. To vote against him because he foreswore the authority of the poet should have been repugnant to every thinking juror. Socrates established that every single juror should have been thinking, not emoting (*Apol* 36a, 39c).

In Plato's depiction, the threat represented by poets to the jury system lies in their absorption in and commitment to spectacle rather than to truth. Poet and audience are mutually implicated in this charge. Socrates knows well what his audience wants from him, but he refuses to deliver. He will not debase himself publicly, through wailing and lamentation and a piteous display of friends and family. "I will do none of these things," Socrates declares, "although in this too I am risking, as I might seem, the extreme danger." The crowd is accustomed to being gratified by an exhibition. But Socrates sticks it to them with an inescapable definition of the judge: "Apart from reputation, men, to me it also does not seem to be just to beg the judge, not to be acquitted by begging, but rather to teach and persuade. For the judge is not seated to give away the just things as a gratification, but to judge them." In this light, poetic authority appears as the real source of tyranny and the poets as the mortal enemies of Socrates. "It would seem that Socrates saw the poets as his most dangerous enemies, as

28. Redfield, "A Lecture on Plato's *Apology*," 99.
29. Abramson, *We the Jury*, 67. Jury nullification is elsewhere defined as "the implicit power to acquit defendants despite the evidence and the law" (Keith E. Niedermeier, Irwin A. Horowitz, and Norbert L. Kerr, "Informing Jurors of Their Nullification Power: A Route to a Just Verdict or Judicial Chaos?" 331).

indeed they would be if they were the creators of the Olympian lore and thus, at the source of the popular orthodoxy, defining the popular piety."[30] Socrates concludes that no one can stand against them and that his only recourse is to say so openly: "Do not be vexed with me when I speak the truth" (*Apol* 34c–35b, 31e). Socrates spoke the truth when he said that emotional gratification has no place in a jury trial. In a more just outcome, the evidence would have a hold on the individual juror or not, but, in either case, the juror would be able to justify his decision

The Sophist in Plato's *Gorgias*

The sophists may have been in the same lineage as the poets (Protagoras claims in the Platonic dialogue of that name that Homer and other poets practiced sophistry but concealed it, "fearing the odium attached"[31]), but they were also rivals, as the sophists wished to topple the poets from their place of cultural dominance and to assume it for themselves. To Socrates, the sophists represented a distinctly new threat. Unlike the poets, who defined the popular piety, the sophists openly taught the secular maxim: "Man is the measure of all things." Socrates' deepest objection to their teaching was indeed that they neglected serious scrutiny of ethical questions.

We have seen that despite the fact that Socrates makes a point of challenging the sophistic assertions of human self-sufficiency, he is commonly associated with them because of his mode of questioning: the source of the philosopher's vulnerability is in the frequency with which he is mistaken for a sophist. Thus if the sophistic threat to Socrates is subsidiary to that of the poets, it is hardly an innocuous one. We turn now to the *Gorgias* to investigate the nature of the ancient menace and to take up more fully the question of why Socrates seems to accept sophistic terms in his encounters with them. To anticipate, Socrates detects the sophistic threat in their intrinsically coercive lan-

30. Joseph Cropsey, *Plato's World: Man's Place in the Cosmos,* 151.
31. Plato *Protagoras* 316d. Protagoras fancies himself the first man to have the audacity to acknowledge openly that he is a sophist and educator. Even if his claim about the earlier poets practicing sophistry is not obviously true, his self-perception as the leading sophist is significant.

guage and in the insidious way this language becomes the yardstick for all political debate. It appears that, similar to scientific discourse in our own time, sophistic language becomes the default choice. Richard Rorty notes that "any academic discipline which wants a place at the trough, but is unable to offer the predictions and the technology provided by the natural sciences, must either pretend to imitate science or find some way of obtaining 'cognitive status' without the necessity of discovering facts."[32] For ancients and moderns, the sophistic perspective becomes easy to assume and difficult to dislodge. Merely to compete, Socrates is obliged to take on the sophists with their weapon, their so-called art of rhetoric. But at the same time, he is intent on exposing their detachment from ethical concerns. Accordingly, Socrates devotes much effort to exposing how the sophists sneak in their valuations through the backdoor as they preach noncommittal from the front.

Socrates knows well that logical reasoning is not sufficient for his purposes. Instead, he makes his interlocutors reveal their characters when he shows in each case that the speaker will not own up to what words imply. His approach is searing, and all psychological. He tries "not to argue them into believing [that virtue always benefits the moral agent] but to maneuver them into acknowledging that, deep down, they have believed it all along."[33] In the end, the psychological victory goes to Socrates, but he fails to persuade the sophists logically, thus demonstrating that even shame will not reform those whom he dubs "the incurables." For our purposes the important lesson is that the only viable strategy when confronting a sophist is to challenge him in dialogue: to make him say in plain terms what he means. Does he mean what he says?

It must be noted from the start that many contemporary readers of Plato, including academics and legal scholars alike, oppose the Socratic

32. Richard Rorty, *Objectivity, Relativism, and Truth: Philosophical Papers,* 35.

33. Richard McKim, "Shame and Truth in Plato's *Gorgias,*" in Charles L. Griswold Jr., ed., *Platonic Writings, Platonic Readings,* 37. Gorgias and Polus, at least, may come to understand that unbeknownst to themselves, they really do accede to the "Socratic Axiom" in McKim's formulation ("virtue is always supremely beneficial *to the moral agent himself* . . . whereas vice . . . is always supremely harmful to the agent" [35]).

position and take up the cause of the sophists. Judge Richard Posner identifies the sophists as his near-kin: "For the everyday pragmatist, as for the sophists of ancient Greece whom he resembles (they are among his ancestors), moral, political, and legal theories have value only as rhetoric, not as philosophy." In this perspective, Platonic philosophy is assumed to be absolutist and foundationalist, as opposed to the easygoing antifoundationalism of the sophist. Similarly, Rorty strives to be "where the Sophists were before Plato brought his principle to bear and invented 'philosophical thinking.'" He himself, in contrast, will be "looking for an airtight case rather than an unshakable foundation."[34]

Alongside many of the contemporary identifications with the sophists, then, is the characterization of Platonic philosophy as dogmatic. That characterization does not sit quite right with this reader. It assuredly does not align well with what we have seen of Socrates' philosophizing, which looks eminently open-ended. In the *Apology,* Socrates has no pretensions toward presenting an "airtight case" for his philosophic activity, never mind "an unshakable foundation." Is this the difference between Socrates and Plato? Or is this the difference between Plato and Platonism? John Dewey notes that "I am unable to find in [Plato] that all-comprehensive and overriding system which later interpretation has, it seems to me, conferred upon him as a dubious boon . . . [his] highest flight of metaphysics always terminated with a social and practical turn."[35] An interpretative morass lies just around this bend. The question at issue is how to read a Platonic dialogue, or, perhaps, the question is how to read. Since that issue is not going to be resolved any time soon, the most we can do is to take note of the controversy and to continue to make our procedure as

---

34. Richard A. Posner, *Law, Pragmatism, and Democracy,* 12; Richard Rorty, *Philosophy and the Mirror of Nature,* 157. Posner adds in that same work, "Plato set the agenda for philosophy . . . by assigning to philosophy the task of discovering by speculative reasoning the truths that would provide secure foundations for scientific knowledge and moral, political, and aesthetic beliefs" (29–30).

35. Dewey, *John Dewey: The Later Works, 1925–1953,* 147, 154–55. Posner cites Dewey in *Law, Pragmatism, and Democracy*—remarkably, to my mind, given his assertions about the agenda of Platonic philosophy to discover foundational truths and his subsequent overwrought claim that Plato "believed that every number, every word, was the projection of a Form that existed in a supernatural Heaven of Forms" (30).

transparent as possible.[36] My predilection is to inhabit the world of the text, to try to connect with the mind at work, by listening as closely as possible to the voices within it. What comes across loud and clear from Plato's *Gorgias* is the claim by Socrates that sophistic rhetoric (and not philosophy) is coercive. Gorgias, Polus, and Callicles each let slip in turn that his own art of rhetoric is prompted by the desire for control and power. What these sophists apprehend in the *Gorgias* is that when they tighten their prose, they tighten their grip. In my reading, Socrates is unbending only in his resistance to their valueless pedagogy.

The *Gorgias* may represent Socrates' most fierce rebuttal to the disingenuous nature of the sophist and the rhetor.[37] The dialogue features a brief but important appearance by Chaerephon, already familiar to us as the one who questioned the Delphic oracle on behalf of Socrates. His opening role is followed by three different performances (in rising degrees of vitriol) in the persons of Gorgias, Polus, and Callicles.[38] Gorgias may be the namesake of this dialogue and, next to Protagoras, the most famous sophist in his own name, but his speaking role here is relatively brief. He is treated with deference and appears to be gracious in his interactions with others. Could this first-generation sophist be responsible for the imperious behavior of his followers? The issue arises almost immediately. If Socrates makes any inroads with Gorgias as he brings to the surface the dubious features of his rhetoric, it may be on account of the coarse behavior of his disciples. As Euben notes, "Gorgias does not recognize the consequences of his 'teaching' until he sees them exemplified in the persons and politics of Polus and Callicles. It is who they are that shows him who he is."[39] The reason that the *Gorgias* is so applicable to the jury

---

36. See my reflections on Plato's Socrates in *Ship of State,* 52–70.

37. I comingle the terms *sophist* and *rhetor* in accordance with Socrates' declaration that they are "pretty close" to the same thing (*Gor* 520a). I follow Nichols's practice in his translation of using *rhetor* in lieu of distinguishing between *rhetorician* (someone knowledgeable about speaking) and *orator* (someone whose leadership stems from his speaking) (Plato *Gorgias* 28n12).

38. Dodds notes that they are "three successive developments of the same force. Polus is the spiritual heir of Gorgias; Callicles the spiritual heir of Polus" (E. R. Dodds, *Gorgias: A Revised Text with Introduction and Commentary,* 5).

39. J. Peter Euben, John R. Wallach, and Josiah Ober, eds., *Athenian Political Thought and the Reconstruction of American Democracy,* 205.

trial in New Haven, and indeed the reason I first made the association between Gorgias and Gene, is because Socrates targets most seriously the rhetoric of this eminently *decent* teacher, not that of his indecent students.

Polus is a troubling indicator of just what happens to the original sophistic teaching in the second generation. Polus is a younger sophist whose name means *colt*. He is appropriately full of spunk but lacking poise and restraint, wholly absorbed by conventional opinion. Polus can be prodded into self-disclosure in a matter of seconds. Callicles is more aggressive and unpleasant, and one of the few interlocutors in the works of Plato whose historical existence is not validated elsewhere. He is not a self-defined sophist but appropriates their teachings in the same casual way he picks up other information that might be useful to him. Callicles seems to be both formed by Gorgias and wholly out of his reach. Whatever vicious thing it is that he comes to embody by the end of the work, Callicles is at several removes from the original sophistic voice and teaching of Gorgias. But Gorgias planted the seed.

The fundamental divide on which the *Gorgias* operates is that the sophist seeks to declaim authoritatively before an audience, whereas the philosopher wants to talk, one to one (*dialegesthai*). We learn that Socrates and his friends have come too late to watch the display (*epideixis*) of Gorgias, for Callicles reports that "Gorgias just a little while ago made a display for us of many fine things." The word is bandied back and forth. Chaerephon pipes in that "Gorgias is a friend of mine, so . . . he will make a display for us now." Callicles intervenes, "What's this? Does Socrates desire to listen to Gorgias?" He invites them to his house where Gorgias "will make a display for you," too. But Socrates balks and counters with an alternative, "would [Gorgias] be willing to talk with us?" He adds pointedly, as for "the other thing, the display, let him put it off until afterwards." Finally, Callicles draws the circle to a close by saying, "There's nothing like asking the man himself, Socrates. And indeed this was one aspect of his display" (*Gor* 447a–c). By not *showing* us Gorgianic rhetoric—presenting it only after the fact—Plato manages to evoke its rigid and stylized nature.

Outside of this Platonic dialogue, a number of actual rhetorical works of Gorgias have survived, including his *Encomium of Helen*. In this work, Gorgias promises to teach to the young a rhetoric that will enable them to "stamp the soul" of their hearers as they wish. In his own name, Gorgias claims that the power of speech "has the same effect on the condition of the soul as the application of drugs to the state of bodies."[40] Gorgias goes on to exercise the infamous sophistic skill of being able to argue either side of an argument and to make the weaker argument the stronger. His tactic in this particular case is to extol the virtues of Helen of Troy. But in truth Helen is merely part of the sideshow. She is an object to be manipulated by the speaker. The real mission of Gorgias is to establish his control over his listeners through his facility in speech. He exploits the misogynistic attitudes of his audience in the process. By coincidence, as Wardy informs us, the word *logos* is grammatically masculine in Greek, whereas *psyche* (soul) is grammatically feminine. This permits Gorgias to blur his references to Paris/*logos* and Helen/*psyche*. Just as Paris overwhelmed Helen (thus exculpating her), so Gorgias marshals *logos* in a way that forces the defenseless audience to acquiesce. "The deliberate feminisation of the *psyche* plays on the Greek cultural assumption that the female as such is a passive object shaped at will by a dominating masculine force . . . the successful orator performs psychic rape."[41] The only reputable position in this sophistic world is to be the manipulator rather than the manipulated. The tightly focused and abstract language of Gorgias has antifemale intimations, in common with other allegedly valueless forms of discourse.

Perhaps Chaerephon eagerly seeks the company of Gorgias in the Platonic dialogue because he seeks to learn the art of seducing without penalty. If so, he will be disappointed on this day. The teaching that follows is not a straightforward matter, largely because of the way that Socrates shakes up the pattern of speech. From the start Socrates interjects the most elementary questions, effectively stopping everyone in his tracks. When Chaerephon and Socrates arrive in the presence

---

40. Gorgias, *Encomium of Helen*, in Aristotle *On Rhetoric* app. 1, 286–87. Robert Wardy makes the provocative suggestion that the display "just missed" was a reading of the *Encomium* (*The Birth of Rhetoric: Gorgias, Plato, and Their Successors*, 58).

41. Wardy, *Birth of Rhetoric*, 43.

of Gorgias, Socrates enjoins his friend to "ask him." Chaerephon is baffled, "What shall I ask?" Socrates responds, "Who he is." Here we are reminded that philosophic activity stems from a wide-eyed absorption in the world. Socratic questions disarm. This is to be the rule henceforth, as the philosopher asks the elemental questions and displays humility in his search for answers. Polus soon breaks in, attempting to barrel through any uncertainties. "By Zeus . . . test me, if you wish!" But Polus is flummoxed by the questions posed to him, and as he is impatient to commence his rhetorical demonstration, he reverts to pat answers. Before long, Socrates calls off the exchange, for Polus isn't answering what is asked, which is "what is the nature of Gorgias's art"—not whether it is a fine one (*Gor* 447c–448a). What Polus would have gotten away with in a rhetorical exhibition is impermissible in conversational exchange.

Socrates is wise to the ways in which the detached speaker may hide behind his words. Unmask thyself, Sophist![42] He counters their neutrality with a proposal that everyone submit to the logos, wherever it may lead. Logos may signify argument, account, reckoning, explanation, or narrative, among many other possibilities suggested in more than five columns of the standard Greek-English lexicon. One should honor logos before honoring oneself, Socrates tells Gorgias, "in order that it may go forward," so that the subject matter may become manifest, not on account of the person speaking, "but so that you may bring your own views to a conclusion in accord with what you set down." To respect the logos properly seems to point the way to the most honest appraisals possible; it should be the rallying cry of every jury. Conclusions should correspond to premises, with nothing accidental or untoward about the procedure. Socrates urges Gorgias to be careful so that they do "not become accustomed to guessing and hastily snatching up each other's words." He should be prepared to pursue every implication and follow every thread—and he should never allow the words to deceive him about the ethical ramifications

---

42. "Socrates draws attention to the Gorgian mode of answering no less than five times (*Gor* 448c, 449b, 449d, 451a, and 451d), and he makes five references to his own methods of speaking and the fact that he is demonstrating them (451a–c, 452a–d, 453c, 453e–454b, and 454b–c)" (Adele Spitzer, "The Self-Reference of the *Gorgias,*" 4).

of his position. Socrates later advises Polus to defer to a good outside of him, to "compel both himself and others not to play the coward but to grit his teeth and submit well and courageously as if to a doctor for cutting and burning—pursuing what's good and fine" (*Gor* 453c, 457e, 454c, 480c). The cure for being tongue-tied by Socrates is for the sophist to take himself down from his distant perch.

The point of supervening importance here is that this logos is not abstract, not disconnected from the person of Socrates. Because Socrates accepts his personal stake, he can toy with his opponents who do not. We might conclude that Socratic psychologizing is more audacious than Socratic reasonableness. Through understanding human motive (and *eros*) so well, Socrates finds ways to make his interlocutors take his words personally. He hits them where it hurts, and this varies by temperament. For Socrates to be effective at inducing the arguments forward, he must consistently put himself on the line, without fear of ridicule or hostility. He welcomes the frankness of the child's perspective, whereas the sophist regards the child's position as a humiliating one to be overcome. Insofar as the sophist recalls the child in his self-definition, he remembers only vulnerability. His great anxiety is the body and how to secure its well-being. His delusion is to imagine that his facility with language answers that vulnerability, that the sophist somehow defines the limits of the logos. This is the presumption that appears with increasing force in Gorgias, Polus, and Callicles. Callicles accuses Socrates of acting like a youth "in the arguments" (*Gor* 482c), and he does, but not in the sense that Callicles can penetrate, for Socrates' youthful character is to be found in simplicity rather than in cynicism.[43]

Socrates appears eager to give utterance to the goodness of the world in his naive way, but he is also respectfully aware of its evil. To apprize good and evil, one must revert to basics. Gorgias, in contrast, allows the basic decency of his own character to shield him from the sight of the burgeoning of an indecent rhetoric. From the start, the indecency comes from an imbalance in the arrangement of human

---

43. Ann N. Michelini remarks that Socrates "completes the reversal of Callicles' social stance, putting his opponent in the position of a child for whom moral understanding must be framed in clear and simple terms" ("*Polle Agroikia:* Rudeness and Irony in Plato's *Gorgias,*" 58).

goods: the overvaluing of the power to acquire and the undervaluing of the need to preserve, evaluate, and measure. The man and his art are out of alignment, so he has uncommon difficulty sorting out the question of who he is. Socrates induces Gorgias to define "the greatest good for human beings" of which he as rhetor is the craftsman. Gorgias answers that it is the power to persuade by speeches, "the greatest good and the cause both of freedom for human beings themselves and at the same time of rule over others in each man's own city" (*Gor* 452d). He promises that the well-trained rhetor can overpower the claims of any expert. Socrates' strategy hereafter is to make Gorgias behold the man behind those words, for either the decency of the person or the indecency of the words must be adjusted.

At first, Gorgias resists saying publicly what might be insinuated in some of his claims. Eventually, though, he agrees to the Socratic terms of making a display of "brief speaking." In the quick back and forth of conversation, things that are revealing have a way of coming out. Before much time has passed, Gorgias has made the claim that the greatest good for human beings and of which he is the craftsman, is "being able to persuade by speeches judges in the law court, councilors in the council, assemblymen in the assembly, and in every other gathering whatsoever, when there is a political gathering. And indeed with this power you will have the doctor as your slave, and the trainer as your slave" (*Gor* 452e). Stated baldly, he worships the power of words for their potential to dominate. Socrates' great talent is to bring to light the contradictory desires harbored in the breast of the sophist.

Polus intervenes after he decides that Gorgias has been shamed into silence. He turns on Socrates and demands to know the solution that he must be concealing. "Since Gorgias in your opinion is at a loss concerning rhetoric, what do you say it is?" Socrates dramatically denies that it is any art at all. Rather, he claims that it is an experience, "of the production of a certain grace and pleasure." Gorgias now intervenes earnestly, for he is puzzled and wants to understand as Socrates goes on to introduce the analogy to cookery. Along with cooking, Socrates says, "I also call rhetoric a part of this pursuit, and cosmetic, too and sophistry, these four parts directed to four kinds of business (*Gor* 462c–463b).

The Socratic divisions are nothing if not provoking, but the interesting turn is when Gorgias becomes Socratic. He asks brief, interested questions, in a spirit of free inquiry. This is a hopeful development in an otherwise grim dialogue. Just as unmistakably, Socrates becomes sophistic, as he builds toward his own *epideixis*. In mockery, Socrates becomes the measure of all things, and he repeatedly draws attention to the objectionable aspects of his sophistic procedure. For instance, his display is strikingly long, which we can hardly fail to notice, because he has been harping on brevity of speech throughout the dialogue. For emphasis, he plays up his verbosity, pledging first that he wants to speak "just as the geometers do"—that is, briefly, to the point, and then doing the opposite and pontificating just like the sophists. The speech is marred further by an excess of divisions; its series of dichotomies confuses. The metaphors are not helpful; they are neither clear nor promising as a means of opening up the argument. "Flattery . . . divided itself into four, and slipped in under each of the parts," he explains inauspiciously. The image of the cook and the doctor and their contest among children reappears later in this dialogue with remarkable force. But here it is tagged on to the end of a long sentence, and it appears wordy even when isolated: "so that, if the cook and the doctor had to contest among children or among men as thoughtless as children which of the two, the doctor or the cook, has understanding about useful and bad foods, the doctor would die of hunger." Some concepts are blurred that might properly remain distinct, as in "sophists and rhetors are mixed together in the same place and about the same things." The speech in its entirety seems convoluted and heavy-handed. It cannot really be absorbed through listening; one would have to diagram it to make sense of it or plot it or turn it into something other than a speech. The most memorable part of the whole episode may be its impact on Polus. "What then are you saying?" he demands to know, after the whole overly technical speech finally draws to a close. "Does rhetoric seem to you to be flattery?" (*Gor* 464c–466a). If Gorgias gets Socratic jokes, they are surely lost on Polus.

With this display of rhetoric, Socrates' ability to declaim in long, complex sentences stands unchallenged. For a long time after the delivery of this speech, no one speaks in anything but clear and direct prose, in the paradigmatic form of Socratic exchange, where positions are revealed and the argument moves forward. By showing that he can successfully mimic sophistic ways, it seems that he has won a place at the table. Socrates can master his competitors in using the language of mastery. Not that either Polus or Callicles is prepared to concede the argument; they remain confident in their abilities to withstand Socratic examination. But everything that follows—and it is surely Socrates' ugliest fight—is in truth directed toward the decent man Gorgias, in the hope that he will come to embrace a more transparent language and show a little humility about what man can measure.

The characters of the interlocutors are most clearly disclosed when they express their views about what constitutes the best life. Polus does not comprehend that there is any other route to happiness aside from the one through power and acquisition. He thinks that the best life begins with the manipulation of words: "What's this?" Polus asks. "Do [rhetors] not, just like tyrants, kill whomever they wish, and confiscate possessions, and expel from the cities whomever it seems good to them?" Polus knows happiness when he sees it: "You see, I suppose, that that fellow Archelaus the son of Perdiccas rules Macedonia?" Polus explains what is obvious to him: as a consequence of his unjust deeds, Archelaus has profited handsomely and earned himself untold pleasures. The happiness of the tyrant is manifest, as clear as the nose on Polus's face. ("Just ask anyone of these men.") In the opinion of Polus, there is nothing to deliberate. But Socrates remains obtuse, denying the assumption that Archelaus, or even the Great King himself, is happy, without knowing how he stands in regard to education and justice (*Gor* 466b, 470d–e, 473e).[44] In the end, Socrates will put Archelaus in his category of incurables. Is Polus as unreachable, in his unthinking worship of that life?

The Socratic alternative to that allegedly happy life is marked by inclusivity. "For I assert," says Socrates, "that the noble and good man *and woman* [*kalon kagathon*] are happy, the unjust and base, wretched." In his commentary, Dodds notes that "this is one of the phrases

---

44. Archelaus and Socrates both die in 399; Archelaus was killed by his beloved and Socrates was executed by his countrymen. Whose life is defended now? Archelaus lost his shine when he lost his life, but Socratic eminence only grows; see *Alcibiades ii,* 141d–e.

'transvalued' by Socrates"—and also used uniquely by him to refer to women.[45] It announces Socrates as being attentive to feminine concerns in a way that is in the starkest contrast to the present company. The sophists lay claim to the macho man, whereas the philosopher stands up for the female. Socrates takes pleasure in countering even the oaths taken by the sophists; to their "by Zeus" he responds with his "by Hera."[46] On numerous occasions, he gives a feminine aspect to his search, from his addresses to man and woman alike to his special honoring of the women's saying: "For the true man must reject living any amount of time whatsoever, and must not be a lover of life. Rather, turning over what concerns these things to the god and believing the women's saying that no man may escape his destiny, he must investigate what comes after this: In what way may he who is going to live for a time live best?" (*Gor* 470e, 500c, 509a, 482b, 512e).

The life of the real man as Callicles presents it is one devoted to mere living and in search of physical security. "The man who will live correctly," he says, "must let his own desires be as great as possible and not chasten them, and he must be sufficient to serve them, when they are as great as possible." Socrates cuts to the chase. Does Callicles really propose "an ungrudging amount" of desires fulfilled as the happiest life—endless scratching for the one who itches? (And why stop with the top of the head?) Socrates will finish the shameless thought that Callicles unthinkingly started. By the time that Socrates is through, holding out the prospect of the life of catamites, "if they have an ungrudging amount of what they want," he makes us apprehend the egoism, misogynism, and distortive impositions of the Calliclean worldview (*Gor* 491e, 494e). From the Socratic perspective, Callicles' emphasis on acquisition implies an unbalanced and adolescent view of human life. He counts and seeks to accumulate, but there is no end to counting. He is shown to be violent and threatening and consumed by the drive to exert strength merely for the sake of exerting strength.

In argument, Callicles does not stick to the sophistic script, any

---

45. Dodds, *Gorgias: A Revised Text,* 242–43 (see also *Gor* 56n50).

46. See *Gor* 448a, 463e, 511c, and 449d. For Socrates' proclivity for taking the female side, see Elena Duvergès Blair, "Women: The Unrecognized Teachers of the Platonic Socrates."

more than he attends to details in his use of other authorities. He is noticeably careless of the traditions of the past, for he seeks only to uphold, not to test, his wisdom. Callicles pretends to call on Pindar for support, but he soon acknowledges that he does not know the ode; likewise, he fails to follow through in his literary references to Zethus and Amphion from Euripides' *Antiope,* which Socrates is more than willing to do. Callicles doesn't really know the text, and Socrates really does. A clear contrast develops between Socrates' receptivity to and awareness of a wide range of literary and historical texts, texts that are suggestive rather than determinative, and Callicles and the sophists' transparent attempts to use their sources to corroborate, and not to enrich, their thinking.[47] Callicles quotes incorrectly. He is oblivious to tradition and impervious to reason: "I don't know what you are saying, Socrates, so ask someone else" (*Gor* 484b–485e, 506b, 505c).

Socrates wickedly leaves off with an old wives tale. He predicts that Callicles will receive the story as a myth, but as for himself, he knows enough to seek its meaning, "for I shall tell you the things I am going to tell as being true." Callicles is too sophisticated to see the reason in tall tales. He is probably unreachable. As such, he provokes in Socrates an aberration from his usual indirect ways; Socrates imagines, finally, that on judgment day "perhaps someone will dishonorably strike you a crack on the jaw and completely trample you in the mud" (*Gor* 523a, 525d, 527a). The point is that such an event shouldn't matter to Callicles. The only thing that matters is to live and die practicing justice.

To make visible the excellence that he embodies, Socrates appeals to a picture of the soul intent on examining "in what way one must live" and on upholding character with firmness. For if the self-examining

47. Ancient and modern sophists have more than a little in common in the way they appropriate texts. Giles Gunn observes that in Rorty's use of literary texts "what disappears is the belief that art, poetry, fiction can sometimes lift us out of ourselves, or compel us into a new relation to ourselves, as when we see or feel experience, or a portion of it, from the partial perspective of someone else" (*Thinking across the American Grain: Ideology, Intellect, and the New Pragmatism,* 115–16). See also the critiques of Posner's *Law and Literature* and *Overcoming Law* by James Boyd White, "What Can a Lawyer Learn from Literature," 2014–16, and Jeffrey Rosen, "Overcoming Posner," 589.

process is endless, still, the seriousness with which one seeks to determine the best life may be discerned, and in time become a fixed quality. Socrates' arguments are "iron and adamantine," and his speech is "always the same." Better to be out of sync with most human beings, he avers, than "being one man . . . be discordant with myself and say contradictory things." The masculine rhetoric of the sophists would seem also to appeal to a single standard. In Callicles' extreme formulation, this would be "the law of nature," according to which the stronger rule the weaker and have more." But it is precisely their lack of examination of this principle that leads to the rhetors' mutable nature.[48] For the strong may be defined in many ways, and whereas Callicles is happy to draw from the conventional sense the impression that his strong man combines might with superior intellectual gifts, in fact, as rhetor, Callicles is committed to valuing a certain kind of knowledge that is entirely separable from power. Not having thought about whether these goods of knowledge and power are commensurable, Callicles simply takes his cue from popular opinion. "In the assembly," Socrates charges, "if, as you are saying something, the Athenian people denies that it is so, you turn around and say what it wishes" (*Gor* 483d–e, 481d). Callicles has no resources for taking up this challenge, except further assertions of the inviolability of his own position. When cornered, he denies everything: it turns out that all along he was only joking with Socrates. It appears that he will say anything to avoid losing face—which he has confused with the soundness of his argument.

Socrates' reaction is singular. "Oh! Oh! Callicles, how all-cunning you are, and how you treat me like a child—at one time claiming that things are this way, and at another time that the same things are otherwise, deceiving me!" (*Gor* 499b–c). Socrates is standing in for the audience: if the rhetor is not called on his behavior, then the audience has accepted the role of mere plaything of the speaker. Behind the rhetor's flattery is only whim. Callicles knows he must win this battle, but he appears to have forgotten why he is fighting it.

48. Gorgias is prepared to argue that his rhetoric is amoral (*Gor* 456d–e) and that the rhetorician "is manifestly one who would never do injustice" (460e). Polus calls upon the many as witnesses (472b), evokes bogeymen (473d), and seeks to ridicule (473e), changing his strategy each time Socrates refutes him.

The *Gorgias* offers a devastating indictment of politics and political power run rampant. Rhetoric lies at the heart of the problem, for the rhetoric of Gorgias the sophist is inextricably linked to tyranny. The rhetoric that had stimulated Athens' rise had burst the limits of meaning and had shattered, leaving the defeated Greeks with the necessity of reconstituting the currency of language. The sophists were dominant, confident, and scathing in their rejection of any alternative to their practice of manipulating mass audiences. The model of political discourse is the one and the many. Or the model is a skilled elite of rhetoricians, deployed to shape the minds of citizens wherever assembled in sizeable numbers. Public opinion is there to be shaped. So rhetoric is a tool for tyranny.

The philosopher's rebuttal denies the relevance of success before a crowd. The Socrates of the *Gorgias* is unable to convince anyone, to change anyone's mind. He exemplifies a life that demands an accounting of self and a more humble measuring of ends. He thereby enables us to take up the task, as Aristotle puts it in his *Rhetoric,* of "discerning the available means of persuasion," where "discerning" is prior to "persuading." Plato displays Socrates at precisely this moment, discerning the means of persuasion that must get beyond the one (rhetorician) and the many (the people) in order to attain a one-on-one communication with any potential reader. It is a matter of moving from the restricting power of rhetoric to the readiness, in principle, to accept or resist persuasion.

Identifying with Emma

During the immediate aftermath of the trial in New Haven, there was, at least, one place where I could ruminate freely about the relevance of an old-fashioned humanities education to a contemporary court case, the Directed Studies program at Yale. Directed Studies is a freshmen program consisting of three yearlong courses in literature, philosophy, and history and politics in which the central texts of the Western tradition are studied. For the first time in a decade with the program, I was asked to teach a literature section. Relinquishing my usual political philosophy syllabus, I looked forward to immersing myself in the works of some literary giants: Shakespeare, Jane Austen,

Tolstoy. The discoveries were every bit as rich as I had hoped, but perhaps the biggest surprise of all was that, lo and behold, there was Plato again, at the center of these texts. Moreover, I became attuned to compelling new instructions about how human beings best deliberate.

A favored topic for a Directed Studies colloquium was the Quarrel between Philosophy and Poetry. The idea of having three professors duke it out on the topic of reason versus inspiration was enticing to students and faculty alike. At the colloquium, however, all of the featured speakers lined up behind Plato, and it wasn't much of a debate. We left wishing for a stronger response on behalf of the poet. We needed Jane Austen.

Before I could begin to share my thoughts in the classroom about Jane Austen and the poets, however, there was an obstacle to overcome: my students hated *Emma*. To be more precise, they found the character Emma distasteful and the book trivial. These were students who whisked through Aristotle and Spinoza and devoured Milton. Indeed, looking back over the syllabi for the entire year from Homer to James Joyce, I had to acknowledge that the only work my students complained about was *Emma*. But I had become convinced that reading *Emma* was superb training for becoming a good citizen and juror.

The students' complaints seemed to relate to the combination of the moral demands made by Jane Austen and the conventional class prejudices and preoccupations exhibited by Emma. To be sure, Emma's form of snobbishness is unlike anything experienced by the typical American undergraduate today. "A young farmer, whether on horseback or on foot, is the very last sort of person to raise my curiosity," Emma instructs her friend Harriet, "The yeomanry are precisely the order of people with whom I feel I can have nothing to do. A degree or two lower, and a creditable appearance might interest me"[49] After readers have made it through *Emma* a few times, this exchange is not offensive but funny, for Emma is caught in the act of a bad mimicry of her true love, Mr. Knightley. She is neither in a position to recognize him yet nor to understand why she is drawn to his discernment. She merely parrots his ability to discriminate, without apprehending his

49. Austen, *Emma,* 25 (hereafter cited parenthetically as *Emma*).

congenial leadership role in the community or her rightful partnership with him in that situation. Before the reader achieves this double vision, Emma may well come across as simply insufferable. Worse yet is her reaction to the marriage proposal made to her by Mr. Elton: "But—that he should talk of encouragement . . . should suppose himself her equal in connection or mind!" (*Emma*, 123). This aristocratic tone is foreign to students in a democratic age, and because it is not acceptable, it is not amusing. Such references to class, like those to gender and race, are hot-button issues for college students. The message is "don't go there."[50]

Although my students could barely stomach *Emma*, some of us among the faculty had portions of *Emma* memorized. During the week that my class was reading *Emma*, I was in my office waiting for a student appointment when the director of the program, Jane Levin, popped in to talk about why our freshmen weren't taking to Jane Austen. We compared notes. "They missed the 'seemed,'" Jane began, and then recited the opening line: "Emma Woodhouse, handsome, clever, and rich, with a comfortable home and happy disposition, seemed to unite some of the best blessings of existence; and had lived nearly twenty-one years in the world with very little to distress or vex her." I responded that my students had not savored her delicious praise of Mr. Elton: very pleasing manners, for a woman "not fastidious." Jane warmed to the game. "Like the charming Augusta Hawkins!" she added, "who, in addition to all the usual advantages of perfect beauty and merit, was in possession of an independent fortune, of so many thousands as would always be called ten." We were off, even though I could never keep up with Jane, who had written her dissertation on Jane Austen and could recite whole pages of dialogue, word for word. We were sputtering with laughter over the deluded Emma "amusing herself in the consideration of the blunders which often arise from a partial knowledge of circumstances" (*Emma*,

---

50. My students are of a generation that has been trained since infancy to reserve judgment and to duck controversy. Some of the other familiar interjections on my college campus are "whatever" and "no problem," all versions of the phrase "agreeing to disagree" that has even the professors complaining about the way students appeal to relativism (see Michiko Kakutani, "Debate? Dissent? Discussion? Oh, Don't Go There!" *New York Times*, March 23, 2002).

3, 31, 162, 101) when our colleague María barged in, my student in tow. "You two are incorrigible," she said with exasperation, pulling Jane out of my office as she pushed the student in. "Whoa!" Jane said. "Right, right, right, I was just leaving."

Is it that *Emma* requires a new translation for a new era? In conjunction with our reading that week in Directed Studies, Jane Levin arranged a special event: a screening of the movie *Clueless,* a Hollywood remake of *Emma*. This was to be followed by a question-and-answer session with Amy Heckerling, the writer and the director of the film. Jane had been successful in luring to our colloquia series a number of philosophers, classicists, and university presidents from Harvard, Princeton, Stanford, and the University of Chicago. But this was of a whole different order. Way cool—even *Phat*. I overheard Jane in the hall when she received Heckerling's letter accepting her invitation. "Whoa! Oh, excellent. Oh, fantastic. Well, this is great. Fantastic. Well, great. Isn't this happy news? Whoa." She showed the letter to María and continued, "Amy Heckerling is just amazing. Oh, totally brilliant. She is fantastic. Right, right, right. Excellent."

The students were more excited still. The movie screening was a much bigger hit than the reading of the book. Of course, the students had all seen *Clueless* before; indeed, they knew many of the lines by heart. Cher, the Beverly Hills version of Emma, slips a Shakespearean sonnet into the mailbox of a teacher, for whom she is plotting a romance with another teacher: "Rough winds do shake the darling buds of May." Cher's sidekick, Deon—each is named for a famous singer who now does infomercials—is impressed by the poetry:

Deon: *Phat*. Did you write that?
Cher: Duh, it's like a famous quote.
Deon: From where?
Cher: Cliff's notes.
Deon: Oh.

As it happened, we had studied that Shakespearean sonnet earlier in the semester. Perhaps the students would see how much could be gained from satire when the original was known. Possibly this lesson could carry over into *Emma* itself. We could hope, anyway. The original Mr. Woodhouse is a doddering hypochondriac who wields no control over Emma and so encourages her willfulness. Cher's father is a fierce litigator with high blood pressure who encourages her to talk her way into higher grades and grills her when she comes home: "What did you do in school today?" On a certain level, it works. "I broke in my purple clogs," Cher reports.

I concealed my own attachment to the film and asked my students if they weren't a little embarrassed to parade themselves as trained mimics. These are students who had been through Plato and who understood the stakes in the ancient quarrel between philosophy and poetry. "Socrates would say that you're indoctrinated," I reminded them. "You are chanting phrases mindlessly, at the mercy of the poet's images that flash by on the screen. What are you doing but handing out honors, praises, and prizes for the one who is sharpest at making out the images and remembering their original order?" That rattled them, at least for a moment. The reference to the *Republic* was unmistakable, and they didn't like hearing themselves described as the prisoners in Plato's cave. "But what about you and Professor Levin?" came the irreverent response. "What is the difference between memorizing lines in movies and memorizing lines in books?" The question wasn't half bad. Everyone who loves *Emma* seems to speak of the magical bond between reader and character, and that would seem to implicate all involved in the terms of Plato's critique. Isn't it a form of self-indulgence to give oneself over to the plot of a novel and to the life of a character?

That question is clarifying, for, in no uncertain terms, readers are not allowed to indulge themselves when they identify with Emma. It is always a chastening experience, as Emma is no ordinary heroine. Jane Austen acknowledges as much, describing Emma as "a heroine whom no one but myself will much like." Tony Tanner lists a small sampling of Emma's faults: "Emma *is* wrong, *does* wrong, can *speak* wrong (Box Hill), *judge* wrong, and can use her power (hers because of her permanently ailing, hypochondriac, dozing father) in a way that can be destructive of other peoples' lives and happiness."[51] When she combines her overactive imagination with her class biases, she makes

51. Tony Tanner, *Jane Austen,* 176.

for an appalling spectacle. But it is the spectacles that Emma creates that are the saving points, because she does not disown responsibility for their disastrous results, and she opens herself to the consequences. She may be self-deceived until her epiphany at Box Hill, but Ermarth notes that even before this, her character is decided and open and therefore subject to self-correction: "Despite her faults, one sign of Emma's superiority is the accessibility of her mind, the fact that her character survives the open scrutiny it bears through most of the book."[52]

Initially, Emma does not see what lies before her, so caught up is she in the world of her own devising. She fancies herself a brilliant matchmaker and a benefactor, intent on "improving her little friend's mind, by a great deal of useful reading and conversation" (*Emma*, 62). They do very little reading ("it was much easier to chat than study"). As for the matchmaking, Emma's self-assured plans for others reveal ever so much more about her own neediness. "Reality comes . . . through such a selective vision, shaped by [her] own capacities and needs, that much of it is simply excluded."[53] What is lovable about such a girl? She relinquishes, finally, the role she had assumed and becomes a judge of her own behavior. For all of her airs, Emma wants others to think well of her. Mr. Knightley reproaches Emma for her behavior, after she makes a cruel joke at the expense of the hapless Miss Bates. Until the moment in which Mr. Knightley tells Emma that "it was badly done," Emma's mood could be described as one of breezy dismissiveness toward the assembled company. But once her (still unrecognized) paragon displays her action to her in a different light, full mortification sets in: Emma recognizes herself in his picture, loathes what she sees, and transforms her very self as a result. Here is a paradigmatic instance of shame becoming partner to virtue, in correcting the transgression and in suggesting how necessary upbringing is for the effect to be possible: another woman might have laughed off the reproach. Emma comes to her senses and realizes that living up to Mr. Knightley's view of her is the most important thing for her to do

52. Elizabeth Deeds Ermarth, *Realism and Consensus in the English Novel,* 152.

53. Stuart M. Tave, *Some Words of Jane Austen,* 215. Tave's chapter on Emma is excellent.

in life. This is the happiest of coincidences: that the ability to judge oneself and the ability to identify one's soul mate turn out to be the same capacity. For Jane Austen did not long suffer the despotic whims of her character. She conjures up the suitable check for Emma: experience and the implausible Mr. Knightley. "I cannot see you acting wrong," Mr. Knightley tells her at Box Hill, "without a remonstrance" (*Emma,* 339). Emma is mortified, repents, and makes amends.

How does this exercise on the part of the author berating her character translate into readers berating themselves? The interplay is mysterious but in the way that literature instructs us in the art of making prudential judgments. Emma is like us. There is no gainsaying this mysterious hold that she has on us, as Lionel Trilling notes, "we come into an unusual intimacy with her. . . . The relation that develops between ourselves and her becomes a strange one—it is the relation that exists between our ideal self and our ordinary fallible self."[54] Her slow growth toward maturity pulls us along because her missteps echo, her mortifications are shared. Such character reforms are scenes from fiction, but such fictions may yet live. Here is Tolstoy's Pierre, in *War and Peace:* "He felt that there was now a judge of his every word and action whose judgment mattered more to him than that of all the rest of the world. . . . whatever he was saying he regarded from [Natasha's] standpoint."[55] The key is the activity that is generated in this identification; it is the very reverse of the passive state that Plato condemned. Austen's genius is to make us connect emotionally with her characters at the same time that she makes us judge them—and ourselves.

"Can movies do this, too?" my students wanted to know. I would hardly deny them this possibility or those pleasures. In the classroom, films surely have their intellectual interest and usefulness. "Just don't try writing your paper for me based on the movie," I added. The great film *Doctor Zhivago* excises the period of Zhivago's decline (and his third marriage); in the film version of *A Farewell to Arms,* Rinaldi becomes the agent separating Catherine and Lieutenant Henry. Who knows why? It is common knowledge that in the film *The Big Sleep,* it is not Raymond Chandler but screenwriter William Faulkner who

---

54. Lionel Trilling, *Beyond Culture: Essays on Literature and Learning,* 43.
55. Leo Tolstoy, *War and Peace,* 985.

gives Marlowe some of his best lines.[56] The perils of passive viewing in that genre look to be homegrown. But I will do anything to send my students back to the books, so long as they learn to distinguish imagination and judgment. Entertainment is much cheaper than the intellectual pleasures of being in harmony with the mind of a great writer. But if intellectual pleasures require more investment, they generally pay off more, too. A close reading of books blurs into a close reading of humanity. For readers, viewers, and jurors alike, the advice of Yogi Berra is always well taken: "You see a lot by observing."

In creating Emma, Jane Austen single-handedly fights off the Socratic challenge to the poets. Socrates charges that the poets, unlike the philosophers, cannot justify their own creations. They enchant and enthrall with their artistic inventions, but they leave their audience bereft of any rational standards to judge the content of those inventions. In Socrates' rendition, the closeness between reader and character impairs the critical faculties of the audience. This closeness indulges readers' emotions and prepares them, generally, to lose their individuality and to be treated as a mass.[57] But identifying with Emma does nothing of the kind. It is an experience of discomfort in which we are reminded of our own propensities to believe in objects of our own imaginative construction. As Arnold Kettle argues, "it is not an exaggeration to say that *Emma* is as convincing as our own lives and has the same kind of concreteness."[58] We recognize the movement from an unchecked imagination to a more grounded judgment. "The judgment makes careful distinctions, usually working with patience and with study, separating facts from errors, discerning just relations and distinguishing proprieties. It is interested in determining truth."[59]

---

56. Who could forget Bogart's inimitable line: "She tried to sit in my lap while I was standing up" (Clive James, "The Country behind the Hill," in Miriam Gross, ed., *The World of Raymond Chandler*, 118).

57. See my "Against Entertainment: Plato and the Poets Revisited," in Todd Breyfogle, ed., *Literary Imagination, Ancient and Modern: Essays in Honor of David Grene*, 177–99.

58. Arnold Kettle, "Emma," in Ian P. Watt, ed., *Jane Austen: A Collection of Critical Essays*, 113.

59. Tave goes on to say that the alternative is, of course, imagination, which is "less concerned with real differences, ranges widely and moves quickly, sees similarities or makes its own agreeable combinations and unities, guided by its feelings. It is interested in finding pleasure" (*Some Words of Jane Austen*, 207).

The combination of the concreteness of a great novel such as *Emma* and the openness of its main character is key to my understanding of a literary rescue. When literature is sufficiently anchored in the particular characters and actions so as to compel our engagement, it may become salutary to our political formation, and it may actually become morally instructive.

Jane Austen's mastery is in inducing us to live the experiences of her characters, without allowing us to compromise our sovereignty or shirk our ethical accountability. This seems to be the clue to her political importance, because as we readers are drawn in, we are continually asked to judge what we see and to reflect upon our own role in this community. Perhaps the preeminent example of this artistry is seen in *Emma*. "It is a vital premise of *Emma,* as a novel," John Bayley wrote, "that we have to live inside such a community, as Jane Austen enables us to live inside the individuals who compose it . . . No question but that both author and reader share in Emma's guilt. Jane Austen's art puts us and herself into a community from which there is no withdrawing."[60] There is no withdrawing from the confines of Highbury or the consciousness of Emma, sometimes with the narrator's searing commentary and sometimes with just unadulterated Emma. So whence does this "guilt" arise? The novel absorbs us into the activity of its main characters, so that we find ourselves in Emma's predicament of playing off a sometimes reckless, always stimulating imaginativeness against our better judgment that lets in the resistance of the real world.

Faulkner's *Absalom!*

I have never been able to persuade my Directed Studies colleagues to add William Faulkner's *Absalom, Absalom!* to the syllabus. The answer invariably is "It's too long." Excuse me, Natasha? Whatever. I resort to assigning this great novel in other courses whenever possible and daydream longingly about a colloquium on Faulkner and the sophists.

Faulkner portrays sophistic characters in nearly everything he writes,

---

60. John Bayley, "The 'Irresponsibility' of Jane Austen," in B. C. Southam, ed., *Critical Essays on Jane Austen,* 5–6.

thus he has a whole lot in common with other authors on our Directed Studies reading list. He may conceal his Platonic lineage, but there is no denying that he is preoccupied with the acquisitive, soulless, Callicles-type character. We saw that Callicles had a rather casual attitude toward the kinds of evidence he brought to bear on his view of the world. This feature interests Faulkner, too, as he takes up the modernist preoccupation with the relation to the past.

On the issue of how people go about reconstructing past events to make them usable and constructive, Faulkner shares more than a little ground with Herodotus. Both strive to evoke living myth and, in the process, to speak to the whole of human consciousness. For Herodotus and Faulkner, the real world extends far beyond what is physically observable; it is an all-enveloping reality "rather than that academic realism which mistakes the material, tangible surface of things for the things themselves."[61] Faulkner's Quentin muses about the past, "Maybe nothing ever happens once and is finished. Maybe happen is never once but like ripples maybe on water after the pebble sinks, the ripples moving on, spreading, the pool attached by a narrow umbilical water-cord to the next pool, which the first pool feeds, has fed, did feed."[62] Quentin's roommate, Shreve, replies that "there are some things that just have to be whether they are or not, have to be a damn sight more than some other things that maybe are and it dont matter a damn whether they are or not" (*AA*, 258). And Faulkner famously said in his own voice, "The past is never dead; it is not even past."

Thomas Sutpen, Faulkner's nineteenth-century landowner, shares the sophistic characteristics of men who cannot comprehend the expansive reality that Quentin explores. Sutpen's type is rather of the absolutists who measure, calculate, and treat human beings as things; they seek endlessly to acquire. For example, Sutpen's plan to create a southern dynasty requires him to "put his first wife aside like eleventh and twelfth century kings did." Sutpen says of her, "I found that she was not and could never be, through no fault of her own, adjunctive or incremental to the design which I had in mind, so I provided for

---

61. Gunter Blöcker, "William Faulkner," in Robert Penn Warren, ed., *Faulkner: A Collection of Critical Essays,* 124.
62. William Faulkner, *Absalom, Absalom!* 210 (hereafter cited parenthetically as *AA*).

her and put her aside." The rationalism of such people distorts their understanding; they simplify the world unduly and thereby miss the greater part of human reality. Sutpen perceives reality as a series of constraints on his own behavior, as when he recounts his boyhood to Quentin's grandfather: "All of a sudden he discovered, not what he wanted to do but what he just had to do, had to do it whether he wanted to or not" (*AA,* 194, 178). This sounds as if Sutpen is making some kind of moral commitment, but for the reader nothing in the situation sustains this view of perceived necessity. First, when Sutpen says this, he is in the midst of hunting down his French architect as if the man were an animal; second, Sutpen's only desire is to hurt others as he himself has been hurt. Readers grow suspicious of all assertions of necessity, just as they do in Herodotus' *History,* for example, when Xerxes is forced by a dream to attack Greece. "There is a vision," Xerxes says, "keeps haunting me in sleep and will not suffer me to do what I would; even now he has threatened me and vanished" (*Hist* 7.15).

A better penetration of the human condition would require the ability to enter into the thoughts and motives and emotions of others. The ability to project oneself into different historical worlds is an imaginative skill. Herodotus' Athenians do this; Faulkner's characters Shreve and Quentin do this. Sitting in their Harvard dorm room in 1910, Quentin and Shreve work out a credible story, through conjecture and interpretation, to solve a murder that occurred in 1865. For the reader, their reconstruction is persuasive, far more so than the existing alternatives. But there is no final check, no way to find out what really happened. As Cleanth Brooks wrote, "*Absalom, Absalom!* is a persuasive commentary upon the thesis that much of 'history' is really a kind of imaginative construction. The past always remains at some level a mystery, but if we are to hope to understand it in any wise, we must enter into it and project ourselves imaginatively into the attitudes and emotions of the historical figures."[63]

The relevance of a jury's reconstruction of a crime to the imaginative reconstruction that takes place in *Absalom, Absalom!* is plain.

63. Cleanth Brooks, "History and the Sense of the Tragic: *Absalom, Absalom!*" in Warren, ed., *Faulkner: A Collection,* 196.

Effects precede causes in what could accurately be seen as a detective novel, as Parker notes, "and the urge to uncover the cause impels the plot and suspense."[64] The story of *Absalom, Absalom!* literally absorbs the reader into its own activity. This is like the situation of the juror, even if in that case there are two authors—prosecutor and defense—vying for control over the narrative, one of whom is more intent on obscuring the line irretrievably and interjecting permanent confusions. But the movement of a real murder case heard by a jury can be seen as having a Faulknerian drive forward in which the audience must participate in the interpretative process. "The judgment in any forensic controversy is not about facts but about what they mean."[65]

In *Absalom, Absalom!* Quentin narrates to Shreve various perspectives of the murder of Charles Bon. The only fact in the case that is indisputable is that Henry Sutpen shot Bon through the heart, but the motive is unclear. Many of the characters who appear—Miss Rosa, Mr. Compson, Grandfather—are much more closely situated to the event in time, place, and relation than are either Quentin or Shreve. Yet they reveal prejudices that blind them to some of the key elements of the story. Miss Rosa's choice of words when she refers to Thomas Sutpen—the demon, the ogre—establish early on that she brings to the story an overpowering resentment, a sense of personal outrage. She missed her childhood, and she was robbed of her marriage; she is monomaniacal in her depictions of these losses and frozen in a single moment of remembrance. Still, we are in no position to dismiss her perceptions. She is partially, but not wholly, unreliable. Mr. Compson is at the other extreme, exhibiting such sardonic distance that readers come to distrust his cynicism. He is much more prone to filling in the gaps of the story with his own hypotheses, and his detachment allows him to see where he has failed—"It just does not explain" (*AA*, 80). Mr. Compson knows that Charles Bon has a Negro mistress and child, but he doesn't know how this would necessarily prevent Bon from a real marriage with Henry's sister. Because he has been unable to make sense of the known facts, Mr. Compson relinquishes hope of

---

64. Parker, *Questioning of Fictions*, 29.
65. Farrell, *Norms of Rhetorical Culture*, 79n50.

any certainty in the matter, and thus he relinquishes any possibility for moral judgment. His own prejudices (especially against women) slip in whenever he is stuck. "Since he doesn't know, the things he makes up reflect his own self. And what he imagines most is Bon. . . . As the character they know least about, Bon gives Mr. Compson the freest range, until his imagined Bon sounds like an aestheticized and idealized version of Mr. Compson himself."[66]

It is not that the characters Quentin and Shreve are somehow without prejudice or that they don't reveal themselves in their retellings. As readers of *The Sound and the Fury* well know, Quentin is absorbed by the issue of incest, and this absorption accounts for more than a little of his drive to understand the motives in this story. Shreve is a Canadian outsider looking in (as a novice anthropologist), curious about the strange mythology of the South unfolding through Quentin's retellings. Their superior penetration is in no sense attributable to their objectivity, at least if that word is taken to imply distance: they come to be on intimate terms with their subjects, and this intimacy is correlated with the soundness of their perceptions. Emotional involvement goes hand in hand with objective judgment. Thus it is more a matter of their receptiveness, their refusal to rest with what "just does not explain." They inevitably push on, conjecturing alternative after alternative until they arrive at an explanation of the given facts that satisfies both of them. It seems from their example that it is possible to lift oneself above one's passions and improve one's awareness of the world. They are willing to struggle, to play the game, that is, to enter into the minds of their subjects, and they do so fully cognizant of the status of their constructions. Quentin "could see it; he might even have been there. Then he thought NO. If I had been there I could not have seen it this plain" (*AA*, 155).

Strikingly, it is when Quentin and Shreve arrive at the most circumstantial portion of the story (a dishonest lawyer is posited to explain how Charles Bon discovered Thomas Sutpen's whereabouts) that they come to full agreement and full conviction. As Waggoner argues, the most circumstantial element is shown to be the most correct, that "the reader is led by the circumstantial solidity of this chapter to feel

66. Parker, *Questioning of Fictions*, 55.

more certain that this sympathetic account of Bon is correct than he is of any other interpretation he has encountered so far in the book."[67] The precise details of the Bon-Sutpen connection do not matter in the sense that their delineation would not advance the reader's comprehension of the murder, but the connection as imagined here already makes sense of the information that Quentin and Shrive possess. In the serious dialogue between Quentin and Shreve, then, the facts are made to reveal their meaning, and the reader is party to the effort. It is a moment of high drama when Shreve asks Quentin why Quentin's father, Mr. Compson, delayed giving him the last piece of vital information, that Charles Bon was not only half brother to Henry Sutpen but also part Negro.

> "He didn't know it then. Grandfather didn't tell him all of it either, like Sutpen never told Grandfather quite all of it," Quentin says.
> "Then who did tell him?" Shreve asks.
> "I did," Quentin replies. (*AA*, 214)

Quentin labored for this insight, but once it is articulated, it is fully persuasive. Thus Robert Penn Warren finds *Absalom, Absalom!* useful for demonstrating that "the great undergirding and overarching meaning of life is in the act of trying to create meaning through struggle."[68] The struggle of the characters in the tale is also the struggle of the readers of the novel.

It is straightforwardly a moral achievement when Quentin and Shreve figure out that the reason Henry killed his half brother was that Bon had "black blood," not because Bon was intent on marrying his half sister ("So it's the miscegenation, not the incest, which you can't bear"). Until this revelation, Henry had been spared the reader's strongest condemnation. The "demon" Thomas Sutpen had overshadowed all others. After all, Sutpen's cold calculus ("that inno-

---

67. Hyatt Waggoner, "Past as Present," in Warren, ed., *Faulkner: A Collection,* 181. Waggoner maintains that this chapter in *Absalom, Absalom!* is the one most instructive to the reader: "we are ready now, prepared by the interchange between Quentin and Shreve, to speculate with them, to invent probable characters and fill in details to make the story, the given incomprehensible facts, plausible" (177–78).

68. Warren, ed., *Faulkner: A Collection,* 14.

cence") is set out in the starkest terms: "that innocence which believed that the ingredients of morality were like the ingredients of pie or cake and once you had measured them and balanced them and mixed them and put them into the oven it was all finished and nothing but pie or cake could come out" (*AA*, 285, 211–12). But Henry now is seen repeating the sins of his father; he had a clear choice to make, and he made the wrong one. The story serves as microcosm for the nation's experience during the Civil War of brother killing brother over racial issues, "when the Old South was faced with a choice it could not avoid, it chose to destroy itself rather than admit brotherhood across racial lines."[69]

Yet it is not simply because of the way *Absalom, Absalom!* exposes racism that it can be said to showcase a kind of ethical reasoning. Faulkner implies that the art of storytelling itself presents the occasion for one's moral presentation. The characters Quentin and Shreve are shown grounding themselves in concrete detail and returning again and again to the given, as a check on their conjectures. When that careful procedure is combined with empathy then their activity of putting together these imaginative reconstructions can be called ethical. And so with readers generally. Turning things over in our minds is how we humans acknowledge our limitations in thought and in action: "At the peak of his powers," Brodhead wrote, "Faulkner's is a world where (as James said of *The Turn of the Screw*) 'nothing is right save as we rightly imagine it'—and where nothing is rightly imagined save as it is imagined again and again."[70] The exercise of that imaginative power and the willingness to test it in dialogue with others is not a morally neutral act. It is a training in the habits of mind of the judge, as Tocqueville saw long ago; these are the habits "that best prepare the people to be free" (*Dem*, 262). This is the activity jurors are called upon to exercise. "It is precisely this experience of their own capacity for moral judgment that lies at the basis of so many jurors' testimony to the personal significance of jury service."[71]

69. Waggoner, "Past as Present," ibid., 182.
70. Richard H. Brodhead, ed., *Faulkner: New Perspectives*, 9.
71. Burns, *Theory of the Trial*, 180.

V

Final Arguments

The normal is so much more simply complicated and interesting.
GERTRUDE STEIN, *The Autobiography of Alice B. Toklas*

Conviction and the Postmodern Juror

Sitting in the holding pen on the ninth floor of the New Haven County Courthouse in November 2001, I remember pondering whether a humanities-centered education from the Committee on Social Thought would be of any use to a jury foreman in a murder trial. I knew that if I were selected as a juror, it would certainly be for a capital case, and that I would end up serving as the jury foreman. At the time, this daydream seemed harmless enough, since, according to all conventional wisdom, I was not a plausible candidate. But as a longtime reader of Plato's *Republic,* I should have been more distrustful of conventional wisdom and taken instruction, rather, from Socrates, as in "be careful what you wish for." Not that I regret my jury experience, which was clarifying and stimulating and changed for good how I connect the passion for stories with the ability to make grounded judgments. And I have drawn the obverse conclusion as well: people who *don't* live comfortably with stories may be unable or unwilling to judge, endangering the criminal justice system that serves to bind our political community. It took a traumatic jury experience for me to apprehend the genuine political usefulness of a humanities-centered education.

As it turned out, my original hypothesis about the beneficial role of a liberal education was fully vindicated; it provides the intellectual skills needed for good judgment-making practices.

Is this kind of liberal education restricted to elite universities such as Chicago, Harvard, and Yale? Hardly. The texts I speak of are possessed by readers inside and outside of the academy. I do not underestimate the difficulty of accessing the text. Nor do I deny that a teacher might be needed to evoke the wonders of the words, but I insist that this teacher could be anyone. (Naturally, it could be no one, too. Even with a devoted teacher, the greatest works can be extraordinarily distant and taxing.) Everyone knows that elite universities may be among the very worst places for escaping conventional thinking. As helpful as my study of classic works has been to me for thinking about unavenged murder, contemporary academic scholarship on these works is often unilluminating because so inextricably aligned with politics of the day.

Freedom in a democratic era depends on viable spaces for individuals to connect and to deliberate. The American jury has this prospect before it whenever jurors' accounts of what happened are stimulated and enriched by the reciprocal action of one narrative on another. Thus as Tocqueville said, "Sentiments and ideas renew themselves, the heart is enlarged, and the human mind is developed only by the reciprocal action of men upon one another. I have shown that this action is almost nonexistent in a democratic country. It is therefore necessary to create it artificially there. And this is what associations alone can do" (*Dem,* 491). Juries serve as Tocquevillian associations that enlarge the heart and develop the human mind. Jurors, so long as they remain with the evidence and break through "the twin strangleholds of methodical rules and arbitrary subjectivism,"[1] must surely be regarded as moral agents.

To be human is to agonize. Ann Molan, in writing about Jane Austen's *Persuasion,* invokes the moral qualities that are exerted every time we allow ourselves to be persuaded, or not to be persuaded. "What the novel presents in [Anne Elliot], and tests, is the quality of her moral being; for . . . the novel constantly insists that this depends in part on

1. Ronald Beiner, *Political Judgment,* 2.

what a person expects from the world, and this influences in turn what the person partly creates, partly finds in his 'persuasions' about the world and himself."[2] The ability to remain open to persuasion just might be one of our best traits as human beings, so long as we watch ourselves so that what we allow ourselves to believe about the world is grounded in more than what we wish to find in it.

I have argued that the institution of the jury can be aligned usefully with the study of great works in the humanities. For anyone familiar with the postmodern turns of some academic humanists in recent decades, this claim may be received with a fair amount of suspicion. In 2002 I told my story to two Yale alums, Rynn Berry, class of 1937, and Sarah Maserati, class of 2001. They both shook their heads in trepidation as I began describing the makeup of the jury. Sarah interjected, "Just wait. The U.S. will bring Osama bin Laden to trial, and they'll put four Yale professors on the jury." Rynn remarked of such a prospect, "Now *there* is a lost cause." Both suggested that for anyone involved in the teaching of the humanities, the deconstructionist influences would be incapacitating, and even obvious evils would go unnamed. After the trial ended, I asked the state's attorney to guess which of the Yale professors had been the problem juror. Dearington responded without missing a beat, "The arts and crafts guy." Now, it was true that one of the holdouts (the lawyer, not the professor) had a very bad case of arbitrary subjectivism, and I do not mean to downplay the dangers from this quarter. But as it turned out, the Yale humanities professors acquitted themselves extremely well in this case, using their experiences in dealing with fallible evidence in their scholarship to guide their thinking in the deliberation room. The scientist, however, was not skilled in the art of making judgments, in negotiating that difficult terrain that Aristotle called the practical realm. He removed himself from deliberations. "Making judgments," Burns wrote, "is one of the ways in which we come to share a world with others."[3]

The great texts that I have appealed to in this book teach us to judge and to share our world with others. In the late night conversations

2. Ann Molan, "Persuasion in *Persuasion*," in Harold Bloom, ed., *Jane Austen: Modern Critical Views,* 156.
3. Burns, *Theory of the Trial,* 213.

of Shreve and Quentin in *Absalom, Absalom!* the two characters are alternately referred to as a single entity ("it might have been either of them [speaking] and was in a sense both: both thinking as one, the voice which happened to be speaking the thought only the thinking become audible, vocal") or as multiplying into four different people ("not two of them there and then either but four of them riding the two horses through the iron darkness and that not mattering either" [*AA,* 243, 237]). The point is the same: with effort, human beings can extend themselves into the minds of other human beings. Of course, this sympathy has limits, and in the modern world, it is possible that these potential connections will continue to dissipate. Tocqueville wrote about this phenomenon under the heading of individualism. "In democratic centuries . . . the bond of human affections is extended and loosened. . . . the fabric of time is torn at every moment and the trace of generations is effaced" (*Dem,* 483). Jane Austen also brings this world to life in her fiction: in *Emma,* in a passing moment, when the prospect of staying single and at home with her father finally penetrates Emma's consciousness; and in *Persuasion,* in a sustained way, where "Anne's lessons do point to the fact (glimpsed at the end of *Emma*) that society is breaking up into smaller and smaller 'circles' and units. This implies—indeed involves—the loss of any sense of a true, authoritative 'center,' and the possible disappearance of any 'common' language (and with that, a shared sense of 'common' values)."[4] The conversations and connections between Emma and Mr. Knightley and between Anne and Captain Wentworth are more authentic than any discussions involving a group or even another person. It is that intimacy that in the best case is re-created between author and reader.

One Case Closed

The family of Nancy McCloskey finally had their day in court. Michael Dearington called me at home to give me the news. In the sum-

---

4. Tanner, *Jane Austen,* 220–21. James Boyd White wrote, "What Emma perceives in her bleak view of future winters, then, is the essential subjectivity and relativity of this world—what we might call its modernity . . . it turns out that in this world—even in this world, one is tempted to say, there is no stable culture, external to the self, on which one can simply rely" (*When Words Lose Their Meaning,* 188).

mer of 2002, he had been preparing to prosecute the McCloskey case for the third time, but by the fall, Anthony Bazier decided to plead out to manslaughter one. Bazier accepted a sentence of fifteen years, making him eligible for parole in nine; he had served four already. So he was looking at five more years, which wasn't much, certainly wasn't enough, but it was over. On January 3, 2003, I returned to the New Haven County Courthouse to hear Nancy McCloskey's sisters speak at his sentencing.

McCloskey's sister Cheryl made the first statement to the court. She referred to her parents, who were both alive and in reasonable health. They visited Nancy's grave every week but hadn't been able to bear the pain of attending either trial. Cheryl said that she herself looked a lot like Nancy, and that sometimes her mother would be taken up short and would say, "You looked just like Nancy when you did that." Nancy's laugh, Cheryl recalled, was always a giggle. She was very nurturing; she believed in her children and stayed home to raise them. Her girls meant everything. She was a great cook. Cheryl said that their parents had always taught her and Nancy not to hate, but now, with Nancy's murder, the family had new cause to understand the meaning of that word. She talked about how Nancy's murder had changed all of them; she turned to face Bazier directly, and she said, "I've had cancer. I've had radiation treatment. But nothing compares to the pain you have caused. You had choices. The choice you made is incomprehensible."

Next, a letter written by Nancy's other sister, Diane, was read to the court. Diane repeated that Bazier had devastated their family, but then she addressed how he stood with his own family. His son, she said, would live knowing that his father was a murderer. She continued, "Nancy and I were extremely close. She was not only my sister, she was my best friend. We used to ask each other how we would cope if one of us died. There is no coping; there is no end to the sorrow, grief, or loneliness."

After listening quietly, the judge spoke with compassion to the family, and he said that he knew that nothing could compensate them for the loss of Nancy. Then the judge asked Bazier if he had anything to say. This would be the first time I had ever heard him speak, but he only said, "Nah."

Later, Dearington thanked me for coming over. "I know the family appreciated it," he said. "They are as content as possible under the circumstances." At least their story got told. Hannah Arendt never tired of citing Isak Dinesen on this point: "All sorrows can be borne if you put them into a story or tell a story about them."[5] Perhaps, it is even true.

The Jovin story, in contrast, remains unfinished, the sorrow still unbearable eight years after the murder of Suzanne. The images do not go away. The feeling that one gets when attending the funeral of someone like Suzanne, a woman of only twenty-one years, is of piercing sadness, God knows. The combination of maturity, promise, and youthful idealism is so poignant, but in Suzanne's case, it was made more excruciatingly so by what consumed her during her final week. She was obsessively writing and rewriting her senior essay about the dangers of Osama bin Laden and terrorism—in 1998, three years before America was changed by the events of September 11, 2001. Her approach was hardheaded and open-eyed: "Bin Laden's technological potential and its disruptive use are one of today's greatest threats to U.S. security," she wrote in one draft. She stayed up all night on Thursday, December 3, 1998, the night before she was murdered, reworking the essay. Then, overtired, she devoted her Friday night to one of her favorite causes, the Best Buddies program in New Haven. The police believe that directly afterward she got into a car voluntarily, with someone she knew. The contrast between her altruism and her goodness and the savage violence of her death is sickening to consider. It is said that her vocal chords were cut, so that she could not scream. As it was, the last thing anyone heard was the bewildered Iphigenia-like cry: "Why are you doing this to me?" That why is simply not answerable.

But on one front we are all answerable, and that concerns the deliberative powers of the common person. It is difficult but absolutely necessary in this circumstance to keep faith with Aristotle: "The true and the just are stronger by nature than their opposites."

The Jury and the American Polity

The jury story I tell is not altogether heartening. The outcome of our deliberations was a bad one, and this was not simply because the jury

---

5. Arendt, *Between Past and Future,* 262.

hung. The case was exceedingly tough: all of our evidence was circumstantial, all of our witnesses were flawed, and the incompetence of some of the police work was jaw-dropping. If the jury had hung on account of the reasonable doubt of one or more of the jurors, justice would have been served. But that is not what happened. We hung as a jury on account of *unreasonable* doubt. So an otherwise ordinary murder in New Haven became a cultural event of significance, as certain jurors presented the refusal to deliberate and the eschewing of judgment as moral positions. This is a morality that American democrats can ill afford in an age of terrorism and religious warfare.

Needless to say, one bad result does not invalidate the jury system any more than one good result assures its reputation. In analyzing that bad result, I have become convinced of the essential soundness of the institution. I do not believe that the jury needs to be reformed in the ways frequently suggested—for instance, by eliminating peremptory challenges during voir dire or by overturning the requirement for unanimity in capital cases. As a juror, I was extremely conscious of the need for unanimity, and I know how much it shaped our interactions, for the better. Nor am I convinced of the pressing need to promulgate information about jury nullification. Jurors will continue to nullify, for better and worse, with or without instruction. My experience did not lead me to fear the power of the state or the discretion of the judge.[6]

This is not to say that all is perfectly in order in the world of the jury, of course. Everyone has a jury joke that suggests the dimensions of the problem. Mark Twain captured elements of its absurdity long ago: "the efficiency of our jury [system] is only marred by the difficulty of finding twelve men every day who don't know anything and can't read." In the aftermath of cases such as the O. J. Simpson trial, Americans feel a deep cynicism about their system of justice. During that trial, Milton Berle quipped that "the case is in the hands of twelve people who didn't have brains enough to get out of jury duty."[7] Some

6. On unanimity, see Akhil Reed Amar, *The Constitution and Criminal Procedure: First Principles,* 170–71. The case for more information on jury nullification is presented eloquently by Abramson in *We the Jury,* 57–95. I agree with Abramson's sentiment that the jury is "the embodiment of nonelite, participatory ideals of democracy" (250). D. Graham Burnett fears state power in *A Trial by Jury,* 162.

7. The Twain quote is cited by Henry G. Miller, *On Trial: Lessons from a Lifetime in the Courtroom,* 3. Alschuler wonders about this attribution and notes

historical features of the jury are difficult to justify. There are plenty
of areas for improvement, and I wouldn't disagree with many of these
piecemeal reforms: jurors should be able to take notes, they should
get the benefit of an opening statement, they should not be actively
disinformed. But the real issues are more fundamental. Americans
need to worry about respect for truth in the courtroom and commonsense reasoning in the deliberation room. The phenomenon of the
nondeliberating juror appears to be on the rise.[8]

I have sought not only to showcase the admirable features of the
American jury but also to track its underside. On the positive side is
the extraordinary combination of the jury's free formation—it is
forced to constitute itself with minimal guidelines—and its respect for
the deliberative powers of the common person—it accepts reasonable
doubt as a self-evident standard of judgment. On the negative side,
the free constitution of the jury is shadowed by the impulse to hand
over decision making to experts, and all too often the commitment to
reason is subverted by an appeal to intuition or to emotion. Without
question, the adverse tendencies appear with more force than the
affirmative ones. Beiner refers to the stranglehold that needs to be
broken for there to be the mere possibility of valid judgments, and
stranglehold is a word that applies fully to the case I have recounted
here: "Judgment allows us to comport ourselves to the world without
dependence upon rules and methods and allows us to defeat subjec-

---

that he has been unable to locate it in Twain ("The Supreme Court and the Jury:
Voir Dire, Peremptory Challenges, and the Review of Jury Verdicts," 154n4). As
a Herodotean, I'll just designate it a "fighting story" and be done with it. The
Berle quote is cited by Dominick Dunne, *Justice: Crimes, Trials, and Punishments*, 244.

8. Rosen supplies the figures to suggest the correlate: that hung juries are increasing significantly. He notes that in Washington, D.C., "between 1992 and
1996, an average of thirteen per cent of all federal criminal trials there ended in
hung juries, compared with only five per cent in 1991" ("One Angry Woman,"
55). Cynicism may well be a root cause. Robin West argues that there is virtually
no debate among legal scholars, lawyers, and judges about what legal justice really means: "There is no tradition, no shared fabric, no mosaic, no family of com-
peting understandings, of what the virtue that for many of us seemingly defines
our professional lives might entail. This prompts ennui, resignation, and, in our
students, a cynicism we deplore but have no clue how to address in a way that
does not expose our own" ("Toward Humanistic Theories of Legal Justice,"
148–49).

tivity by asserting claims that seek general assent."[9] My book is cautionary in its claim that we are susceptible to too much rigidity or too little anchoring in times when science cannot guide us and when we are without the resources of a strong humanities tradition to help us think through our human conundrums. The jury shows these highs and lows in crystallized form, but they appear elsewhere throughout our culture, wherever judgments are called for. Academia, where I live, is full of relevant spectacles.

The appeal to emotion or intuition can be a much more worrisome proclivity than it would appear at first glance, for it easily slides into an appeal beyond the matter at hand, a demand to change standards of procedure according to the end that is desired. This contravenes the most basic sense of the principle of objectivity; in the courtroom, this principle "is embodied in the standardized set of formal procedures and implicit judgment practices . . . and not in any metaphysical criteria of truth or fact."[10] However random one's standards of procedure may be at the outset, whether one is judging the quality of writing or the guilt or innocence of the accused, there should be a transparent and universal application of those standards once discussion is underway. This sounds so elementary, and yet the experiences that I describe show repeated transgressions. Sometimes bypasses are enjoined on account of some default authority, and at other times, they are enjoined on account of special apprehensions or personal theories. Such bypasses have serious undertones. Does everything reduce to personal whim? That is an opening for tyranny, as free from oversight as what Tocqueville wrote about in "the tyranny of the majority."

Americans are not accustomed to hearing themselves described as subjects of tyranny or despotism, but those are precisely the terms that Tocqueville uses in *Democracy in America* when he turns his attention to intellectual matters in the United States. For him, the pressing matter in the age of democratic revolutions is the source of one's belief, for with the demise of political hierarchies, old intellectual authorities are overturned, too. In volume 1, Tocqueville takes note of a

---

9. Beiner, *Political Judgment,* 2.

10. W. Lance Bennett and Martha S. Feldman, *Reconstructing Reality in the Courtroom: Justice and Judgment in American Culture,* 32–33.

pervasive intellectual conformity: "I do not know any country where, in general, less independence of mind and genuine freedom of discussion reign than in America." The problem is intrinsic to democracy, not to America; with so much to decide for themselves, democrats turn to the silent (invisible) authority of majority opinion to help them along. In the process, minority opinion tends not to be heard. But, in Tocqueville's view, this is exacerbated by the American national character, which is confident in its practical abilities, "constantly led back toward [its] own reason as the most visible and closest source of truth" and suspicious of anything transcendent. The end result is a tendency to deny what the majority has not articulated. Tocqueville claims that the public has a singular power among democratic peoples: "It does not persuade [one] of its beliefs, it imposes them and makes them penetrate souls by a sort of immense pressure of the minds of all on the intellect of each" (*Dem,* 244, 404, 409).

This authority of public opinion bears an important relation to the appeal to intuition described above in the way that pressure is exerted on everyone to accede to a view, without anyone actually arguing for it. Its persuasiveness is not established, but it is assumed. "An unexamined life is not worth living," Socrates famously declared, shortly before his fellow democrats put him to death, posthaste. In America, where there is business to be done, the time for examination is short; deliberation only slows action and impedes results. The tendency to submit to what everyone knows is ever present in democracy since an individual can authorize so little about the world and appears insubstantial next to the majority. By necessity, Tocqueville concludes, American democrats rely on a great number of "ready-made beliefs" (*Dem,* 407). There is no simple way to cope with this fact of democratic life. Perhaps the most Americans can hope for, with Tocqueville, is an awareness of how often they advert to invisible authorities and how incumbent on them it is to resist an easy or uncritical accommodation to this practice.

The second default position that I track here (with Tocqueville), and the second opening for tyranny, is the refusal to engage at all where science and its precise measurement cannot go. This is particularly troubling in a trial, if Robert Burns is correct in noting that "the acceptance of a story and the reaching of a verdict seem to be the same human act."[11] This tendency to bracket metaphysical questions is long established in and at the heart of America's own philosophy, pragmatism. More properly, pragmatism is a method, based on the premise that the meaning of an idea or proposition lies in its observable, practical consequences. The pragmatist approaches philosophy "as an outdoorsman," in the words of John Patrick Diggins, in the spirit of experiencing life "as though each morning were a new beginning." Underlying pragmatist thinking is the view that "if we want our conception of an object to be meaningful . . . then we should limit that conception to the real-world behavior the object will exhibit under all possible conditions." As a method of taking guidance from what works, it has a strong correlation with the scientific method. The starting point for the pragmatist is that questions that are answerable may be carved out from those that are not—as if the nonanswerable questions can take care of themselves. At the turn of the twentieth century, William James used a corridor in a hotel as an unproblematic image to illustrate the appeal of this workaday philosophy: "Innumerable chambers open out of it. In one you may find a man writing an atheistic volume; in the next someone on his knees praying for faith and strength; in a third a chemist investigating a body's properties . . . But they all own the corridor, and all must pass through it if they want a practicable way of getting into or out of their respective rooms."[12] The idea is that the occupants of the different chambers will leave each other alone and will live in peaceful coexistence. For much of American history, this view suited the American temperament without engendering any discernible hostility from the outside world. But it appears that in the post-September 11 world, Americans can no longer afford such pragmatic complacency.[13] They need to worry more about what kinds of sinister occupants are in those chambers.

11. Burns, *Theory of the Trial*, 149.

12. John P. Diggins, *The Promise of Pragmatism: Modernism and the Crisis of Knowledge and Authority*, 115; Louis Menand, *Pragmatism: A Reader*, xiii–xiv; William James, *Pragmatism*, 21–22.

13. The contemporary applications of this stance are numerous. There is Richard Rorty, who encourages a "lightmindedness" toward traditional philosophical questions, or John Rawls, who bases his theory of justice on moral intuitions. There is Daniel Dennett, who takes a Darwinist-centered approach that argues for an analog between the ways genes of biological evolution are trans-

William James and John Dewey brought the term *pragmatism* into common usage in the late nineteenth century, but Tocqueville also identified this phenomenon, especially in volume 2 of his *Democracy in America.* Tocqueville describes the philosophic method of the Americans ("born Cartesians") in terms that are in line with their practical know-how and political self-sufficiency: "As they see that they manage to resolve unaided all the little difficulties that practical life presents, they easily conclude that everything in the world is explicable and that nothing exceeds the bounds of intelligence. Thus they willingly deny what they cannot comprehend" (*Dem,* 404). That tendency to isolate what is knowable and ignore what is not leads to an ever-increasing predominance of science as the authority, and in Tocqueville's story, that development goes hand in hand with an increasing centralization of government. What Tocqueville traces is the process of individuals handing over their powers of judgment to the central authority. In other words, Tocqueville's study reminds us that American democrats have long been susceptible to the intellectual tendencies that I relate from my jury experience. Then as now, the jury room is also the place where best to offset those unreflective responses and to encourage self-sufficiency in our critical powers.

Aeschylus on Trial: Is One Life Worth more than Another?

After the trial was long over, I went in search of Aeschylus, an author I knew I needed to know better. By rights, the *Oresteia* should have come first; it is the urtext of murder and vengeance. But I happened upon a chilling line in the secondary literature on Aeschylus that changed my mind about where it belonged: the idea that one life might be worth more than another. Once again, my academic studies veered back toward the real murder cases. The *Oresteia* became the final text.

Aeschylus's *Oresteia,* first performed in 458 BC, is the only trilogy (*Agamemnon, The Libation Bearers, The Eumenides*) to survive intact from the classical Greek theater. It depicts the moment of transition

---

mitted and the way cultural achievements are—that is, without agency, without mind, without purpose.

from the precivilized world of fate and revenge to the civilized world of justice under law. The commitment is mutual: individuals will give up their right to impose justice in the form of death for the murderers of their kin. Henceforth, punishment for capital crimes will be the exclusive responsibility of the state. Familial self-restraint is compensated by the assurance that the state will administer the death penalty whenever it is justified. Revenge is replaced by the rule of law. John Locke, the political philosopher most closely associated with America, makes clear the foundational importance of this bargain in his *Second Treatise of Government.* The rights and liberties that individuals cede to the state are revocable if the government fails to perform the functions with which it was entrusted. But, once given to the state, the right to punish is not recoverable; that power the individual "wholly gives up."[14]

By and large, that core issue of political philosophy, the handing over of power to the state, evoked in the *Oresteia* is dismissed by contemporary scholars. What preoccupies many current readers is Aeschylus the misogynist. The verdict at the end of the trilogy that goes against Clytemnestra and in favor of Orestes is taken to signify that her life is less valued than his. In what amounts to me as the final marker of the corruption of judgment in contemporary times, readers of Aeschylus now ignore the elemental political insights as they disparage his judgment. Real life and literature collide.

Five years after the murder of Suzanne Jovin, I had a conversation with the detective overseeing the still-unsolved case. He reported that he is constantly asked why so much time and energy has been devoted to this one case. What does that say about us, he repeated to me, that we treat this case so differently than we do the others? My question is a variant. What does it say about us that we are prone to asking such a coarse and misguided question? As someone pulled into the lives of both New Haven victims, I can affirm that in each case, it was not possible for unrelated human beings to care any more about the victims. Their stories, however, should not be equalized or quantified or reduced in these ways. Tocqueville could surely illuminate the propensity at work to settle on the lowest common denominator or to

14. John Locke, *Two Treatises of Government,* 353.

seek some yardstick to measure the value of a life. My interest is to stay with the story, to get to where the meaning resides. I return, therefore, to the drama of Aeschylus, which Goethe called the most sublime conception of the human mind, in the hopes of restoring its "untimeliness"[15]—that is to say, its enduring relevance.

Aeschylus and the Hung Jury at the Heart of Civilization

The story of the *Oresteia* is both intricate and profound. "A man returns home and is killed by a woman: a man returns home and kills a woman; it is the same woman, the men are father and son."[16] The house of Atreus has been cursed with endless rounds of murders and vengeance. Each kin-murder requires that another murder be carried out in revenge. The action of the first drama, *Agamemnon,* concerns the killing of the king after his return from the Trojan War (itself a source for multiple stories of retribution[17]), but Agamemnon's murder is set against the backdrop of crimes more ancient. To stay with the immediate past, Agamemnon and Menelaus are the Atridae, the sons of Atreus. Atreus and his brother, Thyestes, had long quarreled over the rule of Argos. Thyestes exacerbated the strain by having an adulterous affair with his brother's wife. Atreus thereupon invited Thyestes to a palace feast, allegedly for reconciliation. But Atreus had in fact murdered the children of Thyestes and proceeded to serve him their remains. After discovering the monstrous deed, Thyestes pronounced a mighty curse on the house of Atreus, before he and his only surviving son (Aegisthus) were exiled from Argos.

Agamemnon (cousin, then, to Aegisthus) was commander of the Greek forces assembled at Aulis to sail against Troy when the curse first descended upon him. The winds from the north prevented the Greek fleet from sailing, and when the troops fell into desperate

15. "I do not know what meaning classical studies could have for our time if they were not untimely," Nietzsche wrote, "that is to say, acting counter to our time and thereby acting on our time and, let us hope, for the benefit of a time to come" (Friedrich Nietzsche, *Untimely Meditations,* 60).

16. R. P. Winnington-Ingram, *Studies in Aeschylus,* 132–33.

17. Robert Fagles notes that Aeschylus referred to his work as "slices from the banquet of Homer," though it was deepened by "even older, darker legends" (Aeschylus, *The Oresteia,* 14).

straits, the seer Calchas was summoned to discover the cause of the god's anger. Calchas declared that the goddess Artemis required the sacrifice of Agamemnon's daughter Iphigenia. Agamemnon was thrust into a choice of dooms. "My fate is angry if I disobey these," Agamemnon protested, in reference to the kings, "but angry if I slaughter this child, the beauty of my house."[18]

Agamemnon sacrifices his daughter, and thus the family curse becomes entwined with the future of the nation as a whole. After the Trojan War, the victorious Agamemnon returns home, where his wife, Clytemnestra, aided by her lover, Aegisthus, kills him, to avenge the killing of Iphigenia. Orestes is then called on to kill his mother, Clytemnestra, in revenge for her killing of his father. Not for nothing has this been called the original dysfunctional family.

Agamemnon gives his name to the first play in the trilogy, but the action is all Clytemnestra's, the woman with "male strength of heart." Her murderous welcome of the king begins with the laying of a carpet for him, rich tapestries to make "a crimson path," such that Agamemnon's foot need not touch the earth. Agamemnon objects. He is not some Asiatic, not one of the gods: "Discordant is the murmur at such treading down of lovely things." Clytemnestra persists, and she shows a dramatic inventiveness: "If Priam had won as you have, what would he have done?" She is strangely persuasive, and the king relents, intending to exercise his will in other spheres. But the queen is always a step ahead, and the atmosphere is heavy; the Chorus cannot shake its foreboding. Before long Clytemnestra appears, standing over her husband's body: "as fishermen cast their huge circling nets, I spread deadly abundance of rich robes, and caught him fast" (*Ag* 11, 911, 926–27, 935, 1381–82). This murder, like all murders in Greek tragedies, takes place offstage. Why does it feel so visceral, then, and so ghastly?

Harold Bloom claims that Aeschylus "possessed a greater insight into the darkness of the war between men and women than any other dramatist before Shakespeare."[19] If so, Clytemnestra is the principal

---

18. Aeschylus, *Oresteia: Agamemnon, The Libation Bearers, The Eumenides,* 206–8. I will cite from this translation while using the notes and commentaries from others, as indicated.

19. Harold Bloom, ed., *Aeschylus's The Oresteia: Modern Critical Interpretations,* 4.

agent. "As he died," she reports, "he spattered me with the dark red and violent driven rain of bitter savored blood to make me glad, as gardens stand among the showers of God in glory at the birthtime of the buds" (*Ag* 1389–92). The darkness of this war is to her taste. Orestes is then called on to kill his mother, Clytemnestra, in revenge for her killing of his father. "Where is the end?" the Chorus of women wail at the close of the *Libation Bearers.* "Where shall the fury of fate be stilled to sleep, be done with?" (*LB* 1074–76).

At the time the *Oresteia* was produced, it was the convention among Greek tragedians to utilize three actors, with a clear distinction in the magnitude of each role, between speaking parts and mutes. "Some of the speaking parts are very slight," Jones emphasizes, "but there are no half measures over their speaking: you do not find characters with only two or three lines to utter. Pylades is the only exception to this rule."[20] Pylades is the companion of Orestes in the *Libation Bearers,* the second play in the trilogy. Pylades serves as a mute from the moment the play opens, when he is seen with Orestes kneeling before the tomb of Agamemnon, until the end, when Orestes finally accosts Clytemnestra. In that pivotal scene, Clytemnestra begins to affect Orestes' resolve, as she bares her breast in supplication. "Oh take pity, child, before this breast where many a time, a drowsing baby, you would feed and with soft gums sucked in the milk that made you strong" (*LB* 896–98). Nothing could be more surprising at this juncture than what Orestes actually does, turning to his silent companion with the plaintive cry, "What shall I do, Pylades?" Pylades speaks. With this deviation, Aeschylus stunned his audience, thereby securing "the most complete arrest of attention, a stopping of dramatic time, for Orestes' direct, inescapable question."[21] What shall I do. Here is the problem of decision. The need is imperative, but the way is murky. The question is inescapable for Pylades (and for us), even though this role was thrust upon him, unexpectedly.

Pylades takes the side of Apollo: "What then becomes thereafter of the oracles declared by Loxias at Pytho? What of sworn oaths? Count all men hateful to you rather than the gods." Orestes concurs with the

20. John Jones, *On Aristotle and Greek Tragedy,* 101.
21. Ibid.

judgment of Pylades. "I judge that you win. Your advice is good" (*LB* 900–903). But is it? Justice—*Dikê* in Greek—is complicated. One claim of right clashes fundamentally with another, even among the gods. As soon as Orestes carries out his task of matricide (sanctioned by Apollo) and is covered with his mother's blood, he begins to see the Furies, the avengers of crime against kin. He flees in search of sanctuary, pursued by these primeval goddesses. The "paradox of *Dikê* continues," in Lebeck's formulation, "there is right and wrong on both sides."[22]

The unendurable situation for everyone may be summarized in the one line of the *Oresteia* that is said to have obsessed Francis Bacon: "the reek of human blood smiles out at me."[23] That is spoken by the Furies, who are describing the experience of physical revulsion when a horrible murder is unavenged. Clear enough. On the other side, the situation is not to be borne, either, because when blood is the only factor in evaluating the seriousness of a homicide, other monstrous crimes go unpunished. Orestes asks the Furies why they didn't hound Clytemnestra while she was still alive. "The man she killed was not of blood congenital." That is unacceptable, too, and Apollo poses this same question to the Furies, charging that they deny that "married love between man and woman is bigger than oaths, guarded by right of nature" (*Eum* 605, 211–19).

The elaborate weavings and trappings of Clytemnestra as she lures Agamemnon to his death suggest that Aeschylus would like us to consider multiple aspects of the crime: her premeditation, her shaping of the story, and her exultation afterward. Through all this, we never forget the innocent Iphigenia. Each character has a moment to pull the reader in wholly to his or her world. Although every present act is complicated by evocations of past grievances, some new twists are more jarring than others. Blood smiles its greeting to different effect.

The settling of Orestes' case should not, then, be considered a victory

22. Anne Lebeck, "The *Commos* in the *Libation-Bearers,*" in Bloom, ed., *Aeschylus's The Oresteia,* 43.
23. In the introduction to his translated edition of Aeschylus's *Oresteia,* Collard wrote that for forty years Bacon was obsessed with the *Oresteia* and that it inspired him to paint the *Triptych.* The haunting line is translated by W. B. Stanford (Aeschylus, *Oresteia,* lxi n. 43).

of the male over the female. Nor is it an establishing of the precedent, as Kuhns wrote, that "the death of the husband shall be counted as more serious than the death of the woman who is his wife." Yet this seems to be the conventional reading. Zeitlin theorizes that "if Aeschylus is concerned with world-building, the cornerstone of his architecture is the control of woman, the social and cultural prerequisite for the construction of civilization." According to Peter French, it is obvious that "Aeschylus did not regard acts of vengeance performed by women as on a moral par with male revenge."[24] This seems to me to distort Aeschylus. However much Clytemnestra's (calamitously) bad form comes into play, she is surely not on the losing side because of her gender. Her role is the most demonic. For all of the equalizing vengeance within the house of Atreus, an occasion arises for qualitative distinctions regarding Clytemnestra's transgression. An artistic assessment of a different order is called for. Her infamous description of the third blow she struck against Agamemnon ("as he died he spattered me with . . . blood to make me glad, as gardens stand . . . at the birthtime of the buds") is pure blasphemy. It is a perversion of the Greek myth of the primeval mating of Heaven and Earth: "In that myth the primal Male came together with the primal Female in the mutual joy of creation. Clytemnestra, however . . . transformed the ancient world's supreme symbol of love between the sexes into her own supreme symbol of hatred."[25] Clytemnestra is "the great artist of ritual," according to Fagles, but her rituals extinguish creation instead of celebrating it. Clytemnestra is condemned through the storytelling. It is her words, her gestures, and her malefic power that generate the ending.[26]

24. Richard Kuhns, *The House, the City, and the Judge: The Growth of Moral Awareness in the Oresteia*, 86; Froma I. Zeitlin, "The Dynamics of Misogyny," in Bloom, ed., *Aeschylus's The Oresteia*, 48; Peter A. French, *The Virtues of Vengeance*, 17.

25. John Herington rightly identifies this act as more terrifying than murder: "a universe divided by open war between the male and the female" (*Aeschylus*, 124).

26. Fagles, "Introduction," in Aeschylus, *Oresteia*, 34. The male-female issues extend considerably further than I can address here. Suffice it to note that Iphigeneia stands as the age-old symbol of the disproportionate suffering of the vulnerable female. This isn't misogynism, this is life. It is one reason women might be particularly concerned with the maintenance of law and adjudication in the political community (and sound judgment in the courtroom).

Orestes, in contrast, is reluctant; he hesitates and seeks reassurance that the god's command of matricide is fixed. He and his sister Electra distinguish themselves by the spirit with which they execute justice, as Herington notes, for they indicate some dim awareness of a kind of justice that will transcend revenge. "They show none of the cruel satisfaction with which the Herald and Agamemnon spoke of the justice dealt out to Troy," he observes, "still less the unholy ecstasy which the king's murder inspired in Clytemnestra and Aegisthus."[27] (This does not mean we like them more.) As Orestes' spokesman, Apollo gives the understated and powerful version. Visually, all is clear: "It was the bath. When [Agamemnon] was at its edge, she hooded the robe on him, and in the blind and complex toils tangled her man, and chopped him down. There is the story of the death of a great man" (*Eum* 633–36). The Furies interrupt this thought by asking about the uncomfortable precedent of Zeus killing Cronus. Apollo becomes so enraged that he explodes in invective. Thus Apollo turns out to be a poor advocate for Orestes, for he cannot control his temper long enough to sustain the all-important visualization of the crime. Nevertheless, the measure of the deed has been taken. Clytemnestra's transgression is worse.

The question to be decided is whether Orestes' transgression is irremediable. Athena, goddess of wisdom and patroness of Athens, intervenes to decide, once and for all, which claim shall be declared just. The issue is to be determined on the basis of a trial, with human jurors and superhuman advocates. This eventuates in a scene that has been called the most surreal in all of Aeschylus: "That a jury of human beings should sit to vote on a case that has divided the powers of Heaven and Earth, the attorneys for the prosecution being daughters of Night and nieces of Fate, while the defense counsel is a son of Zeus and his spokesman!"[28] The moment is one of high definition for Athens, politically speaking; it is a moment of consonance between Attic tragedy and the political life of the Athenian community. "This forevermore shall be the ground where justices deliberate," Athena intones, "Here is the Hill of Ares" (*Eum* 683–85), where, in actuality, the Areopagus Council sits, defending the political community against

27. Herington, *Aeschylus,* 132.
28. Ibid., 147.

the cycle of kin-murder. The powers of this council had been sharply debated in the years before the production of Aeschylus' trilogy, as the democracy assumed its new form. Aeschylus manages to stay political "in the noblest sense of the word," as Lesky argues, not forcing the connections but allowing them to emerge seamlessly.[29]

Notably, in the *Eumenides,* Athena casts her vote in favor of Orestes before the jury's votes are counted: "This is a ballot for Orestes I shall cast. There is no mother anywhere who gave me birth, and, but for marriage, I am always for the male with all my heart, and strongly on my father's side. So, in a case where the wife has killed her husband, lord of the house, her death shall not mean most to me" (*Eum* 735–40). As it turns out, among the mortal Athenians, the vote is split, and it is a hung jury. Athena, therefore, has cast the deciding vote.

What does this mean? Why does Athena act so precipitately? Her announcement is suspiciously swift, suspiciously undefended. Beyond identifying her prejudice that she "is always for the male," she makes no genuine effort to convert anyone to her side.[30] This becomes more startling in retrospect, as we witness her amazing powers of persuasion toward the Furies, who eventually accept the verdict and her offer of a new home and place of worship. Perhaps Athena's power lies more in decisive and symbolic action than in argumentative logic. Like Orestes, she was in an impossible situation, and yet judgment was required. "The matter is too big for any mortal man who thinks he can judge it," Athena declares. "Even I have not the right to analyse cases of murder where wrath's edge is sharp" (*Eum* 470–73). That she actually embraces the gratuitous nature of the vote may signify her acceptance of the irrational prejudice at the core of politics. It need not be debilitating, apparently. By declaring her own position before the jury votes are counted, Athena deflects much of the drama of the situation onto what the mortal outcome will be. In other words, she de-

---

29. Albin Lesky, *Greek Tragedy,* 85.

30. Athena's bias toward the male is nothing next to Apollo's antifemale vindictiveness. It needs to be said that Aeschylus is neither "Athena" nor "Apollo," since so many commentators make that equation. D. J. Conacher wrote, for example, that "there is not the slightest indication on the poet's part that the judgment of Athena and, in particular, the status quo (of male superiority) which it is taken to represent are to be regarded as anything other than satisfactory" (*Aeschylus' Oresteia: A Literary Commentary,* 209). See also Brian Vickers, *Towards Greek Tragedy: Drama, Myth, Society,* 414–16 and note 47.

fines the situation again. It is not the immortal breaking of the tie that gets the stress; it is the mortal making of it. The legitimacy of the vote is established. When all of the clashes between male and female result in this impasse, a dead tie, then the result of a hung jury may be seen as a great achievement.

This is in Athens, of course. In America, everyone knows that a hung jury means no prosecution. Who needs a goddess to tip the scale? But even if Athena's vote is superfluous, her statecraft is not. There is nothing given about the reaction of the Furies. Athena knows well that they are capable of venting their poisons on her land. "Do not be angry any longer with this land nor bring the bulk of your hatred down on it, do not render it barren of fruit, nor spill the dripping rain of death in fierce and jagged lines to eat the seeds" (*Eum* 800–803). She has in sight only what is constructive for Athens. To this end, Athena devotes her full attention to bringing the Furies over to her side. Although it does not look promising when they immediately issue threats to breed cancer and mortal infection, there is cause for hope when their leader pauses to ask "What shall I do?" To feel the force of such doubt is to form oneself politically. The script is not foreordained. There is room for persuasion to maneuver whenever that question pierces the heart.

Athena has intervened to establish the meaning, as she tells both sides what the impending vote will signify. At this moment, she literally grounds the tribunal of justice known as the Council of Areopagus, in order not "to cast fear utterly from [the] city." Hereafter, she explains, this place will be reserved for considering and judging the most terrible crimes. Athena elaborates, "What man who fears nothing at all is ever righteous? Such be your just terrors, and you may deserve and have salvation for your citadel" (*Eum* 698–701). Kevin Crotty argues that throughout the trilogy, the avengers have struggled to control the meaning of their deeds, but that only here are the characters enabled "finally to achieve this narrowing of meaning, and to establish authoritatively a single and agreed-upon significance for an event."[31] This is Athena's great contribution. She locates due process and provides the space for a just terror to preserve the peace.

31. Kevin M. Crotty, *Law's Interior: Legal and Literary Construction of the Self,* 52.

Athena is the supreme embodiment of the creator of the *polis* (the city or political community), and so she is the worthiest of benefactors for Athens. Aristotle wrote in his *Politics* that "the one who first constituted [a city] is responsible for the greatest of goods. For just as man is the best of animals when completed, when separated from law and adjudication he is the worst of all.... For adjudication is an arrangement of the political partnership, and adjudication is judgment as to what is just."[32] Aristotle does not name names, but his description is a good fit for the Athena of the *Eumenides.* Her use of persuasive artistry for propitious ends has already been emphasized. There is nothing idealistic about her accomplishment; she does add Necessity where Persuasion needs buttressing: "I have Zeus behind me. Do we need to speak of that? I am the only god who knows the keys to where his thunderbolts are locked." But she gets the order right, in the name of balance. Her inauguration of due process points the way to a transcendence of the natural state. In the best case, the political community does not lose the connection to nature (this is what turns the Furies into "Kindly ones," the translation of *Eumenides:* "you shall win first fruits in offerings for children and the marriage rite for always" [*Eum* 826–828, 834–366]), but nor is the *polis* driven headlong by nature. Politics buys the time and space for human flourishing.

The political community has this in common with the verdict in the trial of the *Eumenides:* there is compromise and concession at its core. The decision is as much an accommodation as a full resolution. "What the jury offers is a 'good enough' decision that people will settle for, if only because it comports with standards of fairness that are open for all to see," Crotty concludes. "Rather than a substantively satisfying, wise decision, then, the jury offers a 'valid' one. On this view, validity is a kind of disappointed justice: it is what *dikē* becomes after its disruptive effects have finally become unendurable."[33]

I would emphasize again the visual aspect of this conclusion: it is open for all to view with dispassion. Aeschylus shows uncommon respect for the commonsense abilities of ordinary Athenians. Commen-

---

32. Aristotle, *The Politics* 1.2, 1251a30ff.
33. Crotty, *Law's Interior,* 59, 60.

tators have long noted his sympathetic portraits of the ordinary char-acters—the watchman in *Agamemnon,* the nurse in the *Libation Bearers.* But this sympathy extends beyond these individual characters to apply to our more ordinary powers of reflection in extraordinary situ-ations. Perhaps a more accurate way of expressing this is to observe that Aeschylus depicts elemental scenes in a way that is deep but ac-cessible to a wide audience. According to one tradition, "Aeschylus was prosecuted for revealing in his plays some of the mystical secrets, but was acquitted on the plea that he was unaware that they were se-crets."[34]

So many cases come to us without instructions. The *Oresteia* shows us that judgment is possible even in matters that are too big for mor-tals. Aeschylus shines light on a better, more harmonious vision than Athens ever achieved as an actual historical city. His drama touches on the deepest human questions, the inescapable question of what shall I do?

After a run through the *Oresteia,* the question about one life being valued more highly than another looks bad and out of place. Context is needed and details and vision. The trouble is that it may take an Aeschylus to create the vision that others, then, can plainly see.

34. George Thomson, *Aeschylus and Athens: A Study in the Social Origins of Drama,* 229.

Afterword

The true and the just are stronger by nature than their opposites.

ARISTOTLE, *Rhetoric*

Judge: Mr. Foreman, do you have a verdict?

Herodotus: We do, your honor. We find the defendant guilty.

Judge: And was this verdict reached in full and open deliberation? Was there sufficient time and occasion for everyone to be heard?

Herodotus: Yes, sir, on both accounts. We were a little slow in beginning, as we wanted to satisfy Alexis de Tocqueville on the question of space. No six-person tables for the Frenchman! He insisted with great strength that we be granted the use of a seminar table around which everyone could sit comfortably. Miss Stein requested a larger chair and a cushion for Basket, and there were other small items that the marshal was happy to bring to us before we began our proper discussion. I drew the line at requesting bourbon, on behalf of a certain southern gentleman who shall remain nameless.

Judge: Well done, Mr. Foreman. Please go on.

Herodotus: We spent the first few days of conversation setting out the dangers we could foresee, such as falling too quickly for an explanation. Jane Austen was quite fierce on the subject, challenging us with drawing-room questions at every turn. Her novels hinge on the assessment of evidence. We didn't want to predetermine the outcome or prejudge the witnesses, so we spent time talking about the weak-

180

nesses in circumstantial evidence in general and the facts of this case in particular. I don't mind telling you that I had a few things to add here about what stands up to time and what does not, about how time draws the color from most everything that happens. But the jurors were quicky in full agreement on this.

The accused, by law, need not provide a story. A reasonable story about the accused cannot be cast into doubt when it contends with no story at all.

Judge: Your proceedings seem eminently sensible. And it sounds as if there was an unusual amount of camaraderie. You don't have to answer this, but I ask, because the legal community is caught up in the issue. Were there rifts or divisions in your jury, and if so, did these find expression in what different individuals defined as reasonable doubt?

Herodotus: Rifts? Were there rifts? Judge, we had ancients and moderns, we had poets and philosophers, we even had men and women. Of course there were rifts!

The funny thing was, all of these divisions seemed to vanish in conversation. For example, Plato was getting quite the reputation for being implacable and old-fashioned, and some of the modern guys felt a real distance. Plato doesn't talk much, you see, but sure as sin he's not missing anything, either, and sometimes people start to take his silence a certain way. Anyway, one afternoon Wallace and William started going back and forth about blackbirds. Blackbirds! I finally had to intervene. Come on, fellas, I said, no private conversations. We have to stay on track. And Plato said, "They're talking about thirteen ways of *looking* at a blackbird—and it's on point. It's about truth. Faulkner said that maybe the truth comes out when the reader has read thirteen different ways of looking at the blackbird and then has his own fourteenth image." Now suddenly there's dead silence. And Plato says, "How about fourteen ways of looking at Socrates?"—and Wallace starts to laugh, and then Faulkner, and pretty soon Plato himself, and then the whole room breaks up. And it wasn't even that funny, know what I'm saying? Well, so much for ancients and moderns. Did you want to hear about poets and philosophers?

Judge: I'll take a rain check. Tell me about the consensus you reached.

Herodotus: Right. But remember, I'm consolidating different views.

This sounds more unproblematic than the process of reasoning actually was.

We decided that the question we had to answer was whether Anthony Bazier was the right man, whether the police had arrested the same individual whom Cruz and Randall identified. One person, Mr. Octible Jones, said no; it was not the same guy.

Octible Jones descended into the courtroom like those people in the Greek world who said *bar, bar, bar.* (You know, the ones who have come down in your history books as barbarians.) The shock to our jury was that Octible Jones was speaking the same language as everyone else. No one could follow his train of thought. All twelve of us found cause to empathize with everybody, including Randall and Cruz and Young and the cops and the lawyers. But not Octible.

He was a felon who didn't know the word. He was in court because his mother made him. He didn't know what a snitch was, or a rat, but he did know tattletales. Cruz referred to him as Randall's boy, which is demeaning. Jones swore the prosecution had doctored his testimony and was leaning on him to make him lie. He was living in his own Octible world. Faulkner loved him so much as to imagine he had invented him in *Go Down, Moses.* He said no one but himself could invent a voice like that. But Octible told a tale of sound and fury, signifying nothing.

We had to make judgments about a lot of people. We talked about character, about who had it, who didn't, and who had signs of it. Aristotle helped us understand that character is the source of judgment, and judgment can locate the truth.

Dante nervously kept hoping he could sneak out of the deliberation room to make a cell phone call to Virgil for guidance. But eventually he realized that the defendant was eligible for the inferno on more counts than brought by the state of Connecticut. Bazier could be ranked with the lustful, the deceitful, the corrupters, but most certain of all, he was headed for the first ring of the seventh circle: those who commit violence against their neighbors.

Longfellow was surprised and a bit dismayed to see his hero Dante dithering so long about the verdict. Longfellow had exhausted his intellectual and emotional powers for years in translating Dante, and he had summoned the elite of Boston to his house on Brattle Street to hear him read from his translated lines. When Norton or Lowell or any one of them had a polite and mild suggestion, Longfellow put them in their place posthaste: *he* was perfectly clear about the case in front of him. He recalled his Puritan maiden Priscilla Mullins who saw through John Alden's dissembling in an instant. Bazier, as directed by the defense attorney, would never speak for himself, but Longfellow knew that his New England forebears could judge this case without dithering. Indeed they had to. When surrounding tribes threw a snakeskin full of arrows over the stockade wall, you didn't have the luxury of saying that the matter remained too ambiguous to act upon.

Aeschylus was completely clear about the case. Civilization requires judgment. When your daughter is murdered it is the natural duty of the family to exact retribution. Justice came, in the precivilizational world, by the system of blood revenge. But then came a time when it was understood that the better way would be for revengeful kin to give over the duty of justice for killers to the state. This they did. So nothing can be more destabilizing than for the state's justice system to turn away from its duty to judge. When the jury won't make a decision, the basis of the civilizational contract is undermined.

We were left with a core story that held together about the events of December 1, 1998. Each of us is convinced beyond a reasonable doubt that the defendant is guilty.

Judge: Do you have any remaining questions for the court?

Herodotus: We do not, your honor. Miss Stein noted that we were told that the accused identified himself as "cousin to Mother's Kitchen." Miss Stein wanted to know, did anyone ever talk to Mother?

Henry Thoreau agreed that was a question, but not *the* question. "Some circumstantial evidence is very strong," he said, "as when you find a trout in the milk." The precincts of 25 Norton Street was a pail of milk, and Mr. Bazier was the trout.

Miss Stein liked that and said she might use it for the title of a book: *A Trout Is a Trout in the Milk a Trout.*

There ain't nothing more to write about, and I am rotten glad of it.

HUCK FINN

Bibliography

Abramson, Jeffrey. *We the Jury: The Jury System and the Ideal of Democracy.* Cambridge: Harvard University Press, 2000.

Aeschylus. *Oresteia.* Translated by Christopher Collard. Oxford: Oxford University Press, 2003.

———. *The Oresteia.* Translated by Robert Fagles. New York: Penguin Books, 1979.

———. *Oresteia: Agamemnon, The Libation Bearers, The Eumenides.* Translated by Richmond Lattimore. Chicago: University of Chicago Press, 1953.

Alschuler, Albert W. *Law without Values: The Life, Work, and Legacy of Justice Holmes.* Chicago: University of Chicago Press, 2000.

———. "The Supreme Court and the Jury: Voir Dire, Peremptory Challenges, and the Review of Jury Verdicts." *University of Chicago Law Review* 56 (1989): 153–233.

Amar, Akhil Reed. *The Constitution and Criminal Procedure: First Principles.* New Haven: Yale University Press, 1997.

Arendt, Hannah. *Between Past and Future: Eight Exercises in Political Thought.* New York: Penguin Books, 1954, 1968.

Aristotle. *Nicomachean Ethics.* Translated by H. Rackham. Cambridge: Harvard University Press, 1926, 1982.

———. *On Rhetoric: A Theory of Civic Discourse.* Translated by George A. Kennedy. New York: Oxford University Press, 1991.

———. *The Politics.* Translated by Carnes Lord. Chicago: University of Chicago Press, 1984.

Austen, Jane. *Emma.* Oxford: Oxford University Press, 1995.

Ball, Milner S. "All the Law's a Stage." *Cardozo Studies in Law and Literature* 11, no. 2 (Winter 1999): 215–21.

———. *The Promise of American Law: A Theological, Humanistic View of Legal Process.* Athens: University of Georgia Press, 1981.

Bardach, Eugene, and Robert Kagan. *Going by the Book: The Problem of Regulatory Unreasonableness.* Philadelphia: Temple University Press, 1982.

Bates, Frank. "Identification from Photographic Evidence." *Anglo-American Law Review* 6 (1977): 90–98.

Beiner, Ronald. *Political Judgment.* Chicago: University of Chicago Press, 1983.

Benardete, Seth. *The Rhetoric of Morality and Philosophy: Plato's Gorgias and Phaedrus.* Chicago: University of Chicago Press, 1991.

Bennett, Linda L. M., and Steven Earl Bennett. *Living with Leviathan: Americans Coming to Terms with Big Government.* Lawrence: University Press of Kansas, 1990.

Bennett, W. Lance, and Martha S. Feldman. *Reconstructing Reality in the Courtroom: Justice and Judgment in American Culture.* New Brunswick, N.J.: Rutgers University Press, 1981, 1984.

Blair, Elena Duvergès. "Women: The Unrecognized Teachers of the Platonic Socrates." *Ancient Philosophy* 16 (1996): 333–50.

Bloom, Allan. *The Closing of the American Mind: How Higher Education Has Failed Democracy and Impoverished the Souls of Today's Students.* New York: Simon and Schuster, 1987.

Bloom, Harold, ed. *Aeschylus's "The Oresteia": Modern Critical Interpretations.* New Haven: Chelsea House Publishers, 1988.

———, ed. *Jane Austen: Modern Critical Views.* New York: Chelsea House Publishers, 1986.

Bond, James E. *The Art of Judging.* New Brunswick, N.J.: Transaction Books, 1987.

Brann, Eva. *The Music of the Republic: Essays on Socrates' Conversations and Plato's Writings.* Philadelphia: Paul Dry Books, 2004.

Breyfogle, Todd, ed. *Literary Imagination, Ancient and Modern: Essays in Honor of David Grene.* Chicago: University of Chicago Press, 1999.

Brodhead, Richard H., ed. *Faulkner: New Perspectives.* Englewood Cliffs, N.J.: Prentice-Hall, 1983.

Brody, David C. "Facing Allegations of Non-Deliberating Jurors." *Justice System Journal* 25, no. 2 (2004): 239–46.

Brooks, Peter, and Paul Gewirtz, eds. *Law's Stories: Narrative and Rhetoric in the Law.* New Haven: Yale University Press, 1996.

Burnett, D. Graham. *A Trial by Jury.* New York: Alfred A. Knopf, 2001.

Burns, Robert P. *A Theory of the Trial.* Princeton: Princeton University Press, 1999.

Chambers, Henry L., Jr. "Reasonable Certainty and Reasonable Doubt." *Marquette Law Review* 81, no. 3 (Spring 1998): 655–704.

Chandler, James, Arnold I. Davidson, and Harry Harootunian, eds. *Questions of Evidence: Proof, Practice, and Persuasion across the Disciplines.* Chicago: University of Chicago Press, 1994.

Cloud, Morgan. "The Dirty Little Secret." *Emory Law Journal* 43 (1994): 1311–49.

Clowes, Edith W., ed. *Doctor Zhivago: A Critical Companion.* Evanston, Ill.: Northwestern University Press, 1995.

Conacher, D. J. *Aeschylus' Oresteia: A Literary Commentary.* Toronto: University of Toronto Press, 1987.

Constable, Marianne. "What Books about Juries Reveal about Social Science and Law." *Law and Social Inquiry* 16, no. 2 (Spring 1991): 353–72.

Cropsey, Joseph. *Plato's World: Man's Place in the Cosmos.* Chicago: University of Chicago Press, 1995.

Crotty, Kevin M. *Law's Interior: Legal and Literary Construction of the Self.* Ithaca: Cornell University Press, 2001.

Dewey, John. *John Dewey: The Later Works, 1925–1953.* Vol. 5. 1929–1930. Edited by Jo Ann Boydston. Carbondale: Southern Illinois University Press, 1984.

Diggins, John P. *The Promise of Pragmatism: Modernism and the Crisis of Knowledge and Authority.* Chicago: University of Chicago Press, 1994.

Dodds, E. R. *Gorgias: A Revised Text with Introduction and Commentary.* Oxford: Clarendon Press, 1959.

Dripps, Donald A. "Reasonable Doubt: Uncertainty about 'Moral Certainty' Continues." *Trial* 30, no. 7 (July 1994): 83–85.

Dunne, Dominick. *Justice: Crimes, Trials, and Punishments.* New York: Three River Press, 2001.

Ermarth, Elizabeth Deeds. *Realism and Consensus in the English Novel.* Princeton: Princeton University Press, 1983.

Euben, J. Peter, John R. Wallach, and Josiah Ober, eds. *Athenian Political Thought and the Reconstruction of American Democracy.* Ithaca: Cornell University Press, 1994.

Farness, Jay. *Missing Socrates: Problems of Plato's Writing.* University Park: Pennsylvania State University Press, 1991.

Farrell, Thomas B. *Norms of Rhetorical Culture.* New Haven: Yale University Press, 1993.

Faulkner, William. *Absalom, Absalom!* New York: Vintage International, 1990.

Felman, Shoshana. *The Juridical Unconscious: Trials and Traumas in the Twentieth Century.* Cambridge: Harvard University Press, 2002.

Finkel, Norman J. *Commonsense Justice: Jurors' Notions of the Law.* Cambridge: Harvard University Press, 1995.

Fortunato, Stephen J., Jr. "Instructing on Reasonable Doubt after Victor v. Nebraska: A Trial Judge's Certain Thoughts on Certainty." *Villanova Law Review* 41, no. 2 (1996): 365–431.

French, Peter A. *The Virtues of Vengeance.* Lawrence: University Press of Kansas, 2001.

Goldman, Harvey S. "Reexamining the 'Examined Life' in Plato's *Apology of Socrates.*" *Philosophical Forum* 35, no. 1 (Spring 2004): 1–33.

Greenberg, Martin. *The Terror of Art: Kafka and Modern Literature.* London: Lowe and Brydone, 1971.

Griswold, Charles L., Jr., ed. *Platonic Writings, Platonic Readings.* New York: Routledge, 1988.

Gross, Miriam, ed. *The World of Raymond Chandler.* London: Weidenfeld and Nicolson, 1977.

Gunn, Giles B. *Thinking across the American Grain: Ideology, Intellect, and the New Pragmatism.* Chicago: University of Chicago Press, 1992.

Hastie, Reid, and Nancy Pennington. "Explaining the Evidence: Tests of the Story Model for Juror Decision Making." *Journal of Personality and Social Psychology* 62, no. 2 (1992): 189–206.

Herington, John. *Aeschylus.* New Haven: Yale University Press, 1986.

Herodotus. *The History.* Translated by David Grene. Chicago: University of Chicago Press, 1987.

Hill, Melvyn A., ed. *Hannah Arendt: The Recovery of the Public World.* New York: St. Martin's Press, 1979.

Hoffman, Morris B. Review of *Law without Values: The Life, Work, and Legacy of Justice Holmes,* by Albert W. Alschuler. *Stanford Law Review* 54 (2001–2002): 597–625.

Howard, Philip K. *The Death of Common Sense: How Law Is Suffocating America.* New York: Random House, 1994.

Howland, Jacob. *The Paradox of Political Philosophy: Socrates' Philosophic Trial.* Lanham, Md.: Rowman and Littlefield Publishers, 1998.

James, William. *Pragmatism.* New York: Dover Publications, 1995.

Johnston, Lawrence V., III. "The Instruction on Reasonable Doubt: Two Hundred Years of Sophistry Is Enough." *Florida Bar Journal* 72, no. 1 (1998): 61–65.

Jones, John. *On Aristotle and Greek Tragedy.* London: Chatto and Windus, 1967.

Kalven, Harry, Jr., and Hans Zeisel. *The American Jury.* Boston: Little, Brown, 1966.

Kronman, Anthony T. *The Lost Lawyer: Failing Ideals of the Legal Profession.* Cambridge: Harvard University Press, 1993.

Kuhns, Richard. *The House, the City, and the Judge: The Growth of Moral Awareness in the Oresteia.* New York: Bobbs-Merrill Company, 1962.

Laudan, Larry. "Is Reasonable Doubt Reasonable?" *Legal Theory* 9 (2003): 295–331.

Lesky, Albin. *Greek Tragedy.* Translated by H. A. Frankfort. New York: Barnes and Noble, 1967.

Lillquist, Erik. "Recasting Reasonable Doubt: Decision Theory and the Virtues of Variability." *U.C. Davis Law Review* 36 (2002): 85–197.

Locke, John. *Two Treatises of Government.* Edited by Peter Laslett. Cambridge: Cambridge University Press, 1990.

Longfellow, Henry Wadsworth. Review of *Twice-Told Tales,* by Nathaniel Hawthorne. *North American Review* 45 (July 1837): 59–73.

Luban, David. *Legal Modernism.* Ann Arbor: University of Michigan Press, 1994.

Mayer, Connie. "Due Process Challenges to Eyewitness Identification Based on Pretrial Photographic Arrays." *Pace Law Review* 13, no. 3 (Winter 1994): 815–61.

Menand, Louis. *Pragmatism: A Reader.* New York: Vintage Books, 1997.

Michelini, Ann N. "*Polle Agroikia:* Rudeness and Irony in Plato's *Gorgias.*" *Classical Philology* 93, no. 1 (January 1998): 50–59.

Miller, Henry G. *On Trial: Lessons from a Lifetime in the Courtroom.* New York: American Lawyer Media, 2001.

Mulrine, Thomas V. "Reasonable Doubt: How in the World Is It Defined?" *American University Journal of International Law and Policy* 12 (1997): 195–225.

Niedermeier, Keith E., Irwin A. Horowitz, and Norbert L. Kerr. "Informing Jurors of Their Nullification Power: A Route to a Just Verdict or Judicial Chaos?" *Law and Human Behavior* 23, no. 3 (1999): 331–51.

Nietzsche, Friedrich. *"The Birth of Tragedy" and "The Case of Wagner."* Translated by Walter Kaufmann. New York: Random House, 1967.

———. *Untimely Meditations.* Translated by R. J. Hollingdale. Cambridge: Cambridge University Press, 1983.

Parker, Robert Dale. *Absalom, Absalom! The Questioning of Fictions.* Boston: Twayne Publishers, 1991.

Pasternak, Boris. *Dr. Zhivago.* New York: Pantheon Books, 1991.

Pizzi, William T. *Trials without Truth: Why Our System of Criminal Trials Has Become an Expensive Failure and What We Need to Do about It.* New York: New York University Press, 1999.

Plato. *The Gorgias.* Translated by James H. Nichols Jr. Ithaca: Cornell University Press, 1998.

———. *Protagoras.* Translated by Stanley Lombardo. Indianapolis: Hackett Publishing, 1992.

———. *The Republic.* 2nd ed. Translated with a new introduction by Allan Bloom. New York: Basic Books, 1991.

Plato and Aristophanes. *Four Texts on Socrates: Plato's Euthyphro, Apology, and Crito and Aristophanes' Clouds.* Translated by

Thomas G. West and Grace Starry West. Ithaca: Cornell University Press, 1984.

Posner, Richard A. *Law and Literature.* Revised and Enlarged Edition. Cambridge: Harvard University Press, 2000.

————. *Law, Pragmatism, and Democracy.* Cambridge: Harvard University Press, 2003.

————. *Overcoming Law.* Cambridge: Harvard University Press, 1995.

Putnam, Robert D. *Bowling Alone: The Collapse and Revival of American Community.* New York: Simon and Schuster, 2000.

Radelet, Michael L., Hugo Adam Bedau, and Constance E. Putnam. *In Spite of Innocence: Erroneous Convictions in Capital Cases.* Boston: Northeastern University Press, 1992.

"Reasonable Doubt: An Argument against Definition." *Harvard Law Review* 108, no. 8 (1995): 1955–72.

Redfield, James M. "A Lecture on Plato's *Apology.*" *Journal of General Education* 15 (1963): 93–108.

————. *Nature and Culture in the "Iliad": The Tragedy of Hector.* Chicago: University of Chicago Press, 1975.

Rorty, Richard. *Objectivity, Relativism, and Truth: Philosophical Papers.* Vol. 1. New York: Cambridge University Press, 1991.

————. *Philosophy and the Mirror of Nature.* Princeton: Princeton University Press, 1979.

Rosen, Jeffrey. "After 'One Angry Woman.'" *University of Chicago Legal Forum* (1998): 179–95.

————. "One Angry Woman: Why Are Hung Juries on the Rise?" *New Yorker,* February 24 and March 3, 1997, 54–64.

————. "Overcoming Posner." Review of *Overcoming Law,* by Richard A. Posner. *Yale Law Journal* 105 (1995–1996): 581–610.

Roth, Philip. *The Human Stain.* New York: Vintage International, 2000.

Saltman, Michael. *The Demise of the 'Reasonable Man': A Cross-Cultural Study of a Legal Concept.* New Brunswick, N.J.: Transaction Publishers, 1991.

Sheppard, Steve. "The Metamorphoses of Reasonable Doubt: How Changes in the Burden of Proof Have Weakened the Presumption of Innocence." *Notre Dame Law Review* 78, no. 4 (2002–2003): 1165–1250.

Sitarski, Lynne A. "Criminal Procedure—Limiting the Scope of Federal Rule of Criminal Procedure 23(b): A Juror's Doubts about the Sufficiency of the Evidence Do Not Constitute 'Just Cause' for the Juror's Dismissal." *Temple Law Review* 61 (1988): 991–1013.

Smigelskis, David J. "Realizing the Practical Intelligence of American Juries." Review of *A Theory of the Trial,* by Robert Burns. *Northwestern University Law Review* 95, no. 3 (2001): 1015–27.

Southam, B. C., ed. *Critical Essays on Jane Austen.* London: Routledge and Kegan Paul, 1968.

Spitzer, Adele. "The Self-Reference of the *Gorgias.*" *Philosophy and Rhetoric* 8, no. 1 (Winter 1975): 1–22.

Steinberger, Peter J. *The Concept of Political Judgment.* Chicago: University of Chicago Press, 1993.

Stith, Kate, and José A. Cabranes. *Fear of Judging: Sentencing Guidelines in the Federal Courts.* Chicago: University of Chicago Press, 1998.

Strauss, Leo. *Studies in Platonic Political Philosophy.* Chicago: University of Chicago Press, 1983.

Tanner, Tony. *Jane Austen.* Cambridge: Harvard University Press, 1986.

Tave, Stuart M. *Some Words of Jane Austen.* Chicago: University of Chicago Press, 1973.

Thompson, Norma. *Herodotus and the Origins of the Political Community: Arion's Leap.* New Haven: Yale University Press, 1996.

———. *The Ship of State: Statecraft and Politics from Ancient Greece to Democratic America.* New Haven: Yale University Press, 2001.

Thomson, George. *Aeschylus and Athens: A Study in the Social Origins of Drama.* London: Lawrence and Wishart, 1946.

Tiersma, Peter. "The Rocky Road to Legal Reform: Improving the Language of Jury Instructions." *Brooklyn Law Review* 66 (2000–2001): 1081–1119.

Tolstoy, Leo. *War and Peace.* Edited with a revised translation by George Gibian. New York: W. W. Norton, 1996.

Tocqueville, Alexis de. *Democracy in America.* Translated and edited by Harvey C. Mansfield and Delba Winthrop. Chicago: University of Chicago Press, 2000.

Trilling, Lionel. *Beyond Culture: Essays on Literature and Learning.* New York: Viking Press, 1955, 1965.

Vickers, Brian. *Towards Greek Tragedy: Drama, Myth, Society.* New York: Longman, 1979.

Vlastos, Gregory, ed. *The Philosophy of Socrates: A Collection of Critical Essays.* Notre Dame: University of Notre Dame Press, 1971.

———. *Socratic Studies.* Edited by Myles Burnyeat. New York: Cambridge University Press, 1994.

Wardy, Robert. *The Birth of Rhetoric: Gorgias, Plato, and Their Successors.* New York: Routledge, 1996.

Warren, Robert Penn, ed. *Faulkner: A Collection of Critical Essays.* Englewood Cliffs, N.J.: Prentice-Hall, 1966.

Watt, Ian P., ed. *Jane Austen: A Collection of Critical Essays.* Englewood Cliffs, N.J.: Prentice-Hall, 1963.

West, Robin. "Toward Humanistic Theories of Legal Justice." *Cardozo Studies in Law and Literature* 10 (1998): 147–50.

White, James Boyd. *Heracles' Bow: Essays on the Rhetoric and Poetics of the Law.* Madison: University of Wisconsin Press, 1985.

———. *The Legal Imagination.* Abridged edition. Chicago: University of Chicago Press, 1973, 1985.

———. "What Can a Lawyer Learn from Literature?" Review of *Law and Literature: A Misunderstood Relation,* by Richard A. Posner. *Harvard Law Review* 102 (1988–1989): 2014–47.

———. *When Words Lose Their Meaning: Constitutions and Reconstitutions of Language, Character, and Community.* Chicago: University of Chicago Press, 1984.

Winnington-Ingram, R. P. *Studies in Aeschylus.* Cambridge: Cambridge University Press, 1983.

Winograde, Jana. "Jailhouse Informants and the Need for Judicial Use Immunity in Habeas Corpus Proceedings." *California Law Review* 78 (1990): 755–85.

Zitrin, Richard, and Carol M. Langford. *The Moral Compass of the American Lawyer: Truth, Justice, Power, and Greed.* New York: Ballantine Books, 1999.

Index

195